# The 1967 Referendum

## Race, power and the Australian Constitution

**Bain Attwood and Andrew Markus**

Oral history coordination by
Dale Edwards and Kath Schilling

ABORIGINAL
STUDIES
PRESS

First edition published as *The 1967 Referendum, or When Aborigines Didn't Get the Vote*, 1997 by Aboriginal Studies Press, AIATSIS.
2nd edition published 2007

Reprinted 2017, 2021, 2026

Aboriginal Studies Press
is the publishing arm of the
Australian Institute of Aboriginal
and Torres Strait Islander Studies.
GPO Box 553, Canberra, ACT 2601 Phone: (61 2) 6246 1183
Fax:    (61 2) 6261 4288
Email:  asp@aiatsis.gov.au
Web:    www.aiatsis.gov.au/asp

National Library of Australia Cataloguing-In-Publication data:

Attwood, Bain.
The 1967 referendum: race, power and the Australian Constitution.

2nd ed.
Bibliography.
Includes index.
ISBN 9780855755553 (pbk.).

1. Aboriginal Australians — Civil rights. 2. Aboriginal Australians — Legal status, laws, etc. 3. Aboriginal Australians — Suffrage. 4. Citizenship — Australia. 5. Referendum — Australia. I. Title.

323.119915

Index by Michael Harrington

Cover illustration: Aborigines from Victoria and NSW in Canberra, November 1965, campaigning for constitutional change. *Australian*, Newspix/News Ltd.

Aboriginal and Torres Strait Islander people are respectfully advised that this publication contains names and images of deceased persons, and culturally sensitive material. AIATSIS apologises for any distress this may cause.

# Contents

# Acknowledgments

Many have helped make this research possible. We wish to acknow-ledge the assistance of the archivists of National Archives of Australia, State Records New South Wales, the University of Sydney Archives and ABC Archives Melbourne, and the librarians of the State Library of New South Wales, the State Library of Victoria, the National Library of Australia, the Australian Institute of Aboriginal and Torres Strait Islander Studies, Rhodes House Library University of Oxford, and the Matheson Library, Monash University. Marita Cullen and Matt Chrulew provided research assistance. Aboriginal and Islander people generously gave of their time to enable Dale Edwards and Kath Schilling to compile Indigenous perspectives. Ellie Gilbert transcribed and gave permission to reproduce a speech by Kevin Gilbert. Barrie Pittock gave us access to some of his private papers.

Sue Taffe was a very generous colleague. Her writings compelled us to reconsider a good part of our argument but she also provided research advice and assistance and gave useful feedback on the draft of this book. Liz Reed gave us the benefit of her insights into the subject and pushed us to question some of our assumptions and arguments. Mary Edmunds and Geoff Gray provided the impetus by commissioning the first edition of this book.

Rhonda Joyce and Shannon Mattison of the School of Geography and Environmental Science, Monash University, reproduced many of the illustrations. Numerous individuals, organisations and newspapers gave us permission to reproduce material and waived their rights to reproduction fees. Every effort has been made to contact copyright owners for permission to use material reproduced in this book. Please inform the publisher if your material has been inadvertently used without acknowledgment and this will be corrected in subsequent editions.

# Abbreviations

| | |
|---|---|
| AAF | Aboriginal-Australian Fellowship |
| AIATSIS | Australian Institute of Aboriginal and Torres Strait Islander Studies |
| ALP | Australian Labor Party |
| APA | Aborigines Progressive Association |
| APNR | Association for the Protection of Native Races |
| ASS | Anti-Slavery Society |
| ATSIC | Aboriginal and Torres Strait Islander Commission |
| CAR | Council for Aboriginal Rights |
| DAA | Department of Aboriginal Affairs |
| FCAA | Federal Council for Aboriginal Advancement |
| FCAATSI | Federal Council for the Advancement of Aborigines and Torres Strait Islanders |
| MHR | Member of the House of Representatives |
| MLA | Member of the Legislative Assembly |
| NAA | National Archives of Australia |
| NAC | National Aboriginal Conference |
| NACC | National Aboriginal Consultative Committee |
| VAAL | Victorian Aborigines Advancement League |
| WILPF | Women's International League of Peace and Freedom |

# Preface

Forty years ago over 90 per cent of electors voted 'yes' in a referendum to alter two clauses in the Australian Constitution in reference to Aboriginal people. Of the 44 attempts to amend the Constitution only eight have succeeded, and the vote in 1967 is the highest ever achieved. This referendum is commonly regarded as the outcome of a major political campaign for change in Aboriginal affairs, and it is frequently cast as an event of considerable import in Australia's history. Over the years it has been popularly claimed that the referendum gave Aboriginal people the vote, granted equal citizenship, repealed racially discriminatory laws, transferred Aboriginal affairs from the states to the Commonwealth, or that it did all of these things.[1] Indeed, this was how the referendum was represented at the time. Yet, a reading of the Constitution would suggest that the changes endorsed in the referendum could have had none of these outcomes.

Repeal of section 127 provided for Aboriginal people to be counted in the next national census but this did not confer citizenship rights such as the vote. The Australian Constitution, unlike the famous American one, makes no reference to citizenship. It is simply not that kind of constitution. It is instead a compact designed by rulers to meet the needs of government and capital, and so it is concerned with the parliament and its powers, the executive and the judiciary, the states, and finance and trade.[2] Besides, legislative changes made prior to the referendum in 1967 had already seen many Aboriginal people gain or regain the formal rights of Australian citizens.

Amendment of section 51 (xxvi) of the Constitution enabled the Commonwealth to enact 'special laws' for Aboriginal people in particular circumstances but this change did not require any federal government to use that power, and in fact it has been little used in the years since. Nor did this amendment compel a federal government to assume a greater role in Aboriginal affairs, let alone take over responsibility for these from the state governments, as the record of the Coalition government after the referendum testifies. Furthermore, no provision of the Constitution prior to 1967 barred the Commonwealth from enacting 'general laws' affecting Aboriginal people: federal legislation of a general nature (such as welfare provision) applied to Aboriginal people in their status as Australian citizens. Moreover, the Commonwealth could have further enlarged its sphere of influence in this area by using another part of the Constitution (section 96), by which the federal government provides specific purpose or tied grants to the States. In short, the importance attached to the referendum presents something of a puzzle. There is obviously a considerable discrepancy between the way it was and has been represented, and the actual legal changes which were proposed. So, why was the referendum so significant?

The answer is to be found less in the words of the Constitution and more in the stories or narratives that were told about these and the changes demanded by those who campaigned the longest and the hardest for the referendum. In their eyes, the referendum was of the utmost importance, and in the end their account of the proposed changes as a matter of rights for Aborigines and of a greater Commonwealth role in Aboriginal affairs persuaded most Australians that this was so. Representation matters, and their representations came to matter. At a time of powerful movements for political and social change, campaigners for constitutional change raised high expectations of major reform, which were not met by the conservative government in the five years following the referendum. Demands for change increased, and in the end the Whitlam Labor government seized hold of the referendum as a mandate to implement sweeping changes in Aboriginal affairs.

In this book we seek to provide an appraisal of the Constitution's race clauses and the referendum's changes in formal legal terms; to understand the meanings attached to these changes by those who campaigned for them, especially in the ten years preceding the referendum; to explain the approach of the Menzies and Holt Coalition governments and the Australian Labor Party to the calls for constitutional change; to assess the consequences of the referendum; and to delineate the ways in which the terms of referendum have been represented and misrepresented, remembered and forgotten, in the years since.

Since we first researched and wrote a book on this subject some ten years ago, a good deal more work has been done on the campaign for rights for Aborigines in the post-war era as well as on the changes in government policy and practice in Aboriginal affairs during this period.[3] We have revised some of our findings in the light of this research. More to the point, as time passes the way in which historians contemplate the past inevitably changes. New historical sources are located or made available to researchers, for example private papers and cabinet minutes. New methods and approaches are adopted, such as the way we understand power and race. Most importantly, perhaps, new problems and questions are prompted by what is happening around us. In this case, major changes in the approach of the Commonwealth government to Aboriginal affairs have provoked much discussion about matters of race and rights generally. More particularly, there has been debate about the Constitution itself, which has included a controversy regarding the very powers the Commonwealth was granted by virtue of the 1967 referendum's amendment of section 51 (xxvi). Anniversaries or commemoration such as the one this year prompt reflection about the meaning and significance of a landmark event, just as they provide an opportunity to contest powerful understandings of the meaning of an event that has ongoing political importance.

During the last ten years there seems to have been little if any change in popular understandings of the referendum. In the first edition of this book we added our voice to those who had tried to correct misunderstandings of it, though we did not assume our book would have much impact on these. Stories, especially myths, are very important in any society, and their accounts of events are seldom overturned since they have considerable emotional power.[4] In this instance, political leaders, legal figures, government officials, school teachers and journalists have continued to represent or misrepresent the terms of the referendum along the popular lines we have already mentioned.[5] This will undoubtedly continue.[6]

In our opinion, this myth-making constitutes something of a problem. The changes brought about by the 1967 Referendum itself, as distinct from the political and social movement of which it was a product, barely warrant the amount of celebration they usually occasion, and the struggle to redress the disadvantage of Aboriginal people remains as necessary today as it was then. Most importantly, perhaps, one of the principal reasons why the leading campaigners for Aboriginal rights fought to change the Australian Constitution in the 1967 referendum has been overlooked. This amounted to a call for a political program that has arguably never been implemented. The better we understand the past, the greater is the scope for grasping the need for change and the means by which this might be realised.

# 1 The Constitution and the Power of Race

The Constitution of the Commonwealth of Australia was drawn up at a time when Aboriginal people had no political power and most settler Australians presumed they were 'a dying race'. Consequently, the drafters of the Constitution paid little attention to them in their deliberations. In fact, Aboriginal people were barely mentioned during the debates of the federal conventions which determined the terms of the nation's foundational document. In the end, only two relatively substantive references were made to them in the Constitution.

The first, a clause of section 51, related to a power granted to the Commonwealth to enact special laws with regard to racial minorities. This lay adjacent to the same powers the next two clauses in the same section granted the Commonwealth in respect of emigration and immigration (xxvii) and the influx of criminals (xxviii). It read:

> The Parliament shall subject to this Constitution, have power to make laws for the peace, order, and good government of the Commonwealth with respect to...(xxvi) The people of any race, other than the aboriginal race in any State, for whom it is deemed necessary to make special laws.

It has been suggested that the scope of this race power did not include Aboriginal people because in the early discussions about a federation of the colonies New Zealand was part of the picture and it wanted to safeguard its superior treatment of Maori people from a federal authority dominated by Australia.[1]

However, the primary issue under consideration in this section of the Constitution was a discriminatory policy in regard to 'alien races' such as those called Kanakas, Chinese, Indians or Malays who had come to Australia as indentured labourers, not 'native races' such as the Maori and the Aboriginal people. Samuel Griffith, Queensland Premier and later the Commonwealth's first chief justice, explained to the first federal convention, in 1891:

> It is proposed to give some exclusive powers to the legislature of the commonwealth. One of them is to deal with 'the affairs of any race to whom it is deemed necessary to make special laws not applicable to the general community; but so that this power shall not extend to authorise legislation with respect to the aboriginal native race in Australia and the Maori race in New Zealand'. I am sorry that my late colleague and co-delegate for Queensland, Mr Macrossan, is not here to express his opinion on that proposal. I am satisfied, notwithstanding that during all his political career he was a representative of northern constituencies in Queensland — constituencies where the question of black [i.e. 'alien'] labour was burning one — that he would have most cordially supported the proposal, and would have insisted upon the necessity of that power being given to the commonwealth of Australia, and not to the legislature of any particular state.[2]

This reveals the purpose of this 'race power', but it does not altogether explain why its provisions did not encompass a power to pass special laws with respect to Indigenous peoples, a matter to which we will return shortly.[3]

It is clear, however, that the Constitution itself did not determine the fact that the states rather than the Commonwealth would have responsibility for Aboriginal affairs. This was dictated instead by the context in which the Constitution was drawn up or, more specifically, by the unwritten conventions of the day. It has been argued that the framers of the Australian Constitution did not consider granting the Commonwealth substantial powers over Aboriginal people because the federal system they were creating was one in which the former colonies were to retain jurisdiction over most policy areas, such as land settlement, industrial development, labour relations and education. Sir Robert Garran, secretary of the Federal Convention's drafting committee, and Commonwealth Solicitor-General, explained later: 'The federating colonies were very jealous of their powers, and assigned nothing to the Federal Parliament unless they thought it very definitely a matter of federal concern'.[4] In the mid-1960s a legal scholar argued: 'few of the powers given to the Commonwealth had any obvious or direct relevance to aboriginal policy, so that a decision to leave aboriginal questions to the States was rationally defensible'.[5] This argument is perfectly reasonable but it overlooks the fact that the colonies assumed that the Commonwealth of Australia had to have a special power over 'alien races' living in Australia and granted these very powers to the federal government. It is striking that the makers of the Constitution presumed there was no similar need in respect of 'native people'.

Their approach to this matter of jurisdiction differed markedly from that of their counterparts in two other comparable countries. Unlike the Australian Constitution, the constitutions of both the United States and Canada gave their federal governments substantial powers over Indigenous peoples. At the time of federation in these two countries, the national governments had claimed responsibility for vast territories comprising Indigenous-controlled lands from which new states or provinces were to be carved, whereas at the time of federation in Australia the Indigenous people had largely been dispossessed of their lands. The former perceived a need for their federal governments to have considerable powers in Indigenous affairs, the latter did not.[6]

The second specific reference in the Australian Constitution to Aboriginal people appeared in section 127:

> In reckoning the numbers of people of the Commonwealth, or of a State or other part of the Commonwealth, aboriginal natives shall not be counted.

There was little discussion about this clause at the federal conventions. Part of the 'Miscellaneous' chapter of the Constitution, its purpose related not to the national census as such but to a formula for calculating the distribution of funds and the apportionment of parliamentary seats to the states on the basis of the size of their populations.[7] The exclusion of Aboriginal people from this calculus suggests a racial assumption on the part of the makers of the Australian Constitution. The Aborigines did not count, hence they did not need to be counted.

Another part of the Constitution warrants consideration. Section 41 reads:

> No adult person who has or acquires a right to vote at elections for the more numerous House of the Parliament of a State shall, while the right continues, be prevented by any law of the Commonwealth from voting at elections for either House of Parliament of the Commonwealth.[8]

On the face of it, this provision guaranteed the right to vote in federal elections for those who had that right in their state of residence, which included many Aboriginal people since all the colonies had granted them the suffrage prior to federation and only Queensland and Western Australia had withdrawn this.[9] In 1902, the first Commonwealth parliament passed a franchise act which included this clause: 'No aboriginal native of Australia, Asia, Africa or the Islands of the Pacific except New Zealand, shall be entitled to have his name placed on an electoral roll, unless so entitled under Section 41 of the Constitution'.[10] The protection this section of the Constitution should have afforded Aboriginal people had been removed, however, on the Commonwealth Solicitor-General's advice that section 41 only applied to those who had acquired the vote *before* federation.[11] This was an odd construction of it since the Constitution made no temporal reference in respect of the acquiring of the right to vote. Indeed, the Solicitor-General's interpretation was ruled invalid by a junior judge in 1925 when a magistrate's court heard a challenge brought by Mitta Bullosh, an Indian man who was an Australian resident. In response, the Commonwealth lodged an appeal with the High Court. However, it withdrew this for reasons of international diplomacy and decided to legislate instead so that any Australian who was 'a native of British India' was entitled to vote.[12]

This episode reveals much about the racial mentality and racial politics of this time. The Commonwealth assumed that Aborigines were unworthy of rights such as the franchise, and realised that it could deny these since Aboriginal people themselves lacked the power to uphold them and they no protectors in the form of an overseas state. More than twenty years were to pass before the Commonwealth was forced to change its position on this matter. In 1949 it enacted by legislation what had been provided in the Constitution nearly fifty years previously. It amended the Commonwealth Electoral Act so that it stated that anyone who was 'an aboriginal native of Australia' and 'entitled under the law of the State in which he resides to be enrolled as an elector of that State and, upon enrolment, to vote at elections for the more numerous House of Parliament of that State' or 'is or has been a member of the Defence Force' was eligible to vote.[13]

More than a decade later the Commonwealth realised, in an environment in which enormous attention was increasingly focused on racial discrimination, that it had to make further changes. In 1962 the parliament, acting on the recommendation of a select committee which had inquired into voting rights for all Aborigines the previous year, passed legislation that provided all Aboriginal adults with the vote for Commonwealth elections (though it did not require them to register as voters, a requirement of all other Australian electors).[14]

In summary, it is evident that the text of the Constitution prevented neither the Commonwealth from enacting some laws in respect of Aboriginal people nor Aboriginal people from voting. Yet, at least one of the sections of the Constitution — 127 — might be said to be discriminatory since it entailed an act of exclusion. Moreover, it is apparent that the context in which the Constitution was forged, rather than the text of the Constitution, dictated that Aboriginal people were to be the responsibility of the states instead of the Commonwealth, and that the context in which the Constitution was interpreted during the nation's first half-century was one unfavourable to the notion that Aboriginal people were entitled to one of the most important rights of a citizen, namely the right to vote.

# 2 The Commonwealth and Aboriginal Affairs

Before the end of the nation's first decade there were calls for the Commonwealth to play a greater role in Aboriginal affairs. Those who advocated this course during the following decades did so on the assumption that more would be done to advance the interests of Aboriginal people if this occurred. It was the hope of the small minority of settler Australians who took an interest in Aboriginal welfare at this time that the Commonwealth government could set an example for the states in its treatment of Aborigines. Some urged the federal government to recognise Aboriginal welfare as a trust vested in the nation and argued that it should actually assume an Australia-wide responsibility for Aboriginal people.

In 1910 a missionary body, the Australian Board of Missions, called on the 'Federal and State Governments to agree to a scheme by which all responsibility for safeguarding the human and civil rights of the aborigines should be undertaken by the Federal Government'.[1] Early the following year a Sydney-based group of humanitarians and scientists put the case to Prime Minister Andrew Fisher (see document 1, p. 89). Shortly afterwards, a new lobby group was formed under the leadership of Archdeacon CEC Lefroy: the Association for the Protection of the Native Races of Australasia and Polynesia (later called the Association for the Protection of Native Races). It asserted: 'The method of relying upon State and Colonial Governments has been tried from the earliest days of colonisation, and has undeniably failed. The Colonial and State Governments have themselves acknowledged the failure'. The Association claimed there was a well known 'political principle that the wider the area from which the governing power is derived, and the larger the task set, the wider and more statesmanlike the policy is likely to be'. In accordance with this, it contended that the federal government was more likely to tackle the Aboriginal problem satisfactorily than the state governments.[2]

In 1913, a committee on Aboriginal welfare, established by the Australasian Association for the Advancement of Science, urged that 'the Aboriginal problem will only be solved when all that is left of the race is made a single and National responsibility and cared for in a National way'. It argued: 'A national sentiment of sympathy and pity would be created towards this unfortunate race whom we have dispossessed'.[3] In 1911 the Commonwealth had assumed responsibility for the Northern Territory, a region previously administered by South Australia, where an estimated one-quarter of Australia's surviving Aboriginal population outnumbered the combined white and Asian population by a proportion of four or five to one.

Over the following decade or so there was very little public interest in Aboriginal affairs, but when the Association for the Protection of Native Races was reactivated in the mid-1920s it resumed its calls for federal control. Its 'Statement of the Policy and Purposes' provided for 'the Nationalisation of the care of the Aborigines under the Federal Government with a view to one National policy of control and administration, instead of (as at present) six, often greatly divergent methods of treatment'.[4] It soon became apparent, though, that the Commonwealth's administration of Aboriginal matters was badly flawed.[5] Consequently, the reformers' belief that a greater Commonwealth role in Aboriginal affairs would be a force for the good was a matter of conviction rather than something grounded in reality.

In 1928 the secretary of the Association for the Protection of Native Races, Rev. William Morley, urged a royal commission on the Constitution 'to recommend to the Federal Government that the Constitution be amended so as to give the Federal Government the supreme control of all aborigines'. A host of other witnesses, including Bessie Rischbieth, President of the Australian Federation of Women Voters, and JS Needham, Chairman of the Australian Board of Missions, endorsed this demand.[6]

Archdeacon Lefroy, now representing the London-based Anti-Slavery and Aborigines Protection Society, suggested that a special referendum be held on the issue 'so that the people of Australia could consider the matter fairly and squarely, and deal with it worthily of our position as a young nation'. He presented the fullest case for federal control (see document 2, pp. 90–1). For example, he argued: 'The whole of Australia owes a debt of reparation to the aborigines, and the debt should be equally be distributed'.[7] Others agreed that the interests of Aborigines would only be properly considered if they became a matter of national responsibility. Needham stated:

In the mid-1930s the anthropologist and churchman AP Elkin (far right) and the Rev William Morley (second right) led the Association for the Protection of Native Races which spearheaded calls for federal control of Aboriginal affairs for over thirty years. The other members pictured at this Association for the Protection of Native Races meeting in c. 1933–4, are (left to right): Mr DG Stead, Bishop Kirkby and Sir Kelso King. (Courtesy University of Sydney Archives)

> The national honour is involved before the world in the question of justice and mercy to the aborigines and the National Government is the proper guardian of the national honour in this regard, and should be able to speak before the nations of the world with authority and clarity on aborigines treatment.[8]

Edith Jones, President of the Victorian Women Citizen Movement, asserted that Aborigines should be regarded as a responsibility like that the Commonwealth had assumed for the New Guineans under a League of Nations mandate. If this was so, she argued, 'we should have to be more particular in our care of them than perhaps we are now'.[9] Others agreed that federal control would free Aboriginal matters from 'local influences and prejudices'.[10]

A minority of the Royal Commissioners supported these calls for constitutional change:

> The recommendation regarding aborigines is based upon the responsibility of the nation as a whole to care for the aboriginal native races of this country. It is hardly fair that the burden of

caring for the natives should rest upon the States which have small populations but in which the bulk of the natives are, while the more settled States have little or no financial responsibility in the matter. The national Parliament should see that all carried their fair share of burden in respect to the displaced native races, and should accept the responsibility for their well-being.[11]

However, the majority refused to endorse any such change to the Constitution:

We do not recommend that section 51 (xxvi) be amended so as to empower the Commonwealth Parliament to make laws with respect to Aborigines. We recognise that the effect of the treatment of aborigines on the reputation of Australia furnishes a powerful argument for transference of control to the Commonwealth. But we think that on the whole the States are better equipped for controlling aborigines than the Commonwealth. The States control the police and the lands, and they to a large extent control the conditions of industry. We think that a Commonwealth authority would be at a disadvantage in dealing with the aborigines, and that the States are better qualified to do so. At the same time we think that every endeavour should be made to ensure the adoption of the best methods of administration by periodical conferences, and that every encouragement should be given to those voluntary bodies which in many of the States have worked for the improvement of the conditions of aborigines.[12]

The federal government accepted the majority view and did nothing (see document 3, pp. 91–2).

In the mid-1930s calls for a greater Commonwealth role in Aboriginal affairs intensified as Aboriginal bodies, most notably the Australian Aborigines' League (see document 6, p. 93), added their voice to that of humanitarian, scientific and feminist organisations (see documents: 4 and 5, pp. 92–93, and 7, p. 94). Federal control, according to the League's secretary William Cooper, would make possible a uniform national policy financed on an equitable basis by all taxpayers:

We feel it but right that our people should be the responsibility of the Federal Administration…We know that the Commonwealth can discharge its responsibilities and we appreciate that the States cannot for the reason that where the white population is relatively smallest the dark population is largest while in the States with a large and wealthy white population the number of aboriginals is comparatively small: thus the bigger the need, the smaller the capacity to meet it.[13]

In January 1938, at the Aboriginal 'Day of Mourning' held to protest against Australia's sesquicentennial celebrations in Sydney, the Australian Aborigines' League and the Aborigines Progressive Association called for a new deal for Aborigines. They demanded 'a National Policy for Aborigines' and 'Commonwealth Government control of all Aboriginal Affairs'. This was linked to a call for a program that would 'raise all Aborigines throughout the Commonwealth to full Citizen Status and civil equality with whites in Australia' (see document 8, pp. 94–5).

When World War II broke out the push for reform in Aboriginal affairs slowed. However, when proposals to increase Commonwealth powers in a range of areas were raised in 1942, the Association for the Protection of Native Races and other bodies urged the Labor government to alter the Constitution in order to enable the responsibility for Aboriginal affairs to be passed to the Commonwealth (document 10, p. 95). In 1943 the United Associations of Women and other women's organisations issued a Women's Charter which included a call for federal control of Aboriginal affairs.

The principal figures in the Aborigines Progressive Association, Pearl Gibbs (far left), Bill Ferguson (holding the sign) and Jack Patten (to his right), led the call for federal control of Aboriginal affairs and citizenship rights for Aboriginal people at the Day of Mourning held on 26 January 1938 at the Australia Hall in Sydney. (Image courtesy of Australian Institute of Aboriginal and Torres Strait Islander Studies, Jack Horner Collection [Image number N4641])

The following year AP Elkin, Professor of Anthropology at the University of Sydney and President of the Association for the Protection of Native Races, made the same demand. Although he assumed there were three different ways in which 'a national policy for Aborigines' could be realised — what he called parallelism, convergence and unification (document 11, pp. 96–7) — Elkin believed at this time that 'the most hopeful method of getting an overall positive outlook' lay in 'unification': the federal government assuming control and financial responsibility.[14] In Elkin's program for change, like those of the Aboriginal organisations, the demand for a national policy and the call for citizenship for Aborigines were connected to one another. He stated:

> The time has arrived to bring into line the Aboriginal policies, acts, definitions and regulations, which prevail in different parts of the Commonwealth. They should be framed and administered from a national point of view. Moreover, we must remember that the Aborigines are British subjects by birth…that many of them, especially the part-Aborigines, already possess Australian citizenship; and that full citizenship is the destiny of all of them.[15]

In 1942 a constitutional convention called by the Curtin Labor government had recommended that certain powers be transferred to the Commonwealth for five years after the war but all the states failed to pass the necessary legislation to enable this, and so the Curtin government decided to hold a referendum. In 1944 it presented fourteen proposals to the electorate that were designed to enable the Commonwealth to embark on post-war reconstruction without legislative limitation. One of the measures regarded the Commonwealth's power in Aboriginal affairs. What had been a matter of common sense for the framers of the Constitution was now challenged by the government. Attorney-General HV Evatt asserted: 'The Constitution as it stands provides that the Commonwealth can legislate for the people of any special race, but for some curious reason makes an express exception of the Australian aborigines. They are to be left to the States'. In arguing for Commonwealth power, Evatt made the same argument reformers had put: 'Few will deny that the care and welfare of the Australian aborigines should, in principle, be a national responsibility'. The Attorney-General realised that the lack of Commonwealth powers was an anomaly which would be seen to be all the greater in the post-war years when Australia assumed 'special responsibilities towards the native peoples of the South-West Pacific', including those of New Guinea (see document 12, pp. 98).[16] It is apparent that that the federal government now felt more sensitive to international criticism of Australia's treatment of its own Indigenous people. In its case to the electors the government asserted that the Commonwealth had to further 'humanitarian development' in order for Australia 'to live up to the principles of the Atlantic Charter'.[17]

The parliamentary opposition, led by Robert Menzies, lent its support to the particular proposal with regard to Aborigines (see document 12, p. 98), but this was somewhat of a pretence as it was opposed to the extension of Commonwealth power generally. The referendum was supported by only 2 million of the 4.3 million votes cast, and a majority of votes was achieved in only two states (South Australia and Western Australia). It was defeated, it has been argued, partly because all fourteen changes proposed were presented in one package and so the electors were unable to vote on each particular measure.[18]

In the years immediately after the war, constitutional change in regard to Aboriginal affairs continued to find advocates. In June 1945 the National Missionary Council and the Association for the Protection of Native Races had urged Prime Minister Ben Chifley to adopt 'a National Policy for Aboriginal Welfare under the control of the Commonwealth Government' (see document 13, pp. 98–9). Other organisations issued similar appeals. They met with a sympathetic response from Minister for the Interior HV Johnson.[19] At the 1946 Premiers conference he presented the case for 'the principle of unified control', arguing that there was 'a responsibility that Australia owes to this race and a responsibility that we have, without doubt, never fully accepted'. However, Chifley was apprehensive that the Commonwealth would have 'a problem child on [its] hands'. Nor was Johnson able to persuade the state Premiers to endorse a greater Commonwealth role. Consequently, in the referendum proposals put to the electorate later that year, federal control of Aboriginal affairs was omitted.[20] This prompted one frustrated campaigner, Gillespie Douglas, President of the Aborigines Uplift Society, to charge that 'the ministry as a whole is...apathetic or hostile to the idea of taking over the burden of the Aborigines throughout Australia'.[21]

In the late 1940s Aboriginal organisations, such as the Aborigines Progressive Association, now led by Bill Ferguson, and the Australian Aborigines' League, now under the leadership of Doug Nicholls and Bill Onus, continued to call for federal control of Aboriginal affairs and citizenship rights for Aborigines, while federal Labor parliamentarian Kim Beazley snr pressed Chifley to hold a referendum to give the Commonwealth greater powers in Aboriginal affairs.[22] In the early 1950s an attempt to form a national organisation to fight for Aboriginal rights finally bore fruit when the Council for Aboriginal Rights was founded in Melbourne,[23] and it began to push for an overthrow of laws contravening the United Nations' Universal Declaration of Human Rights (see document 14, pp. 99–100). The winds of change in race matters were beginning to blow more strongly. However, a push for constitutional reform to achieve change in Aboriginal affairs awaited a concerted campaign.

# 3 The Federal Council for Aboriginal Advancement and Constitutional Change

Calls for the Commonwealth to assume responsibility for Aboriginal affairs all but disappeared from public discussion in the course of the 1950s. When they returned, however, they were closely connected, as they had been in the 1930s and 1940s, with calls for citizenship rights for Aboriginal people. This led to a campaign in which a move to federal control, the repeal of racial discriminatory laws and the securing of citizenship rights came to be regarded by many campaigners as a series of reforms which naturally belonged together. Most particularly it came to be assumed that amendment of the Australian Constitution was necessary in order to realise these changes and that it would necessarily lead to these changes. Indeed, the case for constitutional change came to be plotted in this way so often that it came to be simply accepted as common sense by many campaigners and their supporters.

The well-known socialist and feminist campaigner Lady Jessie Street was largely responsible for construing the matter of constitutional change in this way, and this influenced other campaigners, among whom was Faith Bandler. (Bandler has come to be the foremost public narrator of the story of the 1967 referendum and has come to be regarded by many as one of the leading advocates for change.)[1] How and why did this happen? In 1954 Street, living in London, had joined the Anti-Slavery Society as its Australian representative, and in 1956 she urged it to take a case to the United Nations Commission on Human Rights regarding the treatment of 'Australian Aborigines' as a minority people. In order to gather information for this she drew up a questionnaire on Aboriginal conditions and prepared to visit Australia to conduct a survey.

Soon after her arrival in Sydney in December 1956, a major controversy broke in the eastern states regarding the plight of Aboriginal people in the Warburton Ranges in Central Australia. They had been

Jessie Street, returning to Australia in December 1956 for several months, reactivated the campaign for constitutional change. She is pictured here with her husband, Sir Kenneth Street (obscured), Chief Justice of New South Wales. (Courtesy *Sydney Morning Herald*)

driven off their lands as a result of the Commonwealth government's decision to allow the British government to test atomic bombs in the area.[2] Two months previously, Bill Grayden, an Independent Liberal MLA, had persuaded the Western Australian parliament to appoint a select committee to inquire into their conditions, and in December it had released a report deploring what it had found. Adelaide churchman Charles Duguid, Shirley Andrews of the Council for Aboriginal Rights, Doug Nicholls and Bill Onus of the Australian Aborigines' League, Doris Blackburn and Anna Vroland of the Women's International League of Peace and Freedom, Brian Fitzpatrick of the Council for Civil Liberties, and members of the Communist Party of Australia soon added their voice in protest. In January 1957, a 'Save the Aborigines' committee was formed in Melbourne, which organised a large public meeting the following month. This passed several resolutions among which was a demand that 'full human rights be guaranteed the remaining Aboriginal tribes' and a demand for a referendum 'to ensure that the native people of Australia become a Commonwealth responsibility'.[3]

Shortly afterwards Grayden led another parliamentary group to the Warburton Ranges. Nicholls joined this expedition and was dismayed by what he witnessed: 'I wish I hadn't seen the pitiable squalor, the sights of my people starving — the most shocking sights I have ever seen. Never, never can I forget'.[4] The expedition shot a film in order to document the appalling state of the Aboriginal people they encountered. It had a profound impact when it was screened in public meetings and on television soon afterwards.[5] One newspaper editor called it 'the most horrible film made in Australia'.[6] For some, the

# WE WANT TO STOP THIS:

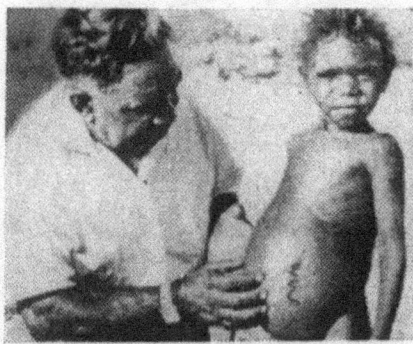 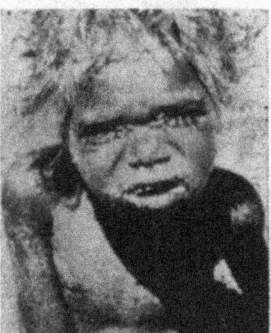

Pastor Nicholls, M.B.E., examining a child on the Warburton Reserve.

Flies! But too weak to bother.

# HELP US—TO HELP THEM!

A leaflet produced by the newly formed Victorian Aborigines Advancement League used these images from the film shot in the Warburton Ranges in February 1957. One journalist observed upon seeing the film which was called 'Manslaughter' when it was screened in television: 'You can read about it without feeling anything much except wonder that such conditions exist; but you can't see it without realising the horror of it...There was a child...so weak that he could not brush from his face the flies that were crawling over it in their thousands. Flies in his eyes, in his nose, in his mouth, his whole face a moving mass of flies...If I hadn't seen it I wouldn't have believed it. And the child with the distended, enormous stomach of beri-beri...I have seen nothing more shocking, nothing more damning, than this film.' (Courtesy VAAL) images were reminiscent of what they had seen in newsreels of Nazi concentration camps such as Bergen-Belsen. In the case of several of Prime Minister Robert Menzies' constituents, they were moved to register their 'horror, concern and shame at the appalling plight of the original Australians', and to demand that 'the government do something about this disgraceful blot on our national conscience at once'.[7]

In the light of the Warburton crisis, Street was convinced that the time was ripe to press the Commonwealth government for change. Writing to Thomas Fox-Pitt, the secretary of the Anti-Slavery Society, in the first week of March, she told him:

> This is the psychological moment as far as considering measures for the treatment of aborigines is concerned. The Grayden report of the Parliamentary Select Committee in West Australia has received great publicity throughout the commonwealth and there is wide public feeling that some thing should be done to ameliorate conditions.[8]

Street believed that constitutional change was required in order to effect this. In the letter to Fox-Pitt we have just quoted she immediately went on to tell him:

> Almost without exception, the people whom I have spoken to believe that the aborigines who are living near civilisation and who are subject to our laws, should be given full citizen rights and treated on equal terms with white Australians. This, of course, would require an amendment to the Constitution which specifically excludes aborigines from the enjoyment of the rights and the application of laws and regulations which apply to other Australians.[9]

In the first half of the twentieth century the legal rights of Aboriginal people were severely limited by racially discriminatory Commonwealth and state legislation that had been enacted over many decades, beginning in the mid-nineteenth century in southeastern Australia. Although there was considerable variation between the states and within states at the whim of local administrators and officials, there was much that was common across Australia: the majority of the Aboriginal people could not vote; receive social welfare such as the old-age pension and unemployment benefits; move freely from place to place; choose their place of residence; make basic decisions concerning their own lives such as where to work, what to do with their earnings and any property they acquired, and whom they might marry; and act as the legal guardians of their children.[10] As we have noted, though, the basis of this racial discrimination was *not* to be found in the text of the Constitution.

Several letters written by Street in March 1957 reveal that she had undoubtedly misunderstood the nature of the Australian Constitution — it made no reference to the rights of any Australian citizens — and that she was clearly mistaken about the sections pertaining to Aboriginal people — 51 (xxvi) and 127. The day after she wrote to Fox-Pitt, she penned a letter to Fitzpatrick in which she recollected that there were 'two articles of the Constitution' regarding Aborigines, 'one which precludes aborigines from citizenship in Australia and the other I think which vests control of the aborigines in the individual States'. (An anthropologist Fred Rose had told her of the constitutional references to Aboriginal people but he had misled her or she had misunderstood what he had told her.)[11] Street also told Fitzpatrick of her plans to discuss with Minister for the Territories Paul Hasluck 'the holding of a referendum to vest powers over aborigines in the Commonwealth Parliament and to make aborigines eligible for all rights to which white Australians are now eligible'.[12] Fitzpatrick provided Street with the relevant sections of the Constitution but this seems to have made little if any difference to her approach to the matter. After a meeting with Hasluck she told Fox-Pitt and Andrews: 'I discussed with him the possibility of a referendum to amend the Constitution to vest powers over all the aborigines with the Commonwealth Parliament, and to extend all legal rights as enjoyed by the white population to the aborigines'.[13]

Street claimed Hasluck was favourably disposed to her suggestion of a referendum (see document 15, p. 100). There are several reasons to doubt this (see document 18, pp. 101–2). As far as section 127 was concerned, he saw no value in troubling oneself about 'the meaning and intention of an obscure section of the Constitution'; and as far as section 51 (xxvi) was concerned, he claimed that government had all the powers it needed to address the needs of Aboriginal people. Hasluck would have realised that Street's take on section 51 (xxvi) was not strictly correct as far as the powers of the Commonwealth were concerned. The Commonwealth did not have power under the Constitution to pass 'special laws' in regard to Aboriginal people qua Aborigines, but it *did* have powers insofar as it could pass general laws that applied to Aborigines in respect of their status as Australian subjects. It would soon use this power to pass legislation in order to enable Aboriginal people (except those who were 'nomadic' or 'primitive') to receive a range of federal social welfare benefits to which other Australians had long been entitled.

This said, Hasluck would have been sympathetic to Street's call for a greater federal role in Aboriginal affairs. More to the point, he might have grasped the logic of her call to amend section 51 (xxvi) as a way of achieving this: the Northern Territory excepted, the states had been responsible for Aboriginal affairs since federation and it was frequently claimed that the Commonwealth could not intervene in Aboriginal affairs because of the existence of section 51 (xxvi). Strictly speaking, this interpretation of the Constitution was erroneous but it had acquired the power of a convention and so was simply accepted. Given this, it might be argued that it was unremarkable that Street assumed that amendment of this particular section of the Constitution was necessary in order to enable the Commonwealth to assume greater responsibility for Aboriginal affairs. The controversy over the Warburton Ranges added force to this assumption as it had been claimed by authoritative figures that the Commonwealth could not intervene in this crisis because its hands were tied by the Constitution.[14] In 1956 the Western Australian Commissioner of Native Welfare, SG Middleton, had told Street 'Yet our very Federal Constitution prevents our National Government from taking any legislative measures whatever in relation to the majority of them' and went on to quote section 51 (xxvi) of the Constitution.[15]

It is important to note, however, that other reformers did not accept that constitutional change was necessary in order for the Commonwealth to play a greater role in Aboriginal affairs. In June 1958 AP Elkin, once a supporter of constitutional change (see document 11, pp. 96–7) but now rather complacent about the changes he and other reformers had helped to secure in Aboriginal affairs, told a group of campaigners who had been greatly influenced by the account Street had given of the Constitution and Aboriginal matters: 'Having had a long experience in these matters, I don't think that it is of much concern whether the Constitution is altered or not. The good work will go on and legal obstacles will be overcome in administration and with good sense'.[16]

It is much harder to make sense of the connection that Street continued to make between constitutional change and citizenship rights, given that the Constitution made no reference to either citizenship or rights. It might be argued that the logic of the story Street came to tell ran along these lines: citizenship was not only a matter of civil rights determined by legal arrangements but of social and economic rights that were usually determined by political arrangements, and she held the latter to be the most important; Aboriginal people suffered social and economic disabilities and these could best be redressed by the Commonwealth but the Constitution apparently barred it from playing a greater role in Aboriginal affairs; if the Constitution was amended, the Commonwealth could assume greater responsibility, the social and economic disabilities would be overturned, and Aboriginal people would become citizens in effect.[17] This is to suggest that Street came to accept that the Constitution made no reference to citizenship in a formal sense but that she persisted in casting constitutional change in terms of 'citizenship' and 'rights' because she presumed they would gain the economic and social rights associated with being a citizen once the Commonwealth assumed greater power in Aboriginal affairs, and/or because she knew that 'citizenship' was a powerful tool in a symbolic sense.

This explanation of why Street connected changes to the Constitution to the granting of citizenship or rights to Aboriginal people makes sense but it overlooks the fact that Street continued to assert that the Constitution *did* make reference to citizenship in its provisions and that these barred Aboriginal people from those rights. In September 1959 Hasluck had to correct her on this matter by pointing out that Aboriginal people were citizens in a formal (though, he admitted, meaningless) sense by dint of the 1948 Nationality and Citizenship Act (see document 20, p. 103), which had conferred the status of citizen automatically on all born in Australia but without bestowing any rights on these citizens; two years later she wrote to the Minister again: 'I suggest that you give consideration to holding a referendum to give all aborigines in any part of Australia full citizen rights'; in February 1963 she informed Fox-Pitt: 'the Australian Aborigine and all who are registered as such…are deliberately excluded by the Commonwealth from having any political rights'; and several months later in a letter to Shirley Andrews and others she made reference to the Constitution in these terms: 'Section 51 (Clause xxvi) and Section 127…specifically deprive Aborigines of the status and rights of citizens'.[18]

Narratives are often created in order to make sense of something — to account for 'how the world is' — and they tend to succeed or fail according to whether they are perceived to perform this work by the story teller or/and their audience. A good narrative commonly leads to the suspension of disbelief, and its credibility does not hinge upon whether it is correct or incorrect on matters of fact. There is a deep-seated human will to believe, and the sincerity and competence of a storyteller counts for much.[19] In this case, Street's narrative, first created in the absence of a copy of the Constitution, made sense: it seemed to provide a satisfactory explanation of why Aboriginal people were denied citizenship rights and why the Commonwealth was unable to do more in Aboriginal affairs; there was no doubt about her commitment to the cause, and she certainly had authority. Indeed, Lady Jessie Street was something of a steamroller, according to her biographer, Peter Sekuless. She brooked no contradiction. 'Well, there you are girl, go and get yourself a referendum', she told Bandler.[20]

In April 1957 Street, Fitzpatrick and a lawyer, Christian Jollie Smith, worked together on a petition that called for a referendum to alter the Constitution. In a copy of a draft Street had drawn up beforehand, which has since won fame as a result of an account Bandler has repeatedly given,[21] there is a preamble in which Street once more expressed her peculiar understanding of the Constitution:

> Believing that many of the difficulties encountered today by aborigines arise from the discriminations against them in two Sections of the Commonwealth Constitution which specifically exclude aborigines from the enjoyment of the rights and privileges enjoyed by all other Australians whatever their country of origin.[22]

Fitzpatrick, if not Jollie Smith, would have realised that this statement was incorrect. The preamble was redrafted so it read:

> THE HUMBLE PETITION OF the Electors of the State of New South Wales respectfully sheweth — The Aboriginal Residents of Australia suffer under disabilities political, social and economic, and that these in important respects are not remediable without Amendment of the Constitution of the Commonwealth, and that Aborigines are entitled to human rights equally with other Australians.[23]

If the petition (see document 16, pp. 100–1) thrust upon the Aboriginal-Australian Fellowship, which had recently been formed in Sydney by Pearl Gibbs, Bert Groves and Faith Bandler, merely implied a causal relationship between constitutional change on the one hand and federal control, the end of racial discrimination and citizenship for Aboriginal people on the other, this imaginary chain of events was explicated in an explanatory leaflet drafted by Jollie Smith. In a sense, this told the same story about the relationship between Commonwealth control, reform in Aboriginal affairs and the protection of Aboriginal rights that had been told by campaigners for some time, but it assumed a particularly simple form here as a consequence of Street's distinctive take on the Constitution (see document 17, p. 101).

The Aboriginal-Australian Fellowship's petition was launched on 29 April 1957 at a meeting held in the Sydney Town Hall. An estimated 1500 people attended this. Many were Aboriginal, perhaps as many as a third. Nicholls was in the chair. Onus and Groves, the poet Dame Mary Gilmore, Labor MHR Eddie Ward, and secretary of the Australian Workers' Union Tom Dougherty were among those who spoke; Aboriginal singers Harold Blair and Nancy Ellis performed; and the Warburton Ranges film was screened. The meeting was hailed as a huge success. A little more than a fortnight later, the first of many petitions calling for a referendum to change the Constitution was presented to the House of Representatives by Labor MP Les Haylen.[24]

Over the next several months, Street, Duguid, Andrews and Victorian Aborigines Advancement League secretary Stan Davey planned a conference in order to found a national organisation to campaign for Aboriginal rights. (This had been envisaged by some reformers for ten or more years.) The meeting took place in Adelaide in February 1958.[25] The Federal Council for Aboriginal Advancement was to become the most important force in the campaign for constitutional change. At its founding, it was an organisation whose leadership largely comprised white men and women, most of whom were socialists or Christians, though its membership was relatively diverse politically.[26]

At the outset, the organisation adopted several principles which it described as 'the basis for a common policy for the advancement of aborigines throughout the Commonwealth'. The guiding philosophy

Four Aboriginal men were among the 26 people who attended the conference which created the Federal Council for Aboriginal Advancement in February 1958. Pictured here (left to right), Jeff Barnes, Doug Nicholls and Bert Groves represented South Australia, Victoria and New South Wales respectively. Bill Onus was an observer. (Courtesy *Advertiser*)

of the Council was non-discrimination and its first principle, which its founders obviously regarded as primary, was 'Equal citizenship with other Australian citizens'. To attain this goal, it was agreed that the organisation's affiliates, which were state-based organisations (such as the Council for Aboriginal Rights and the Aboriginal-Australian Fellowship), would focus on calls for two particular changes. These were reported shortly afterwards in the Victorian Aborigines Advancement League's magazine, *Smoke Signals*, in this way: '(1) For the repeal of all legislation, both Federal and State, which discriminates against the aborigine. (2) For the amendment of the Federal Constitution to give the Commonwealth power to legislate for aborigines as for other citizens'.[27] The former reveals that the organisation's founders realised that the basis of discriminatory laws lay in federal and state legislation; the latter, however, might suggest that they did not grasp the nature of the legislative powers the Commonwealth already had according to the Constitution, namely the power to pass 'general laws' laws rather than 'special laws' in respect of Aboriginal people.

The original minutes of the conference, which do not seem to have been reported publicly at the time, might shed some light on why the Council's founders were calling for constitutional change. The relevant section reads:

> Amendment to the Commonwealth Constitution to give the Commonwealth power to legislate for Aborigines as with all other citizens and because of their special disabilities legislation on the lines of the rehabilitation scheme to be enacted to assist integration of the Aboriginal people, in the interim 'special disabilities' grants to Aboriginal welfare.[28]

This is a rather confused or confusing formulation. Nevertheless, it might be argued that 'special disabilities legislation' was a reference to the clause (section 51 (xxvi)) that gave the Commonwealth power to enact 'special laws' for races other than Aborigines, and that the Commonwealth's 'special disabilities legislation on the lines of the rehabilitation scheme' was a reference to the Commonwealth using its power to enact 'special laws' for returned servicemen, which is to say that it amounted to a call for the Commonwealth to have the same kind of power to pass legislation specific to another group of Australians, namely Aborigines.[29] It is difficult to be really sure that this is what these reformers meant, though.

The murky nature of the demands for constitutional change probably owes much to fact that it was very difficult at this time for reformers to advance, or perhaps even conceptualise, legal provisions or legislative measures that discriminated in *favour* of racial groups such as Aboriginal people. It was an age of fervent anti-racism in which a doctrine of universal inclusion, called 'assimilation', reigned supreme.[30] Consequently, laws that distinguished or differentiated between people on the basis of race were seen as necessarily bad: necessarily because laws made on this basis had been conceived and implemented in the past in order to discriminate *against* Aborigines, and it was these racist laws that reformers hated and wanted to overthrow. In this context it is not surprising that campaigners invariably cast their demand for Aboriginal advancement by calling on government to treat Aborigines in the same way as other Australians were treated. This is to say that these campaigners tended to conceive of equality for Aboriginal people as an ideal that would be realised by governments applying *non*-racial principles and treating everyone the same, rather than by their applying principles that treated people of 'the aboriginal race' differently. The Federal Council's slogan of 'Equal citizenship rights with other Australians' tended to constraint any formulation of an approach which sought to make distinctions between people on the grounds of race.

Soon after its founding, the organisational apparatus of the Council was established in Melbourne. It remained there for the next ten years and relied on the work of Labor MHR Gordon Bryant, Andrews, Davey (who became the Council's secretary), and Council for Aboriginal Rights president Barry Christopher. They took over responsibility for the campaign for constitutional change begun by the Aboriginal-Australian Fellowship, and drew up another petition. Like the members of the Aboriginal-Australian Fellowship and earlier advocates of constitutional change, these spokespersons saw a greater Commonwealth role as *the* prerequisite for realising change in Aboriginal affairs: as the government which represented Australia in the eyes of the world and which had the greatest resources, it was the means of ending racial discrimination and overcoming racial inequality. These reformers also posited a relationship between constitutional change, Commonwealth responsibility for Aboriginal affairs and the amelioration of Aboriginal people's disadvantage, but they shed Street's claim of a relationship between constitutional amendment and rights or citizenship for Aborigines (see document 19, pp. 102–3).

In the course of 1958 the Federal Council gathered nearly 26,000 signatures on this petition, which Bryant presented to the federal parliament.[31] In the same year a joint parliamentary committee on Constitution review decided that section 127 be deleted (on the grounds that it was liable to be misconstrued overseas as racially discriminatory);[32] and the following year the Australian Labor Party's federal conference adopted the alteration of section 51 (xxvi) and the removal of section

President of the Victorian Aborigines Advancement League and Labor MHR, Gordon Bryant was one of the key Federal Council leaders and played a major role in all its campaigns for a referendum. He was apparently drawn to the Aboriginal cause after seeing the Warburton Ranges film. (Courtesy VAAL)

127 as the party's policy. Over the next few years ALP frontbencher Kim Beazley snr and his younger colleague Bryant kept the issue of constitutional change before parliament, calling in particular for a referendum on section 51 (xxvi) (see document 22, pp. 104–5).

In the early 1960s, historians Sue Taffe and Jennifer Clark have observed, it became apparent to the Commonwealth government that there was a surging interest in Australia's race politics, particularly its Aboriginal ones: the Soviet Union was championing decolonisation abroad, the new African nations were paying attention to the plight of the colonised elsewhere in the world, African and Asian nations now constituted an important bloc in the United Nations, and the international body served as a forum to air matters of race and racism. Australia was getting bad press. In particular, questions were being asked about the civil rights of the Indigenous people here. Aboriginal affairs could no longer be regarded as merely a domestic matter; it was now an international one. Since the nation state was held responsible for the treatment of Indigenous people, it became increasingly clear that the fact that responsibility for Aboriginal affairs largely lay in the hands of the states and not the Commonwealth was a serious problem. Calls for a greater Commonwealth role were made from a growing number of quarters.[33]

In the course of the 1960s, the political scientist and historian John Chesterman has observed, both international pressure and domestic activism led Commonwealth and state governments to grant civil rights to Aboriginal people. Indeed, these forces fed one another: the growing interest in Aboriginal affairs abroad was exploited by local campaigners and their work raised international awareness of the Aboriginal situation.[34] This was to prove a crucial factor in the fight for constitutional change.

# 4 The 1962–3 Petition Campaign

In 1962 affiliates of the Federal Council for Aboriginal Advancement pressed the organisation at its annual conference to take up the matter of constitutional change again. It was agreed that it should conduct a more ambitious petition campaign for a referendum as part of 'a comprehensive Action Programme' to advance the Aboriginal cause. In deciding upon this strategy, the Federal Council had several aims. It wanted to publicise the basic principles underpinning its work but it especially wanted to put the legal discrimination Aboriginal people suffered 'more clearly before the public' in order to persuade Australians of the need for reform in Aboriginal affairs. To this end, it published a leaflet that listed the legal disabilities Aboriginal people suffered in the mainland states and the Northern Territory:[1]

**Rights enjoyed by Aborigines on settlements & reserves in five States & the Northern Territory**

|  | NSW | VIC | SA | WA | NT | QLD |
|---|---|---|---|---|---|---|
| Voting rights (State) | Y | Y | Y | N | Y | N |
| Marry freely | Y | Y | Y | N | N | N |
| Control own children | Y | Y | N | N | N | N |
| Move freely | Y | N | N | N | N | N |
| Own property freely | Y | N | Y | N | N | N |
| Receive Award wages | Y | N | N | N | N | N |
| Alcohol allowed | N | N | N | N | N | N |

The Council's campaign was co-ordinated in Melbourne by a petition committee comprising the Council's most important white leaders: Shirley Andrews, Gordon Bryant, Barry Christophers and Stan Davey. They all had a sound grasp of the implications of the constitutional changes the Council was seeking. This was apparent in their consideration of section 51 (xxvi). The campaign committee considered a proposal to recommend the repeal of this clause, just as Jessie Street had originally recommended,[2] which would have removed the Commonwealth's power to 'make laws for the peace, order and good government of the Commonwealth with respect to the people of any race other than the aboriginal race in any state for whom it is deemed necessary to make special laws', but it opted instead to call for its amendment through the deletion of the words 'other than the aboriginal race in any state'.[3] What was the Council's rationale for retaining this section of the Constitution given that they knew that original intent of those who had framed it was racist in the sense that it was to be used to discriminate against non-white peoples? By amending rather than repealing section 51 (xxvi), the Council leaders believed, the Commonwealth would be able to introduce special laws that would discriminate in *favour* of Aboriginal people. As Bryant put it, the Commonwealth could pass legislation that would 'give special benefits and assistance to Aborigines without depriving them of their basic rights'.[4] This call for special rights was obviously more emphatic than the ambiguous articulation of such a right at the Federal Council's founding conference just a few years earlier.

Andrews, who assumed the greatest burden in running this campaign, was initially opposed to the petition campaign since she believed that it distracted the Federal Council from more important matters. As she told Street in June 1962: 'It seems to me to be putting the cart before the horse to be concentrating exclusively on the legal aspects of discrimination and ignoring the economic ones'.[5] At much the same time she confided to fellow Communist Party member Brian Manning: 'If all Aborigines become full citizens overnight, and they were not entitled to any special financial aid, they would be expected to start from a position behind the lowest paid of other workers'.[6] In other words, Andrews saw repealing discriminatory laws and thus winning 'equal rights' for Aboriginal people as only the first step in Aboriginal advancement. She was only able to reconcile herself to the onerous work she performed for the petition campaign by regarding it as part of a broader campaign for 'social justice' for Aboriginal people and by pressing the case for the federal government enacting 'special Aboriginal legislation' to meet the needs of Aborigines as an oppressed group of people.[7]

The Federal Council realised that it had to justify a demand that obviously amounted to a call for special rights for Aboriginal people rather than just the same rights that other Australians enjoyed. Whereas the latter was grounded in a universal and non-racial principle and entitlement to those same rights was due to any individual who was a member of the group called the Australian nation, the former was

Shirley Andrews, who largely played a backroom role in the Federal Council's work, performed a large share of the organisation's work in its 1962–3 petition campaign. (Courtesy Sue Taffe)

grounded in a principle that distinguished between people on the basis of race and entitlement to those special rights was due only to those who were members of the group called the Aboriginal race. In presenting its demand for special rights, the Council appealed to international conventions, in particular the principles of the International Labor Organisation convention on Indigenous peoples. This, Andrews explained, 'advocate[d] a completely equal status [for Aborigines] with other sections of the population and, at the same time, such special measures as are required for "promoting the social, economic and cultural develop-ment of these populations and raising their standard of living"' (see document 25, pp. 108–9). More often than not, though, the Federal Council's leaders referred to national practices instead, in particular the provision of special grants to returned servicemen and women. The Commonwealth Repatriation Act, Bryant argued, was 'a good working model' for legislation 'to cater for the special needs' of Aboriginal people. This was a sensible ploy in a community that honoured, more than anyone else, those who had fought in overseas wars.[8]

For the most part, however, the emphasis in the Federal Council's petition campaign was upon Aboriginal people being treated the same as other Australians. Apart from the assumption that this was necessary in order to win the support of settler Australians, calls for special laws for Aboriginal people troubled some of the Council's Aboriginal leaders. In their experience, 'special laws' stood for racism, inequality and inferiority. They looked forward to the day they were no longer under special Aboriginal legislation they called 'the Act'. Andrews sought to reassure them that the special legislation the Council had in mind could advantage them (see document 25, pp. 108–9).

Although the members of the Federal Council's petition committee knew the precise legal meaning of the constitutional changes they were demanding, they simplified the complex matters at stake when it came to representing these to the public, especially in their most widely distributed material. In part, this approach was required because political campaigns require a simplification of the issues, in part because the matters at stake were especially complicated because of the varying state and territory policies and practices.[9] This, however, does not change the fact that they simplified matters in a particular way. First, they cast both the clauses of the Constitution that were exclusionary in reference to Aboriginal people (section 51 (xxvi) and section 127) as discriminatory (see document 23, pp. 105–6), even though in the former case Aboriginal people were not encompassed by the special powers bestowed on the Commonwealth to enact discriminatory laws against non-white races. (Arguably, this claim was a function of the continuing influence of liberal anti-racism: any sign of a people not been treated the same as another was cast as an example of racial discrimination.) Second, they cast the changes as a move 'Towards Equal Citizenship for Aborigines' (see illustration p. 31). And third, they asserted that the Commonwealth had no power to make laws in regard to Aboriginal people (see document 23, pp. 105–6), and that a change in the Constitution would transfer responsibilities to the Commonwealth (see document 24, pp. 106–8). Some campaigners repeated Street's claims. For example, Faith Bandler asserted that the constitutional changes would give Aboriginal people 'full citizenship rights and nothing less'. This implied that citizenship rights were simply a function of the changes to the Constitution the campaigners demanded.[10] Some Council spokespersons (such as Bandler) probably accepted Street's account of constitutional change and repeated it unknowingly, others (such as the petition committee members) probably accepted and repeated it knowing that 'citizenship' and 'the Australian nation' were words that moved hearts and minds.

The campaign for a referendum was launched at a meeting in Sydney in October 1962. Aboriginal speakers were given top billing since the Council wanted to raise their profile and increase the participation of Aboriginal people in its work. They included representatives of most states or territories, among whom were Federal Council President

## National Petition

## TOWARDS EQUAL CITIZENSHIP FOR ABORIGINES

TO THE HONORABLE THE SPEAKER AND MEMBERS OF THE HOUSE OF REPRESENTA-
TIVES IN PARLIAMENT ASSEMBLED:—

The Petition of the undersigned citizens of the Commonwealth respectfully showeth:—

THAT, in view of the fact that the Commonwealth Constitution discriminates against the Aboriginal people
in two Sections (as set out below), it thereby limits their right to "peace, order and good Government
under the Commonwealth Parliament", and

THAT such discriminations in effect give support to other laws and regulations which deprive Aborigines of
equal wages and employment opportunities and deny them the right to own and develop their
remaining tribal lands, and

THAT they have an inferior legal status compared with other citizens of the Commonwealth.

Your petitioners humbly pray that the Commonwealth Government remove Section 127 and the discriminatory
words in Section 51 (as underlined), by the holding of a referendum at an early date.

And your petitioners, as in duty bound, will ever pray.

| Name | Address |
|------|---------|
|  |  |

*Section 51:* "The Parliament shall, subject to this Constitution, have power to make laws for the peace, order and good
Government of the Commonwealth with respect to:—

*Clause xxvi:* "The people of any race, **other than the aboriginal race in any State,** for whom it is deemed necessary to
make special laws."

*Section 127:* "In reckoning the number of the people of the Commonwealth or of a State, or other part of the Commonwealth, aboriginal natives shall not be counted."

Authorised by Mr. Stan Davey, general secretary for the Federal Council for Aboriginal Advancement, on behalf of
34 affiliated organisations from all Australian States and Northern Territory.

The Petition should be returned to P.O. Box 59, Coburg, Victoria, by February 28th, 1963.

GREENSBOROUGH PRESS PTY. LTD., BEEWAR ST., GREENSBOROUGH.   JF 2065.

The petition drawn up by the Federal Council for Aboriginal Advancement in 1962 for its second
campaign for constitutional reform. (Courtesy AIATSIS)

Joe McGinness and three of its state or territory secretaries: Davis Daniels, Doug Nicholls and Kath Walker (who changed her name to Oodgeroo Noonuccal in 1988). The last named was made the campaign's national co-ordinator and undertook an Australia-wide speaking tour.[11] A broad range of bodies were approached to support the campaign: political parties, unions and labour councils, churches and religious bodies, service clubs, women's associations, sporting clubs, schools, and elderly citizens councils.[12] The petition committee set a target of 250,000 to 300,000 signatures but the campaign was limited by the Council's meagre funds. Nevertheless, it gathered an estimated 103,000 signatures in 94 separate petitions. It was able to present these to parliament in a more or less constant stream.[13] The Council felt sure that the campaign had resulted in a general public much better informed about the racial discrimination that Aboriginal people suffered.[14]

In September 1963, Prime Minister Robert Menzies agreed to a request, brokered by Bryant, to meet a Federal Council delegation and hear its plea for constitutional change. McGinness claimed later that they had received 'a very sympathetic hearing' but Andrews doubted it was more than smart 'public relations work' by a wily politician. After the meeting Menzies was rather surprised to be told he was breaking the law when he offered Walker a drink.[15] Bandler later claimed this

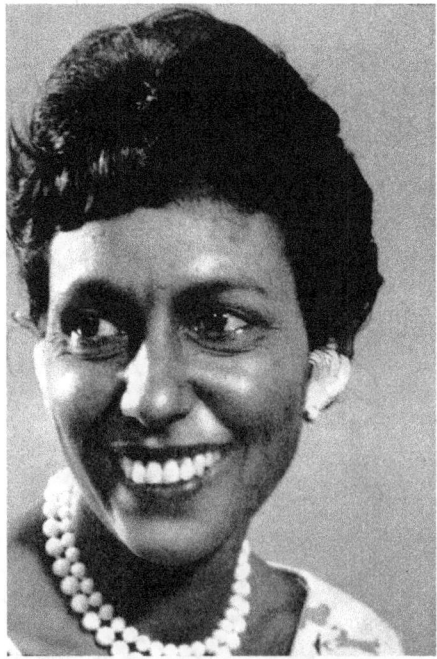

In 1962, Kath Walker addressed numerous meetings throughout Australia to promote the Federal Council for Aboriginal Advancement's campaign for constitutional change. (Courtesy VAAL)

was 'the turning point' in the campaign for constitutional change, a moment which prompted Menzies 'to give the situation of Aborigines more thought'.[16] (Bryant formed the same opinion.)[17] Yet, for the time being at any rate, the government refused to act.

The Australian Labor Party's leader, Arthur Calwell, was more sympathetic. In August 1964 he introduced a private member's bill to amend section 51 (xxvi) and repeal section 127. The debate reveals the range of reasons the Federal Council and its allies sought these changes and why others opposed change. Calwell largely made the case by focusing on how these two clauses were *perceived*. First, in respect of Aboriginal people he asserted in reference to section 51 (xxvi): 'These words [other than the aboriginal race in any State] are regarded by many aborigines as an insult, and, as they see the meaning of the words, they are entitled to their views'; and he argued in reference to section 127: 'our Constitution...protects our rights and liberties...but the aborigines do not share the rights'. Second, in respect of the international arena, he claimed these sections rendered Australia vulnerable to the charge of racial discrimination. In most of Calwell's speech, therefore, his call for constitutional change was in accordance with the principle of non-discrimination. At one point he asserted: 'Today, we regard the aboriginal as an Australian citizen, and any argument about his race is irrelevant'. Yet, at the close of the speech he seemed to reveal that he was aware that Aboriginal leaders had not embraced an assumption held by most anti-racist liberals, namely that the rejection of racial *discrimination* necessarily meant the rejection of racial *difference*. He stated:

> The aborigines are not a dying race; they are not being absorbed, or assimilated, however you like to describe it, and there are many educated and sophisticated aborigines who want to see their race preserved intact, who do not want it absorbed by the majority of Australians.

This recognition of Aboriginal people's sense of themselves as Aboriginal did not lead Calwell to make a case in his speech for constitutional change in terms of any principle that rested on racial differentiation, though remarks he made when he interrupted government speakers during the debate make it clear that he knew there was a demand to amend section 51 (xxvi) so that the Commonwealth could pass special racial laws to discriminate in a way that would benefit Aboriginal people.[18]

Kim Beazley snr, who had long been an advocate of constitutional change and was close to Bryant and the Federal Council, pressed this matter more overtly. He, too, made the case for constitutional change in terms of the way those clauses of the Constitution were regarded as discriminatory by Aboriginal people and by people around the world but he made it clear that he was not opposed to discrimination per se:

> It depends on the nature of the discrimination. Almost all our laws are discriminatory...The Repatriation Act is discriminatory because it legislates for a special category of persons with a special category of needs...I do not run away from the word 'discrimination' simply because most people construe the word as meaning hostile discrimination. I claim that aborigines have special needs.[19]

Beazley had spoken at the end of a debate in which government members had asserted their commitment to the programme of assimilation. They saw this as grounded in a non-racial principle. (They were, like most, oblivious to the fact that this programme aimed to absorb Aboriginal people into a community that was actually conceived in distinctively racial terms rather than universal terms since it assumed and asserted that white Australian ways were the norm everybody else should follow.) As such, they rejected any constitutional change that would mean Aboriginal people were treated differently or 'racially'. The Attorney-General Billy Snedden asserted:

> to remove the words [other than the aboriginal race] is to give the Commonwealth power to legislate throughout Australia for aborigines as a race. It is my view that this is contrary to Australian thinking, that there is no thinking in Australia which desires that the Commonwealth should have the power to legislate for the aboriginal race. I believe — and I think that the Australian people believe — that the aboriginal race should be assimilated in his status and that there should be no necessity for special laws for him...Even beneficial discrimination is discrimination. We want to move to the stage where there is no special legislation, whether it is beneficial or disadvantageous. We do not want to turn back the clock, and by taking those words out of placitum (xxvi) there would be a turning back of the clock.

Given this, Snedden rejected the claim that 'those words' were discriminatory. Similarly, he asserted that section 127 did not discriminate against Aboriginal people. He was prepared to concede that they gave offence, but held that there was no pressing need for a referendum to repeal this.[20] Constitutional change would have to wait.

# 5  The Coalition Government and the Demand for a Referendum

For many years the Menzies Coalition government resisted calls for a referendum to change the Constitution's provisions in reference to Aboriginal people. In 1965 it finally decided some action was necessary but it proposed the smallest of changes. In April that year, shortly after the Student Action for Aborigines' 'Freedom Ride' protest in country New South Wales had exposed racial discrimination to a degree no previous protest in Australia had done,[1] Prime Minister Robert Menzies informed the federal parliament that the government had decided to hold a referendum which would include a proposal to repeal section 127 though not one to amend section 51 (xxvi).[2] This provoked much public discussion: major newspapers supported changes to both sections, the organisation Abschol circulated a petition calling for the abolition of section 51 (xxvi), and the federal parliament debated the government's proposal.[3]

The Cabinet minutes reveal the inherently pragmatic approach of the government to the matter. In February 1965 Attorney-General Billy Snedden had submitted a proposal recommending a referendum to alter section 24 of the Constitution so as to change the number of senators relative to the number of members of the House of Representatives (which became known as the nexus issue). He believed it would be a mistake for the government to proceed with this unless it also put a proposed to repeal section 127. This was so, he told Cabinet, because public opinion in Australia had come to regard section 127 as racially discriminatory. He thought, moreover, that the inclusion of a question regarding section 127 would help the task of getting support for the government's proposal regarding section 24. In support of repealing section 127 he pointed out that the Constitutional Review Committee had recommended this several years previously; asserted that the original reasons for this section no longer held; argued that Aboriginal people should be counted as they now had the vote;

and suggested that it would win international approval. In respect of the last consideration, he observed: 'There would assuredly be international approbation of any move to repeal section 127, as it savours of racial discrimination. Its repeal could remove a possible source of misconstruction in the international field' (see document 26, pp. 109–11).[4] The Cabinet accepted Snedden's recommendation.[5]

In February Snedden's submission to Cabinet had also recommended that the government include in the referendum a proposal to amend section 51 (xxvi), by omitting those words 'other than the aboriginal race in any State'. Yet, it is evident that he had no interest in the Commonwealth acquiring a new legislative power as a consequence of this. Rather, he merely argued that this proposal should be included in the proposed referendum because its absence could prejudice the success of the other proposals. The public, he told Cabinet, had become convinced that this part of the Constitution was racially discriminatory. He himself rejected this construction of the section but implied the government had to accept that this had become a popular view. Snedden advanced no other substantive reason for proposing this constitutional change. Indeed, he informed his colleagues that it was very unlikely the government would want to use the new powers it would obtain by the amendment of this section of the Constitution (see document 26, pp. 109–11). The Cabinet rejected Snedden's recommendation as it did not accept the section was racially discriminatory.[6] The Attorney-General returned to the matter in August 1965, warning Cabinet that there would be much dissatisfaction if the government did not include a proposal for this change in the referendum: 'I believe the Government would be criticised, albeit mistakenly, for lacking sympathy for the aborigines... On the other hand, to delete the words would...meet the wishes of those making the representations and would appeal to the broad public conscience'. Cabinet once more rejected his submission.[7]

In November 1965 the government introduced a bill to provide for a referendum that comprised a proposal to amend section 24 and repeal section 127. In reference to the latter, the Prime Minister told parliament: 'the matter can be simply put by saying that section 127 is completely out of harmony with our national attitudes and with the elevation of the Aborigines into the ranks of citizenship which we all wish to see'. Menzies explained his government's decision to reject the calls to amend section 51 (xxvi) by omitting 'other than the Aboriginal race in any state' in much the same terms. First, he rejected the claim that this provision was discriminatory so far as Aboriginal people were concerned. Indeed, he regarded this as a curious interpretation of those words; in his opinion they protected Aborigines against racial discrimination. Second, he suggested that it would not be in the best interests of the Aboriginal people for the Commonwealth to have the power to pass 'special laws'. This was so because it would enable a federal government to create a body of laws that could deny Aboriginal people what other Australians had. Third, he argued that this amendment would be contrary to the goal of treating Aboriginal people the same as everyone else; in other words, it would undermine the programme of integrating Aborigines into the national community (see document 29, pp. 113–14).

The limited terms of the referendum proposed by the Coalition prompted Federal Council members from Melbourne, Sydney and Brisbane to descend on Canberra in November to press their case for constitutional change and to support a private member's bill a Liberal backbencher proposed to introduce in the federal parliament. WC Wentworth urged changes to the Constitution that had much the same purpose as those demanded by the Federal Council but they took a somewhat different form. He thought it was unwise to amend section 51 (xxvi) by omitting those words 'other than the Aboriginal race of any state'. First, he pointed out that this change did not stipulate whether the discriminatory laws should be favorable or adverse. As this might suggest, he was fearful this amendment would leave Aborigines vulnerable since the Commonwealth government would be able to make laws that discriminated against Aboriginal people. Second, Wentworth contended that this change might mean that the Commonwealth would acquire new responsibilities in Aboriginal affairs but its powers would merely be concurrent with those of the states. In view of these considerations, Wentworth recommended the repeal of section 51 (xxvi) and its replacement with a new section stipulating that the race power could only be used to pass laws for the advancement of Aboriginal people, and he proposed a new section be created in the Constitution in order to prohibit racial discrimination in Australia (see document 30, pp. 4–15).[8]

In the course of 1965–66, there was something of a shift in the principal reason the Federal Council for Aboriginal Advancement (now the Federal Council for the Advancement of Aborigines and Torres Strait Islanders) demanded constitutional change. They increasingly saw the amendment of section 51 (xxvi) in terms of it providing the Commonwealth with the power to discriminate in the favour of Aboriginal people rather in terms of providing the power to override the state laws which discriminated against them.[9]

In part this was a function of its recognition that the regime of racist legislation, both federal and state, had largely been dismantled.

In November 1965 activists from New South Wales joined Doug Nicholls and Kath Walker in 'a silent vigil' outside the federal parliament in order to press the case for constitutional change. They held placards pressing the Federal Council's call for constitutional change to help overcome racial discrimination and achieve equality. Here, they hold placards which read (left to right): 'Give us equality in all States: Include section 51 in the referendum'; 'Two sections discriminate: End the two'; 'Give us equal rights throughout Australia'; '1900-1965: Aborigines still unequal under Constitution'; 'Don't stop short of full equality: Amend section 51'; 'Justice... End discrimination now'; 'Aborigines a national question...'; 'Sections 127 and 51 discriminate: Referend 'em both'; 'Don't just count us: Let us count.' (Courtesy *Australian*)

In 1959 the Commonwealth had extended entitlement to pensions and unemployment and maternity allowances to all Aboriginal people except those classed as 'nomadic or primitive', and in 1966 this final discrimination was removed. In 1957 Victoria became the first mainland state to remove all forms of racial discrimination from its statutes when it repealed sections of the Licensing Act, which prohibited supply of alcohol to Aborigines, and sections of the Police Offences Act, under which it was an offence for a white person to 'wander or lodge in company with any of the Aboriginal natives of Victoria'. In 1963 New South Wales removed its last discriminatory laws, and in 1966 South Australia followed suit. This meant that only Queensland and Western Australia retained discriminatory laws at the time of the 1967 referendum. A large number of Aboriginal people still lived 'under the Act' in these states but even there some changes had taken place: Western Australia had given Aboriginal people the vote in 1962 and Queensland in 1965, though the latter reserved the right to strike someone off an electoral role whom they deemed to be incapable of exercising the vote.[10] Many of these changes owed much to the pressure the Federal Council had exerted on governments, as Chesterman among others has argued.[11]

The shifting emphasis within the Council's articulation of its demand for constitutional change was probably also facilitated by the Coalition government's take on the nature of the amendment the organisation proposed to the race power. Menzies' rejection of the

Federal Council's interpretation of the key phrase in section 51 (xxvi) as racially discriminatory, as well as his assertion that those words actually protected Aboriginal people against racial discrimination, seems to have prompted, even forced Council spokespersons such as Gordon Bryant to contemplate further how they might best represent the organisation's proposal to the electorate. At any rate, the Federal Council now had more reason to represent the Commonwealth's acquisition of the race power as a measure that would give it the power to discriminate for Aboriginal people (see document 27, pp. 111–12).

The Federal Council's Legislative Reform committee, which was initially chaired by Lorna Lippmann, was critical to the increasing emphasis the organisation placed on section 51 (xxvi) as a tool for positive discrimination.[12] In April 1965 it released 'Principles of Legislation for Aborigines and Torres Strait Islanders' which stated: 'Aborigines have suffered grave disabilities (segregation, wage and other discrimination, lack of education facilities)...Legislation must accept this fact and plan for special compensatory facilities'.[13] In the same month Bryant issued a leaflet in which he made the case for changing section 51 (xxvi) largely in these terms. He emphasised that the Commonwealth had the power to act in favour of other groups in the community but that it had no such power in respect of Aboriginal people: 'For the foreseeable future, the Commonwealth would be expected to DISCRIMINATE IN FAVOUR of the Aborigines by special beneficial legislation' (see document 27, pp. 111–12).

In February 1966 Lippmann conceded that a future government would be able, under the amendment the Federal Council sought, to pass laws discriminating against Aboriginal people. Aboriginal leaders such as Kath Walker were concerned enough about this to call for the repeal of section 51 (xxvi) (see document 28, p. 112). However, Lippmann argued that it was unlikely this nightmare would ever occur: 'The climate of public opinion is strongly against racial discrimination in Australia, and Commonwealth governments have shown themselves to be more susceptible to public opinion and better informed than are state governments'.[14] She none the less played safe by sending a circular letter to federal parliamentarians in which she cast the Federal Council's amendment as a measure that would enable the federal government to 'take positive steps to improve the lot of Aborigines and to negate discriminatory laws'.[15]

In the same month Lippmann presented to the Federal Council a petition calling for constitutional change that had been drawn up by a Labour MHR, AS Luchetti. After the Council agreed to endorse it, Barrie Pittock, who soon assumed the role of convenor

Lorna Lippmann (right), Shirley Andrews (middle) and Jessie Street (left) at one of the annual conferences of the Federal Council for Aboriginal Advancement held in Canberra. (Courtesy Sue Taffe)

of the Council's Legislative Reform, made some minor changes to its wording and began circulating the petition. Unlike the earlier Federal Council petitions, this only referred to section 51 (xxvi). It followed Wentworth's proposed legislation by calling for changes to be made in the Constitution in order to grant the Commonwealth power to make laws for the advancement of Aboriginal people and to prevent the making of laws discriminating against any Australian (see document 31, p. 136).[16]

In February 1966 the Coalition government decided it would not proceed with the referendum to amend section 24 and repeal section 127, though it had endorsed this move just a few months previously.[17] A month earlier Harold Holt had succeeded Menzies and he was determined to do some things differently in order to distinguish his prime ministership from his predecessor's. He soon overhauled Australia's racially discriminatory 'White Australia' policy and signed the United Nations International Accord for the Elimination of All

In June 1966, the Federal Council, Abschol and Student Action for Aborigines organised a protest in Sydney against the postponement in the constitutional referendum. Their emphasis differed from that of the Federal Council's Legislative Reform committee, which was led by Melbourne campaigners. The protestors distributed leaflets headed 'WHY ARE WE DEMONSTRATING', which read: 'Today, 30th June, is Census Day. Today the white population of Australia will be counted. But Aborigines are excluded from the Commonwealth Census by Section 127 of the Constitution: "In reckoning the numbers of the people of the Commonwealth or of a State or other part of the Commonwealth, Aboriginal natives shall not be counted". Why should the descendants of the original inhabitants of Australia suffer this insult? Because the referendum which was to remove this grave discrimination has not been held. Every fair-minded Australian must deplore this law. Please write to your Federal member protesting against the injustice of this provision and demand the referendum be held'. Pictured here are the Rev. George Garnsey, Faith Bandler, her daughter Lilon, and an unidentified woman protesting outside the Commonwealth Bank in Martin Place in Sydney. (Courtesy *Australian*)

Forms of Racial Discrimination. He seems to have been reluctant to proceed with a referendum that did not propose changes to section 51 (xxvi), all the more so perhaps because some churchmen and lawyers had pressed the case for amending section 51 (xxvi) in January and February and Wentworth's private member's bill had attracted much publicity since November the previous year. Yet, in March Holt informed Lippman that the government's position on the matter had not changed.[18]

In February 1967, however, the Holt government decided to proceed with a referendum that now included the proposal to amend section 51 (xxvi).[19] This did not reflect any fundamental change of heart. The previous month Attorney-General Nigel Bowen had presented much the same arguments for this course of action as his predecessor Billy Snedden had put: removing words in the Constitution 'alleged to be discriminatory against aboriginal people' would meet the demands of those 'urging action with respect to aborigines' and 'would be welcomed by a very large section of the Australian people'. Bowen made it clear that he was not proposing a new dispensation in the Commonwealth's approach to Aboriginal affairs: the government would not assume a greater administrative role in Aboriginal affairs but would just continue to play a role in formulating policy jointly with the states.[20] A key member of the Cabinet was nevertheless opposed. Charles Barnes foresaw the possibility that 'the Commonwealth would have to take to take responsibility for Aboriginal welfare throughout the Commonwealth...or be subjected to increasing criticism for not doing so'.[21]

The government decided to proceed but only on the basis of an agreement that the administration of Aboriginal affairs would remain in the hands of the states. A Cabinet minute reflects the government's lukewarm acceptance of the need to include the proposal to amend the race power:

> In deciding to adopt this further proposal [to amend section 51 (xxvi)], the Cabinet felt that, notwithstanding the original intention in inserting the words in question, which was to safeguard the position of people of Aboriginal race [sic], the words had been widely misinterpreted and there is a general impression that they are discriminatory. It took the view that if the referendum was carried the Commonwealth's role should not be to legislate itself but rather to participate with the States in the forming of policy.[22]

In presenting the proposal for the referendum to parliament Holt observed that the Coalition had been persuaded there was a popular and deeply rooted opinion that sections 51 (xxvi) and 127 of the Constitution were discriminatory and that it had decided to remove these so there would no grounds for any one to claim that racial discrimination continued to exist in Australia.[23] No doubt this was so. Yet, it seems evident that the government was once more intent on using the Aboriginal proposal in the referendum to bolster the chances of success for its proposal regarding the nexus issue. This political tactic did not escape the attention of observers at the time. The *Age* pointed out that two very different matters were being put in the one referendum and suggested that the government was 'hoping that support for an uncontentious proposal' would have 'a carry-over of Yes voters for the less popular one'.[24]

One cannot but conclude that the Coalition government's belated decision to go ahead with the referendum was a self-interested, even

"If they break the nexus between the Upper and the Lower Houses, will they rent one to us?"

This cartoon, published in the *Bulletin* a week before the referendum, drew attention to the government's preoccupation with the proposal to alter the ratio of members of the two houses of parliament rather than the proposal to alter the sections of the Constitution referring to Aborigines. It appeared alongside an editorial comment which concluded: 'We have been too tight-fisted in handling the special problems of the Aborigines, but, even more important, we have been too tight-minded.' (Courtesy *Bulletin* and Les Tanner)

cynical one. It wanted to maintain the status quo in Aboriginal matters, shore up its position at home and protect Australia's image abroad. During the campaign, Holt made it clear that his government had no plans to play a new role in Aboriginal affairs or take a new direction in Aboriginal policy, though he did pledge that were the race power to be used by the Commonwealth it would be to the advantage of Aboriginal people.[25] The government's lack of commitment to the true goals of the referendum is evident in its lacklustre campaigning.[26] In the Prime Minister's speech launching the 'yes' case only nine of 36 paragraphs, or approximately two of its ten minutes, were devoted to the Aboriginal issue (see document 41, pp. 124–5). The rest was reserved to spruik for the nexus issue. (This was in stark contrast to the speech that Calwell's successor as the leader of the Labor Party, Gough Whitlam, gave (see document 42, pp. 125–6).) The task of campaigning for a 'yes' vote on the Aboriginal proposal would clearly be left to others.

# 6 The Campaign for the 'Yes' Vote

The task of campaigning for a 'yes' vote for the Aboriginal question in the referendum on 27 May 1967 was primarily assumed by the Federal Council for the Advancement of Aborigines and Torres Strait Islanders, though it had considerable support from churches, the Labor Party and trade unions. It conducted the campaign in much the same terms as it had framed its 1962 petition campaign. In other words, it equated the constitutional changes proposed with the Commonwealth assuming a greater Commonwealth role in Aboriginal affairs, the overthrow of racially discriminatory laws and the winning of rights or citizenship for Aborigines. This was so even though by 1966 the vast bulk of racially discriminatory legislation had been repealed and most Aboriginal people had been granted the set of legal rights associated with citizenship. Why did the Federal Council and its allies represent the constitutional changes in this manner?

For some of the principal figures in the campaign it seems to have become an article of faith. Those such as Faith Bandler, the Federal Council's New South Wales campaign director, had been greatly impressed by Lady Jessie Street and profoundly influenced by her assertions about the provisions of the Constitution regarding Aborigines. It seems she and some of her fellow members in the Aboriginal-Australian Fellowship such as Jack Horner, took Street to be saying that these literally denied Aborigines citizenship rights, sanctioned racially discriminatory laws, and barred the Commonwealth from taking responsibility for Aboriginal affairs. They certainly spoke as though they did.

Alongside these figures' apparently limited grasp of the legal terms of the constitutional changes at stake, however, we must place their understanding of the referendum's emotional import. Those such as Bandler had an especially strong personal investment in the matters at stake in the referendum. As her biographer, Marilyn Lake, has rightly observed, there are often 'subjective, personal investments in one's choice of "fundamental principles"' and 'it is important to remember the emotional bases of powerful political mobilisations'. (For Bandler, the daughter of one of those 'Kanakas' in regard to whom section 51 (xxvi) of the Constitution had been devised in order to equip the Commonwealth with the powers to control, the campaign for the referendum was primarily a fight for the inclusion of blacks in the Australian nation on the same terms as whites.)[1] There is perhaps no better way of appreciating the enormous hopes that campaigners invested in the referendum than viewing an ABC television programme, *The Day of the Aboriginal*, screened a week before the poll. At the end of this, members of the Aboriginal-Australian Fellowship raise their voices and sing: 'We are going/We are going/We are going/To Freedom...27th of May/Each one say/YES YES YES/For Freedom' (see document 34, pp. 119–20). It is difficult to listen to this and not be moved. ('Vote yes for freedom' was a version of 'We are going to Freedom' that folk singer Gary Shearston had written by adapting a poem by Kath Walker, and was similar to the song 'We Shall Overcome' performed most often and most notably by African-American civil rights activists.)[2]

The bulk of the Council's leadership, which comprised Shirley Andrews, Gordon Bryant, Barry Christophers, Stan Davey, Joe McGinness and Barrie Pittock, better understood the nature of the constitutional clauses at stake in the referendum. They knew citizenship was not a matter treated by the Constitution; they knew Aboriginal people were already Australian citizens by virtue of the 1948 Nationality and Citizenship Act; they knew nearly all of the discriminatory laws had been repealed by federal and state governments; and they knew the constitutional changes proposed would not force a federal government to take charge of Aboriginal affairs. Yet, they still represented the referendum as a matter of federal control, the repeal of racist laws, and citizenship for Aborigines.

Arguably, this occurred because they believed that the Commonwealth government was the primary means of providing a form of citizenship for Aboriginal people which entailed social and economic rights and so was more meaningful or real than citizenship in terms of political or civil rights, and because they were convinced that they had to secure a massive 'yes' vote in the referendum in order to create a mandate for a federal government willing to play a greater role in Aboriginal affairs. At the same time, though, it can be suggested that the way they represented the referendum was determined by the fact that they had inherited a political narrative or tradition which had long tied the calls for a greater Commonwealth role in Aboriginal

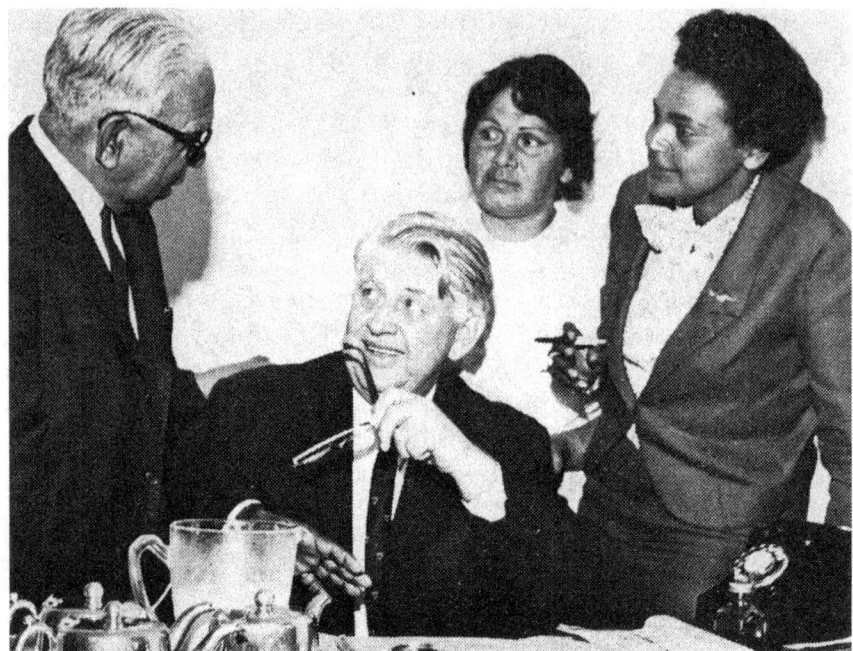

In April 1967 a Federal Council deputation canvassed federal MPs at Parliament House to seek assurances that they would support the Aboriginal question in the referendum. Pictured here in Gordon Bryant's parliamentary office are (left to right) Doug Nicholls, Gordon Bryant, Winnie Branson and Faith Bandler. (Courtesy *Canberra Times*)

affairs, the overthrow of racially discriminatory laws and rights for Aborigines to constitutional change. In other words, they, too, were true believers.[3]

It is clear, however, that these leaders were conscious of the importance of making an emotional appeal to the voters. Davey advocated a campaign that would be 'a call to the nation' and Bryant insisted that it 'must stir the people's hearts and minds'.[4] More particularly, they realised that 'citizenship' had a strong emotional pull for most voters, all the more so in a white nation that was now ashamed of its international reputation for racism and highly attuned to the demands minority groups were making for civil rights. Moreover, it made sense to represent these constitutional changes in terms of the common rights of citizenship rather than the exclusive special rights which they hoped would be granted Aboriginal people following the Commonwealth's winning of the power to make 'special laws'.

The Federal Council began preparing for the referendum soon after the Commonwealth parliament had passed the relevant legislation (see document 32, pp. 116–17). A 'national campaign directorate' was established in Melbourne, and Bryant and McGinness were appointed as its heads. The Council had meagre resources but it had financial support from some of its allies. In a whirlwind of activity, it lobbied politicians, held public meetings, organised rallies, distributed leaflets, stuck handbills and posters, and sold badges and buttons. Most importantly, perhaps, it bombarded the media, and won much favourable publicity in newspapers and magazines (see documents 38–40, pp. 121–4) and on radio stations and television channels.[5]

In adopting a strategy to persuade voters that the referendum's Aboriginal question was a matter of 'the greatest importance',[6] the Federal Council necessarily simplified the nature of the matter at stake. The name it chose for its campaign committee — Aboriginal Rights 'Vote Yes' — reveals the essence of the way it went about promoting the 'Yes' case. Its publicity materials suggested to the punters that this matter concerned rights for Aborigines. Leaflets called upon electors to 'Right wrongs: Write Yes for Aborigines on May 27' (see illustration below); posters urged voters to 'Vote Yes for Aboriginal Rights' (see illustration p. 50); and songs were recorded to exhort the electorate to 'Vote "Yes" to give rights and freedoms'. Other promotional materials had the same emphasis. Council spokespersons urged the press to encourage electors to 'vote yes to the question of Aboriginal rights' and to 'vote yes to give the Aborigines full citizenship rights'.[7]

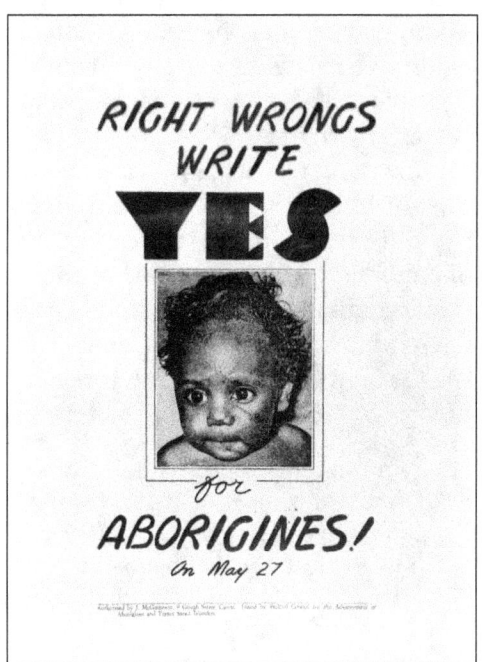

For its leaflets the Federal Council chose images of Aboriginal children to symbolise a new future for Aboriginal people and to make an emotional appeal to white Australian voters. (Courtesy Jack Horner Collection, AIATSIS)

More specifically, in respect of the amendment of section 51 (xxvi), the Council's publicity materials claimed a 'yes' vote would see the Commonwealth assume responsibility for Aboriginal affairs and adopt major programs to tackle Aboriginal people's disadvantage. Its background information notes stated: 'Aborigines are a national responsibility. We must see to it that the National Parliament is able to accept that responsibility'; a national publicity officer asserted: 'At present...the Commonwealth Parliament has no power to pass laws to benefit them even though it has this power for every other person who lives in Australia or in an Australian Territory'; a national press release, asking the question, 'what will be the positive results if the referendum is passed', answered: 'the Commonwealth will be able to pass laws relating to Aborigines'; one state campaign secretary, Jack Horner, told newspaper readers that this change meant the federal government would 'take formal responsibility for Aborigines', and Bandler told the press: 'by voting yes, you give this responsibility to the national Parliament and make possible a real programme of equal rights and equal opportunity for Aboriginals'.[8]

In reference to the repeal of section 127, the Federal Council largely represented this as a matter concerning the inclusion of Aboriginal people in the nation. This clause made 'the original Australians' feel they were 'a race apart in the land of their birth' and it insulted them by implying they were not worth counting, indeed the national census enumerated the number of sheep and cattle but not the number of Aboriginal people. The Federal Council also claimed, though, that the repeal of this clause actually meant that Aborigines would be 'treated equally with other Australians' and would be recognised 'as Australian citizens by right'.[9]

In trying to persuade voters to vote 'yes' the Council appealed to a set of liberal principles. It emphasised individual rights and equality, and presented the referendum as a means of realising the vision of a modern progressive nation that integrated all peoples as citizens undifferentiated by race. Only occasionally did the Council cast the referendum as a means of enabling a federal government to grant special rights to Aborigines;[10] for example, in some 'background notes' prepared by the National Directorate, it was stated:

> In view of the special disadvantages of lack of capital, education and 'know-how' suffered by the Aborigines, the well known principle of justice that 'it is as unjust to treat unequals equally as to treat equals unequally' is a strong argument for special legislation to enable Aborigines to overcome their disadvantages (see document 33, pp. 118–19).

In stressing the theme of equal rights, the historian Charles Rowley observed afterwards, the Council tried to appeal to a view that Australians were developing themselves and the kind of nation of which they wanted to be a part.[11] This was evident in several of the slogans the Council considered for the campaign, such as: 'Towards an Australia Free and Equal: Vote Yes', and 'Let's Be Counted — Vote Yes' (see document 32, pp. 116–17). Its publicity materials urged Australians to 'give Aborigines a fair go'. One spokesperson suggested to voters: 'When you write Yes...you are holding out the hand of friendship and wiping out nearly 200 years of injustice and inhumanity'. Another encouraged the use of this rhyming slogan: 'If to Aborigines you would be fair, put a YES in the bottom square'. Other campaigners told electors: 'As a nation we have a chance to show our willingness to really help the Aboriginal people'.[12]

The Federal Council sharpened this play on the nation's sense of pride by invoking the spectre of international condemnation. They warned of the harm that would be done to Australia's standing in the world were the referendum to be defeated. One leader claimed: 'the image of Australia throughout the world is at stake'; a campaign ditty, to be sung to Waltzing Matilda, went: 'Vote Yes, Australia, Vote Yes, Australia, The eyes of the world are upon us today'; and the national campaign directorate asserted: 'The eyes of the world — particularly African and Asian eyes — will be on Australia on May 27th. A "no" vote to the Aboriginal rights question will brand this country racist and put it in the same category as South Africa'.[13]

The terms in which the Federal Council represented the referendum was largely endorsed by the media. In respect of the amendment of section 51 (xxvi), the *Age* forecast: 'A Yes vote will pave the way for improving their health, education and housing; it will give them opportunities to live normal lives'; and the *Sydney Morning Herald* proclaimed: 'In simple terms the object of these constitutional changes is to provide the Commonwealth with more definite power to give positive and practical aid to the Aboriginal people'.[14] In respect of the repeal of section 127, the *Age* framed this in terms of 'the case for allowing the Commonwealth to treat Aborigines as a people' and 'the Aborigines' right to be called Australians'; the *Sydney Morning Herald* in terms of 'the referendum on the status of the Aborigines' and 'the referendum on Aborigines'; and the Melbourne *Herald* in terms of 'the referendum on whether discrimination against the aboriginals should be ended'.[15]

In turn, it seems that the vast majority of voters came to regard the referendum as being about citizenship rights for Aborigines and the advancement of Aboriginal people. A Morgan Gallup poll

**VOTE YES**

FOR

**ABORIGINAL**

**RIGHTS**

AUTHORISED BY JOE M<sup>c</sup> GINNESS 9 GOUGH ST CAIRNS
PRINTED BY RISING SUN PRESS 192 CANTERBURY RD.
CANTERBURY VIC.

The poster most commonly used in the Federal Council's campaign. (Courtesy Gordon Bryant Papers, National Library of Australia)

administered a week or so before the referendum found 22 per cent of those questioned believed that the 'chief effect' of the poll would be 'equal rights' for Aborigines; and a further 14 per cent expected the constitutional changes would produce, among other outcomes, improved 'status' and 'Aboriginal freedom'. More particularly, many voters had come to believe the referendum concerned the right to vote (see document 47, p. 133), notwithstanding contrary sources of information such as a pamphlet providing the official 'yes' case (see document 43, pp. 126–7). The greatest number of those polled believed that the principal outcome of changing the Constitution would be 'better opportunities' and 'improved conditions' for Aborigines.[16] In the light of all this, it is hardly surprising some commentators felt compelled to point out that the constitutional changes proposed were a matter of neither '"civil rights"' nor '"freedom now"' (see document 49, p. 135). At the time it was claimed that confusion about the terms of the referendum was widespread (see document 45, pp. 129–30). An earlier advocate of constitutional change, AP Elkin, thought it necessary to pen a long opinion for a leading newspaper explaining to the poor misguided voters the precise nature of the constitutional changes at stake in the referendum (see document 45, pp. 129–30).

Many newspapers called for support for the referendum by projecting a vision of a future in which a coming generation of Australians might enjoy a world free from racial discrimination. This carefully staged photograph of two boys in a Chippendale lane appeared on the front page of the *Sydney Morning Herald* two days before the plebiscite. The caption was: 'Racial discrimination — what's that?' (Courtesy *Sydney Morning Herald*)

The Federal Council's Aboriginal leaders largely echoed the non-Aboriginal leaders' representation of the constitutional changes under consideration. They emphasised that the Commonwealth would assume responsibility for Aboriginal affairs and spoke in terms of the ending of racial discrimination and the winning of citizenship rights.[17] However, the referendum had a special meaning for most Aboriginal campaigners. It held out the prospect of a vote that could herald their acceptance by a country which had always spurned them even though (but more probably because) they were its original peoples. Bill Onus, the Victorian campaign state director, urged Australians to 'vote yes to give Aborigines full citizenship rights' and argued that the matter at stake was 'a fundamental question of human rights' (see documents 36 and 37, pp. 120–1). In one speech he pondered: 'In this year of our Lord, nineteen hundred and sixty seven, we cannot help but wonder why it has taken the white Australians just on 200 years to recognise us as a race of people'.[18] Charlie Leon, Aboriginal-Australian Fellowship president, affirmed that Aboriginal people wanted to become a part of their own country.[19] Chicka Dixon, the acting president of the Sydney organisation the Foundation of Aboriginal Affairs, asserted: 'For most Aborigines [the referendum] is basically and most importantly a matter of seeing white Australians finally, after 179 years, affirming at last that they believe we are human beings' (see document 46, pp. 130–2). Harriet Ellis, the Aboriginal convenor of a trades hall vote yes committee, declared that a yes vote would help to 'eliminate an inferiority complex' among Aboriginal people.[20]

Aboriginal leaders invested much personally in a favourable outcome. Bert Groves, president of the recently revived Aborigines Progressive Association, stated that a yes vote would realise 'a long cheri-shed dream' (see document 40, p. 124). Some appeared to fear the worst; Doug Nicholls claimed: 'Something will die inside Aboriginal people if the referendum fails'.[21] It seemed important for Aboriginal leaders to believe that white Australians could be moral beings. Charles Perkins, one of the Federal Council's vice-presidents, remarked: 'For myself as an Aboriginal, it is a moment of truth — whether the white people really are interested in our welfare or rights' (see document 35, p. 120). Onus commented: 'if we lose this, then it will most certainly be an indictment against the Australian people'.[22] McGinness warned: 'The patience of Aboriginal people is becoming exhausted'. Dixon suggested that 'a crushing rejection' would mean 'bad blood between black and white for the foreseeable future' (see document 46, pp. 130–2).

There was, however, a more fundamental difference between the approaches of the Aboriginal and non-Aboriginal campaigners. For ten years many non-Aboriginal activists had questioned the policy of assimilation. However, none made it the subject of debate during

BREAKING THE NEXUS

This cartoon suggested that voting 'yes' to the Aboriginal question could hardly be expected to free Aborigines from the forces that had oppressed Aboriginal people for 180 years. (Courtesy Bruce Petty and *Australian*)

Bill Onus and other Federal Council leaders, including general secretary Stan Davey (to Onus' right), prepare for a lunchtime procession through the streets of Melbourne on the last day of the referendum campaign. (Courtesy *Herald* and *Weekly Times*)

the referendum campaign. By contrast, several Aboriginal leaders expressed serious criticisms of it in the lead-up to the poll. Groves expressed the desire of Aboriginal people 'to be part and parcel of the community' at the same time as he made it clear they wanted 'to do this without losing [their] identity as Australian Aborigines'. The policy of assimilation, he stated bluntly, reflected 'a failure to accept a minority race on the basis of equality', indeed, he went so far as to call it 'a modified method of extermination' (see document 40, p. 124). Other Council leaders like Kath Walker were no longer so committed to the campaign for civil rights. She would soon lead a charge for rights for Aborigines on the basis of their status as the country's Indigenous people, rather than calling for the rights of Australian citizens.[23]

In the opinion of the Federal Council's Aboriginal rank and file, the priority the organisation had given to the fight for constitutional change was misplaced. Aboriginal-Australian Fellowship member Ken Brindle later told Bandler: 'I couldn't see how it would benefit us...I was more informed than the average Aboriginal, but I couldn't understand it';[24] Leon later recalled that the thoughts of Aborigines 'were always on housing and jobs' and other bread-and-butter issues. At a symbolic level, too, it seems that many Aboriginal people regarded the referendum as relatively unimportant. The right to drink was a more significant marker of equality than the right to be counted in the national census. Sydney Aboriginal figure Mum Shirl later remarked: 'As far as being a citizen, it wasn't even a word I even thought about'.[25]

# 7 The Poll and its Consequences

The Federal Council and its allies were acutely aware that few constitutional referenda had ever been approved in Australia. Only four of the 24 previously held had been passed. One of these had been a constitutional amendment concerned with a similar matter of federal government responsibility for the people's welfare but the campaigners felt they had little reason to be sanguine regarding this one. Besides, they did not simply want a majority of states to vote in favour of the Aboriginal question; they demanded a huge 'Yes' vote so they could pressure the Coalition government to act.

In the tradition of Australian referenda, the two questions facing the voters in the polling booth were formulated in general terms. In the case of the changes in reference to Aboriginal people in the Constitution, voters were asked:

> Do you approve the proposed law for the alteration of the Constitution entitled — 'An Act to alter the Constitution so as to omit certain words relating to the People of the Aboriginal Race in any State and so that Aboriginals are to be counted in reckoning the Population'?[1]

No formal case was made for a 'No' vote (see documents 43, pp. 126–7 and 48, p. 133) and no one campaigned for one, though a small number presented arguments for it.

The result of the Aboriginal referenda was a resounding 'Yes'. All states voted in favour of the proposition, and of the formal votes 90.77 per cent were 'Yes' and only 9.23 per cent 'No'. Contrary to the expectations of the sceptics, the electors proved they were capable of distinguishing between the two issues presented to them. Support for the Aboriginal question did not carry over to the nexus one: it only won a majority in one state and a national 'yes' vote of 40.25 per cent.

The Federal Council and its allies took their appeal to as many venues as they could. Its president, Joe McGinness, joined a silent demonstration outside the Norwood Oval in Adelaide before the football match of the day. (Courtesy *Melbourne Diocesan Historical Commission, Catholic Archdiocese of Melbourne*)

There was some variation between states, and more between electorates. The highest number of 'No' votes was recorded in those places where Aboriginal people were the most visible.[2] Across Australia, the 48 rural electorates returned a 13.15 per cent 'No' vote, compared with only 7.5 per cent in the 74 urban electorates.

**Table 1: Returns by state[3]**

|                   | % voting 'No' |
| ----------------- | ------------- |
| Western Australia | 19.05         |
| South Australia   | 13.74         |
| Queensland        | 10.79         |
| Tasmania          | 9.79          |
| New South Wales   | 8.54          |
| Victoria          | 5.32          |

**Table 2: The ten electorates with highest 'No' vote[4]**

| Electorate (State) | | % voting 'No' |
|---|---|---|
| Kalgoorlie (WA) | Rural | 29.04 |
| Kennedy (Qld) | Rural | 23.45 |
| Canning (WA) | Rural | 22.75 |
| Perth (WA) | Urban | 20.85 |
| Moore (WA) | Rural | 20.82 |
| Leichhardt (Qld) | Rural | 19.44 |
| Cowper (NSW) | Rural | 19.12 |
| Grey (SA) | Rural | 18.64 |
| Angas (SA) | Rural | 18.24 |
| Gwydir (NSW) | Rural | 18.21 |

No results survive for individual polling booths except for some incomplete figures published in newspapers. These show there was a majority 'No' vote in a very small number of booths.[5] The subdivisions which returned a high 'No' vote are listed in Table 3.

**Table 3: Subdivisions recording high 'No' vote[6]**

| Division (State) | Sub-division (town) | % 'No' vote |
|---|---|---|
| Leichhardt (Qld) | Georgetown | 62.92% |
| Grey (SA) | Streaky Bay | 39.43% |
| Kennedy (Qld) | Charters Towers | 38.73% |
| Kalgoorlie (WA) | Kalgoorlie | 34.35% |
| Fisher (Qld) | Wondai | 29.05% |

The meaning to be attributed to these figures requires some consideration. It is hardly surprising that there was some degree of opposition, given the high level of bigotry existing in many parts of Australia. In this context, the striking feature of the referendum is not the high 'No' vote in some localities, but the fact that there was a 'No' vote of over 20 per cent in only five electorates and that the highest 'No' vote in an electorate was less than 30 per cent. This was by far the strongest endorsement of a referendum in Australian political history, a fact which has to be taken into account in any evaluation of the campaign's significance.[7]

The poll result was greeted joyfully by the campaigners. Evelyn Scott, later a chairperson of the Council for Aboriginal Reconciliation, has remembered: 'There was screaming when I heard it on the radio...

**SIMPLE REQUEST – SIMPLE ANSWER**

Some newspapers received letters expressing concern about the Commonwealth assuming power to pass special legislation in regard to Aboriginal people but they unequivocally declared their support. This cartoon appeared in Queensland's *Courier-Mail* (Courtesy Estate of Ian Gall and the *Courier*)

You just couldn't believe the percentage of the national vote'; and Faith Bandler has reminiscenced: 'We went *mad* with excitement'.[8] News of the huge 'Yes' vote seems to have had a profound impact on some Aboriginal people. Rodney Hall has recalled seeing Aboriginal people in Brisbane the next morning, going into town to assert that they now *could* go into town:

> There were black people on the streets in a way that we had never seen them...It was so touching. People were up, had washed their children, combed their hair and got themselves up in their very best gear and walked out in the streets of Brisbane, down Queen Street where they never went.[9]

In the wake of the poll, the campaigners for the 'yes' vote tried to use the huge vote as a weapon to press the Coalition government to act. For the Federal Council, Gordon Bryant proclaimed the vote as 'an overwhelming endorsement of the view that it is time for national action' and urged 'immediate action in a number of fields' so that 'effective help' could be given to Aboriginal people, and Stan Davey issued a statement that presented a five-point plan to the government headed by a demand 'To establish a national policy on Aboriginal

In Western Australia, the state most opposed traditionally to the Commonwealth assuming more power, Aboriginal leaders gathered at the Aboriginal Centre in Perth on the night of the referendum to follow progress of the poll. Pictured here (left to right) are George Abdullah, Jack Davis and Charles Pell. (Courtesy *West Australian*)

affairs based on the needs and desires of Aborigines and Torres Strait Islanders' (see document 52, pp. 6–7).[10] WC Wentworth argued that the referendum vote was so 'overwhelming' that the government 'would now have to consider some immediate action to make it effective'; and Gough Whitlam claimed that 'the overwhelming vote' had removed the Constitution as 'an alibi' for the Commonwealth's refusal to play a greater role in Aboriginal affairs.[11]

How can the massive 'Yes' vote be explained? It might be argued that voters were compelled by a sentiment that something had better be done for Aboriginal people. In the wake of the vote, Bryant claimed:

> The average voter at the time of the referendum in May may not have known very much about the Aboriginal question and probably had the idea, based on a good Australian tradition, that the Aboriginal people of this country had not had a fair go. Most voters probably had vague ideas that the Aboriginals had not full citizenship rights and might not be able to vote. Doubtless some voters were misinformed on many matters, but most were directed by their consciences and sense of social justice to take

the view that something ought to have been done to better the lot of the Aboriginal people.[12]

The historian Charles Rowley more or less concurred with this assessment. He saw the vote as the expression of 'a changing public opinion', arguing that there was a general feeling that there was something that was seriously wrong, a genuine concern about this, a belief that the matter had been neglected for too long and a conviction that it was up to the Commonwealth to provide a solution.[13] The authors of later accounts have agreed. This, we should remind ourselves, was age of reform and revolution in which there was enormous sense of optimism that the world could be put right, even made anew, through the power of protest and by the authority of government.[14]

At the same time, though, one might construe the vote more specifically as an affirmation of the government's program of assimilation whereby Aborigines would be incorporated into the nation and so could no longer remind white Australians that they had been dispossessed and despoiled. In much the same spirit, it can be argued that voting 'yes' was regarded, consciously or unconsciously, by white Australians as a means of redemption. In a context in which white Australia's racist policies and practices had been exposed to an unprecedented degree, it was an opportunity to remove the traces of racial discrimination from their nation's constitution and proclaim that Australia really was the country of the fair go.

Prior to the vote, some commentators feared the consequences of something like this happening. John Moses on ATN 7's 'Seven Days' observed:

> The great danger is that we'll look at the referendum as a kind of sop to the national conscience, that we and our governments will sit back and say smugly to ourselves and the world 'The slate's clean. There's no difference now between Aborigines and us. The Constitution applies equally to black and white'. If this happens it will be as shameful a thing as we've ever done. For the way Aborigines are living now, here and now, in this affluent, selfish nation is a national disgrace.[15]

By 27 May, as we have shown, the referendum had come to promise a good deal for its supporters: the Commonwealth would assume control of Aboriginal affairs, sweep away racial discrimination, grant citizenship rights to Aborigines, and realise equality for the Aboriginal people. As such, there was an enormous discrepancy between the account the campaigners had given on the one hand and the take the Coalition government had on it on the other. This became apparent very soon after the referendum took place.

Its approval by the electorate, even in the extraordinarily sweeping manner achieved, barely affected the Coalition government's approach to its role in Aboriginal affairs, despite the concerted efforts of the Federal Council and its allies to capitalise on this (see document 52, pp. 136–7).[16] The day after the referendum Holt departed on a four-week tour of the United States and Europe. Some sympathetic commentators pointed to the problem they had highlighted during the campaign. In an editorial the *Australian* called upon the government to set out 'its view of its new constitutional position in this field' and to provide 'an assurance that the matter does not rest in mere changes in the constitution' (see document 53, pp. 137–8).

At a party a fortnight after the referendum, members of the Aboriginal-Australian Fellowship, the sponsor of the first petition calling for a referendum, toasted the Federal Council's New South Wales campaign director Faith Bandler who had won enormous publicity for the 'Yes' vote. Those pictured here are Lilon Bandler (front centre), Hans Bandler (far left second row), Edna Blackshaw (right of Faith Bandler), Elizabeth Mattick (far right second row), Rev. Alf Clint (behind Blackshaw), Harriet Ellis (back row, second from left), Bert Groves (far left back row), and Aboriginal and Torres Strait Islander students at Tranby College in Sydney. (Courtesy *Australian Women's Weekly* and Jack Horner Collection, AIATSIS)

In weeks and months after 27 May, it became increasingly evident that more pressure was needed if substantive change was going
to be achieved (see documents 54 and 55, pp. 138–9). The Holt
government prevaricated for several months before addressing the
matter. When it did, consideration of national and international
opinion were once again uppermost in its decision making. The
Prime Minister told Cabinet in August: 'We must take into account
the place the Aborigine question occupies in Australia's international
relationships, and also the fact that the electorate will undoubtedly
look increasingly to the Commonwealth Government as the centre
of policy and responsibility on Aborigine questions'. Yet, Holt and
the Cabinet were of the opinion that the government 'should not
magnify the Aborigine problem out of its true reality', and remained
of the opinion that it need not take any new initiatives in policy, let
alone administration. Indeed, it was believed that the government
should continue to leave administration of Aboriginal affairs to the
states. Nevertheless, the Cabinet recognised that a few crumbs at
least had to be tossed to the advocates of change, and so it agreed to

See any bright new changes coming up for me in the near future?''

The massive 'Yes' vote achieved, those calling for a change in the approach to Aboriginal
affairs immediately shifted their attention to the Holt government's stance. This cartoon
appeared in the Australian two days after the poll, alongside an editorial asking 'Were the
voters cheated?' (Courtesy *Australian*)

establish a small office, numbering only two or three people, whose function would be merely advisory. This was to become the Council for Aboriginal Affairs.[17]

In September 1967 Holt revealed in Parliament the government's intention to more or less maintain the status quo in Aboriginal affairs.[18] The Federal Council and its allies were dismayed. Bandler condemned the government for being 'apathetic and petty' and complained it was 'giving power back to the States'.[19] The *Sydney Morning Herald* dismissed the government's new office for Aboriginal affairs: 'The decision makes a mockery of the referendum in May. It is as if the electorate had never made any moral commitment to do a great deal more for Aborigines'.[20]

In the short term, therefore, the referendum had utterly failed to realise the hopes of its champions. Yet, over the next several years the Council for Aboriginal Affairs, comprising a top ranking public servant (Nugget Coombs), a leading anthropologist (WEH Stanner) and a highly rated diplomat (Barrie Dexter), used the massive 'Yes' vote of the referendum to press the Holt, Gorton and McMahon governments to consider new policies and play a new role in Aboriginal Affairs,[21] and the promise of the referendum was properly fulfilled when the Labor Party came to power in November 1972.

Labor interpreted the referendum as a moral mandate to take responsibility for Aboriginal affairs in Australia. In the speech that launched Labor's election campaign, Whitlam asserted: 'In 1967 we, the people of Australia, by an overwhelming majority imposed upon the Commonwealth the constitutional responsibility for Aborigines and Torres Strait Islanders'.[22] The story the Federal Council had told regarding constitutional change in its ten-year campaign for a referendum authorised this new role for the Commonwealth, just as it hoped it would.

In assuming a new role for the Commonwealth in Aboriginal affairs, it should be noted, the Whitlam Labor government chose to interpret the referendum in a particular way. Its mandate was actually equivocal since two rather different conceptions of Aboriginal rights and Aboriginal policy had been evident in the campaign in May 1967. In the first, which dominated the public representations of the 'Yes' case, the emphasis was upon an approach to Aboriginal affairs that envisaged that equality for Aboriginal people would be achieved by spurning any distinctions between people on the basis of race and thus granting Aboriginal people the same rights as other Australian citizens enjoyed. This confirmed the thrust of the assimilation programme that sought to include and incorporate Aboriginal people as *individuals* in the Australian nation, thereby erasing their sense of themselves as Aboriginal. In the second, which informed the program of the Federal Council but was seldom articulated in the case made for the 'Yes' vote, the emphasis was upon an approach to Aboriginal affairs which envisaged that equality for Aboriginal people would be achieved by distinguishing between people on the basis of race and by granting Aboriginal people special rights for a temporary but not indefinite period in order that ameliorative programs could be implemented to address their disadvantage. Implicit in this approach was an assumption that Aboriginal people would retain their sense of themselves as members of a *group*. This entailed a rejection of assimilation, or at least of the way this program was seen by most white Australians.

In the aftermath of the referendum, a third conception of Aboriginal rights and Aboriginal policy became prominent, though it had been emerging for some time. This overlapped at the same time as it departed from the one we have just discussed. It, too, distinguished between the rights of Aboriginal and settler Australians, but it did so on grounds which rested on a notion of difference between Aboriginal and settler Australians that was considered to be permanent rather than temporary in nature: Aborigines were the Indigenous people of the country and in accordance with this unique status they were entitled to a distinctive set of rights. These were special rights on a basis that departed from any of those granted to any settler Australians. In the second and third conceptions of Aboriginal affairs and Aboriginal rights, demands for rights to land as well as to capital and culture came to the fore.

The Labor Party embraced, albeit to a limited degree, the latter two conceptions of Aboriginal rights and Aboriginal policy and began to interpret the referendum as a mandate for these shortly after the poll. This was in keeping with the changes in the way the Federal Council and its allies had been conceiving of these. Thus, in 1968 Whitlam told the House of Representatives:

> The referendum was not designed merely to remove discrimin-ation against Aboriginals; its purpose was to give the National Parliament and the National Government authority to grant especially favourable treatment to overcome the handicaps we have inflicted on them...This was more than a mandate. It was a virtual command by 5,700,000 Australians that the national Government take a lead to promote health, training, employment and land rights for Aboriginals...What is needed is a policy of equal rights *and* special privileges.[24]

Once in power, the Australian Labor Party sought to implement policies in keeping with the latter conceptions of Aboriginal rights and policy, as did its successors (both Coalition and Labor) for the next twenty years, though perhaps more in keeping with the third rather than the second conception. We will return to this matter later.

In the meantime, we want to focus on the implications of the fact that the Whitlam government asserted the primacy of the Commonwealth in Aboriginal Affairs upon coming to power. This has led many commentators to assume that there was a necessary relationship between the amendment of section 51 (xxvi) of the Constitution and the Commonwealth assuming control of Aboriginal affairs. However, this is not so. Several observations are in order. First, amendment of section 51 (xxvi) in itself did not require the federal government to take charge of Aboriginal affairs, as the record of the Holt, Gorton and McMahon governments between 1967 and 1972 reveals. Second, the Commonwealth could and did take charge of Aboriginal affairs by means other than the amendment of section 51 (xxvi). It is apparent that Whitlam Labor government seldom actually used the legislative power provided by amendment of section 51 (xxvi). For most of its reforms, it proceeded through administrative rather than legislative changes, and negotiation with the states. Constitutionally, it relied upon the power the Commonwealth had to make financial grants under specific terms and conditions (section 96) and overrule states through the external affairs provision (section 51 (xxix)) and the power of states to transfer functions to the Commonwealth (section 51 (xxxvii)). In other words, it is apparent that the extension of the Commonwealth's role in Aboriginal affairs was not solely dependent on amendment of section 51 (xxvi), even though this undoubtedly guaranteed the federal government's ultimate authority because the Constitution stipulates, in the cases of conflict on matters in which powers are concurrent or shared between the Commonwealth and the states, that Commonwealth's law will prevail.

The referendum, we conclude, was vital to the changes which occurred in Aboriginal affairs, not so much because it amended section 51 (xxvi) of the Constitution but more because it helped create a climate of opinion that provided a federal government with a mandate for change. The referendum bestowed upon the Whitlam government and its successors the moral authority required to expand the Commonwealth's role in Aboriginal affairs and to implement a major program of reform. Without this mandate, the Whitlam government could never have done what it did. Here lies the primary historical significance of the referendum.

# 8 Remembering and Forgetting the Referendum

The passing of time has seen the nature of the constitutional changes approved by the 1967 referendum recede from historical consciousness, only to be replaced by a myth that uncannily represents these in the same terms as the original campaign. The referendum, moreover, is commonly described as 'historic' and 'momentous', a 'turning point', and a 'landmark' event, and it is frequently taken as a reference point in considerations of Aboriginal affairs.[1] By the twenty-fifth anniversary the referendum had become the subject of much commemoration and by the thirtieth a cause for enormous celebration.[2] Its growing historical significance can be seen in the remarks of an Aboriginal activist who was sceptical about its importance at the time. Twenty years after the event, Ken Brindle told Faith Bandler:

> You ask me now why I didn't get too enthusiastic over the referendum? To tell you the truth I really didn't understand it... You were more far-sighted...[I]f I knew then what I know now, you wouldn't have been able to stop me...No Aboriginals knew what benefits they'd derive from changing the federal Constitution, but if they could have foreseen the present situation they would have worked for it too...Now when I sit down and see what it brought about, I say: "Thank Christ for Bandler and [Shirley] Andrews and their mob".[3]

Insofar as the myth recounted in recent years can be traced back to the way the Federal Council represented the referendum during its ten-year campaign, it seems apparent that accounts that have been informed or provided by Bandler have played a part. In her personal history of the Federal Council, *Turning the Tide: A Personal History of the Federal Council for the Advancement of Aborigines and Torres Strait Islanders*, published in 1989, Bandler acknowledged:

Change following the referendum was disappointingly slow. Our early euphoria died down. The government, despite putting the referendum to the people of Australia, had themselves been lukewarm about it...Meanwhile, the lives of Aborigines virtually remained the same...Aboriginal people had cause to wonder whether much had been achieved at all.

Yet, she asserted elsewhere in the same book:

In 1967, major political and social change occurred. A referendum was held from which flowed Commonwealth responsibility for Aboriginal affairs, changing forever the social and political relationship between Aborigines and non-Aborigines...The benefits of the referendum were manifold. Acknowledgement of Aboriginal citizenship and the rights inherent in this status as well as funding from the Commonwealth government, removed many of the barriers which previously had kept Aborigines 'out of sight and out of mind' for mainstream Australia.[4]

In re-presenting the terms in which the Federal Council had demanded constitutional change between 1957 and 1967 — in other words, by retelling the story that it told at the time — Bandler's history makes it very difficult for readers to grasp the actual nature of the referendum and its outcome, that is, to realise that the changes brought about by the referendum did not flow from altering a clause or two in the Constitution but were instead the outcome of the way the champions of constitutional change had construed

A decade after the 1967 referendum, many Aboriginal people were frustrated by the slow pace of change, as this poster for National Aboriginal Week suggests.

those clauses and the consequences of their amendment or repeal. In Bandler's narrative the referendum comes to stand in for, or to symbolise (in the way that myth usually does), something much more complex and diffuse.

More recently Bandler has described the referendum as 'the greatest victory the Aborigines have had or ever will have'.[5] Perhaps this is a necessary fiction that she, among others, has found necessary to create in the absence of the very outcomes these erstwhile campaigners for racial equality hoped to achieve. There are probably other reasons for this claim. First, Bandler's remembrance of the referendum campaign for the referendum is informed by a bitter memory of its aftermath. Much to the dismay of Bandler and others, Aboriginal leaders such as Kath Walker and Doug Nicholls rejected the non-Aboriginal leadership of the Federal Council and articulated a perspective of the future in which distinctions between people on the basis of 'race' and an emphasis on Aboriginality were central (see document 56, pp. 139–40).[6] Second, the referendum, despite or more probably because of its rather elusive significance, is a victory easier to celebrate than the outcome of one of the Federal Council's other major campaigns: its achievement of equal wages for Aboriginal workers in the Northern Australian cattle industry.[7] In the wake of that victory, white employers actually sacked most of their Aboriginal stockworkers and then tried to push Aboriginal people off their traditional lands. (The Federal Council could not prevent the former but it did try to foil the latter.)[8]

The fundamental terms in which Bandler celebrated the referendum have been repeated by most of those who have since written about it. In part, this is due to the tendency of many writers, including academic historians, to provide accounts of the past in terms of major events, rather than rendering the past as a complex process of change that seldom has any obvious beginnings or endings. In part, it is because many have made the mistake of reading the past backwards, in this case assuming that the Commonwealth's assumption of the major role in Aboriginal affairs was the necessary outcome of the changes to the Constitution demanded by the campaigners. Yet, none of this explains why so much has been made of this particular event rather than some other one.

Why and how an event is commemorated depends, of course, upon those who are intent on remembering it. The referendum is obviously an attractive choice for those in search of something positive to remember in the terrible history of the white treatment of Aboriginal people in this country. It probably only takes pride of place, though, because Australia has nothing better to celebrate, such as a historic treaty, like that enjoyed by its trans-Tasman neighbour, New Zealand. In lieu of a more telling agreement, the massive 'Yes' vote for Aborigines has been made to stand for the beginning of reconciliation between Aboriginal and settler Australians. Its resounding endorsement by the voters reassures because it seems to have been inspired by so-called Australian principles such as equal treatment and the ideal of a unitary nation undivided by race, rather than the principle of special rights for Aboriginal people and the ideal of a more pluralistic nation.

By representing the referendum as the moment when Aborigines were granted 'citizenship rights', celebration of it serves other func-tions. Its focus on the political rights Aboriginal people were granted distracts attention from the substantive economic and social rights typically associated with citizenship in a flourishing democracy which they have never gained. Remembered in this way, a sharp but artificial distinction is drawn between the past and the present (see document 59, pp. 143–4). Conservatives can acknowledge the unfortunate aspects of the past at the same time as they can proclaim that these do not influence the present or are simply the preoccupation of so-called black armband historians.[9] The referendum seems to play a more redemptive role for liberals, an imaginary historic point of transition from a bad old racist regime to a good new non-racist one. It stands as proof of the humanity of settler Australians.

The referendum has also been invoked as a benchmark of settler Australian goodwill towards Aboriginal from which there should be no regress. Hence, so-called backlashes are often measured against the resounding 'yes' vote of May 1967.[10] In all these references, though, the relatively large 'no' vote in the referendum in the rural areas, where there were the highest or most visible populations of Aboriginal people, is conveniently forgotten.

Some Aboriginal leaders and their supporters used the twentieth and twenty-fifth anniversaries of the referendum to make a comparison between the dreams of 1967 and nightmarish contemporary reality in order to call for greater commitment and more resources in tackling the disadvantage of Aboriginal people (see document 57, pp. 140–1). In 1987, Charles Perkins spoke of the slowness of progress; and in 1992 Lowitja O'Donoghue spoke of how little had been achieved (see document 58, pp. 141–3), Pat Dodson of the urgent need for further change, and Pat O'Shane of how far the cause of 'real citizenship' had to go. On the later occasion they were joined by Labor Prime Minister Paul Keating who spoke of Australia's failure to rise to 'the challenge which the triumphant referendum required us to meet'.[11]

In 1987 and 1992 some Aboriginal leaders used commemorative occasions as an opportunity to challenge the long-standing political arrangement between the Australian state and Aboriginal people. On 27 May 1987 Michael Mansell interrupted a National Press Club luncheon, at which Minister for Aboriginal Affairs Clyde Holding was musing upon the need for a treaty or contract between Aborigines and other Australians, in order to present the case for a sovereign Aboriginal nation and to suggest that white Australia could retain all existing freehold and leasehold land but the traditional owners of the land should retain their rights to the rest.[12] On 27 May 1992 Kevin Gilbert, at a day of protest and mourning held at the Aboriginal Tent Embassy, lamented the day Australian citizenship was imposed upon Aboriginal people (see document 60, pp. 144–6).

The oral testimony of Aboriginal people reveals that many do not regard the referendum highly. Some are of the opinion that it made little difference to their lives, that there is still a long way to go before equality is achieved, and that they still have to struggle for basic rights (see documents: 80 and 81, pp. 161–2; 88 and 89, p. 164 and 91, p. 165). For example, Emily Walker has stated: 'I don't really think that the referendum achieved anything' (see document 87, p. 160).

For some Aboriginal people, though, the referendum is highly significant. With considerable vehemence, many assert that they 'got the rights in 1967' or were allowed 'to go to places that we never went before, such as pictures [and] swimming pools' (see document 76, p. 160). How can we interpret these statements? It is important to grasp the ways in which they could be historically true, not in the sense that the referendum bestowed legal rights upon Aborigines (since we know this did not occur) but rather because it served to change the nature of race relations. This could have happened in at least two ways. First, since the referendum highlighted and challenged racial discrimination, local governmental authorities might have been persuaded to abandon long-standing rules (such as barring Aboriginal children from municipal swimming pools); second, the referendum might have provided Aboriginal people with the necessary impetus to assert the legal rights that they already had on paper by enabling them to overcome their own fears and be bold enough to do things like taking up seats in the same section of the cinema as everyone else (see documents 72–74, pp. 158–9). In other words, the referendum helped Aboriginal people become real Australian citizens because it alerted them to their rights and gave them the confidence to exercise these. As Leisha May Eatts has recalled: 'I didn't know that I could vote in the referendum and believed that the referendum had to pass for us to vote. But I started to vote after the 1967 referendum' (see documents 76 , p. 160 and 78, p. 161).

There is another way statements such as 'we were given citizenship rights in 1967' might be explained. In oral testimony it is often the case that a long and complex train of occurrences are unwittingly compressed into a single one. So, for example, the gaining of the citizenship rights is condensed into a single moment — the 1967 referendum — rather than remembered as something that actually took place over several years. A further way of interpreting such shorthand statements has been suggested. Historian Heather Goodall has argued that statements of this kind owe something to the fact that 'when they have spoken out, Aborigines have been met not simply with arguments to the contrary, but usually by flat denials of their accusations, accompanied by denigration of Aboriginal truthfulness and of their ability to judge their own conditions'. 'This,' she contends, 'has influenced the form of recollections': they have become more simplistic, 'the subtleties and complexities worn away over the years of trying to put a case in the face of indifference and denial'.[13]

In this particular case, anthropologist Barry Morris has argued, 'getting the rights' or 'having the rights' might be a statement that Aboriginal people make in a context where they have those rights in an abstract sense but in reality are being denied the enjoyment of them.[14] The Aboriginal leader Noel Pearson has suggested that the demand Aboriginal people on Palm Island recently made for a judicial review of the death of Mulrunji Doomadgee in police custody might amount to 'an angry insistence that Australia delivers on the promissory note of the 1967 referendum: that equality of citizenship means there must be just treatment under the rule of law'.[15] (The Commonwealth acceded to this demand, appointing a retired judge, Sir Laurence Street, one of Jessie Street' sons. He advised the Queensland government that there was sufficient evidence to bring a charge of manslaugher against a police officer.)[16] The assertion by Aboriginal people that 'we got the rights in 1967' has much the same purpose as the demand for those rights by campaigners in the 1950s and 1960s: to challenge the status quo and bring about much-needed change.

# 9 Reconciliation and Constitutional Change

Our consideration of the 1967 referendum has led us to conclude that this event helped to bring about some much-needed change in Aboriginal affairs but that it was not the watershed or turning point it is often represented to be in respect of Aboriginal rights. Or, if it can be regarded as a watershed or turning point in this regard, its nature was very different to the one claimed by the myth of the referendum. Arguably, its symbolic recognition of citizenship rights for Aboriginal people created a context in which campaigners for Aboriginal rights, especially those who were Aboriginal, were more able to conceive or articulate a claim for a different kind of rights and even a different kind of relationship between Aboriginal people and the Australian nation, than they had been for a very long time; and it gave momentum to a campaign for these.[1]

In the wake of the referendum Aboriginal and non-Aboriginal campaigners increasingly demanded the kind of special rights that many had long assumed Aboriginal people had an entitlement to, namely Indigenous rights: the rights of a people who are 'the people of the land' or the first peoples of the land. The claim to Indigenous rights primarily comprised a demand for rights to land and to compensation for land of which they had been dispossessed — what were increasingly called 'land rights' in the years following the 1967 referendum — but also the right for Aboriginal people to sustain their own culture and identity and to manage their own affairs — what was increasingly known from the early 1970s as 'the right of self-determination'.

The demand for Indigenous rights for Aboriginal people had (and has) a basis very different in principle to the one made for citizenship rights. Whereas the demand for citizenship rights rested upon a claim to a status to which all members of the nation were believed to have an inherent right in their capacity as human beings and Australians, the demand for Indigenous rights rests upon a claim to a status to which only Indigenous people are believed to have an inherent right in their capacity as the descendants of the original people of the land. In other words, it was and is rooted in a claim to a particular kind of historical difference: Aboriginal people were and are the first peoples of this country, and non-Aboriginal people were and are not.

Indigenous rights are a special right but they have a different basis, in principle if not always in policy and practice, to those special rights which might be claimed by those who are deemed to have a particular need or have performed a particular service. (The failure to distinguish properly between special rights on the basis of Indigeneity and special rights on the basis of disadvantage as well as a tendency to privilege the former rather than the latter lies at the heart of the failure of much government policy and practice in Aboriginal affairs.) Special rights are considered, at least theoretically, to be rights that people claim as individuals (rather than as members of a group), and entitlement to these rights is held to be temporary in the sense that they cannot be transferred to or inherited by one's descendants (as, for example, in the case of a returned soldier). By contrast, Indigenous rights are unequivocally group rights in the sense that these are rights people can only claim on the basis of being a member of an Indigenous people, and entitlement to these rights has an ongoing or permanent rather than a temporary basis.

In the years following the 1967 referendum, the upsurge in demands for Indigenous rights as well as self-determination for Aboriginal people, growing criticism of the racial dimensions of the policy of assimilation, a genuine concern to address the chronic disadvantage of Aboriginal people but also a realisation that the implementation of a programme of special rights to redress Aboriginal disadvantage and achieve a higher level of integration of Aboriginal people in national life would prove enormously costly, and an ongoing apprehension about international criticism of Australia's treatment of Aboriginal people prompted federal governments, first of all the Coalition, then Labor, to first contemplate a change in the nature of the Commonwealth's Aboriginal policies and finally to abandon 'assimilation' and adopt 'self-determination'.[2] The task was one of both redressing and managing Aboriginal people's historical difference. The Commonwealth accepted the permanent presence in Australia of Aboriginal groups (or communities) that their predecessors had long sought to undermine, even destroy, and they tried to nurture these as a locus of Aboriginal culture and identity (Aboriginality). Under this new dispensation, Aboriginal people were recognised by successive governments as members of a group or a people (though not of a nation), and were granted special rights to some parcels of land (but seldom compensation for dispossession) on the grounds that they were culturally different and had suffered historically because of racial discrimination. Governments sought to nurture Aboriginal leadership in order to create a partner in governance and administration by creating new forums for political representation and establishing new forms of bureaucracy. They also sought to nurture Aboriginal culture by funding programmes in art, theatre, dance, music, literature, history and so forth. In doing this they championed Aboriginality as an integral part of the nation's fabric.[3]

In the 1970s and 1980s, however, federal governments only had partial success in tackling the problem of Aboriginal historical difference. Two factors were uppermost. First, Aboriginal people had suffered nearly two hundred years of dispossession, destruction and discrimination, and this had (and has) affected generation after generation of families and communities, resulting in considerable loss of capacity. This crisis could not be resolved in one generation, let alone two. Second, Aboriginal campaigners not only continued to demand recognition of Indigenous rights to land and capital but also acknowledgement of Aboriginal people's status as a sovereign group, which entailed a different relationship between Aborigines and the Australian nation–state. It became increasingly apparent that government was reluctant to meet the demand for Indigenous rights to any great degree and that it was unwilling to contemplate any claims in regard to sovereignty. Consequently, in the early 1990s the Hawke Labor government proposed a formal process of national reconciliation between Aborigines and other Australians, which resulted in the formation of the Council for Aboriginal Reconciliation.

By this time profound changes in the racial or cultural make-up of Australia and Australia's relationship with Britain and its Asian-Pacific neighbours had prompted a renewal of calls for Australia to become a republic. By necessity, this put calls for changes to the Australian Constitution back onto the political agenda. Most advocates of change seem to have had three premises. First, the Constitution was the nation's founding document and thus had set the framework for the way the nation was constituted politically and legally; second, a nation which has changed so much in the course of a century needs a new foundation stone in the form of an altered constitution; third, the lack of a written statement of the rights of the people had resulted in an arrangement that has worked well for the protection of the rights of the majority (of) people but poorly for minorities, especially Aboriginal people, and so there is a need to amend the Constitution.

Not surprisingly, Aboriginal leaders took an especial interest in constitutional change,[4] encouraged by the High Court's 1992 Mabo decision which had changed the way in which the law of the land told the story about the historical relationship between Australia and the Aboriginal people.[5] Indeed, they invested the Constitution with the most profound importance for their political struggle. They saw it as the fundamental or basic law of the nation and thus a means by which the Aboriginal relationship to the nation might be determined. At an international conference regarding the position of first peoples in national constitutions, held in Canberra in 1993, it was asserted:

> Recognition in the Constitution, as fundamental law, has clear symbolic value. It is appropriate for the Constitution to reflect fundamental constitutional relationships within the Australian polity. In the absence of historic treaties, which exist in most comparable countries, the Constitution may be the best vehicle to recognise the status of the Aboriginal people.[6]

The Constitution, of course, was silent about the relationship between Aboriginal people and the Australian state, at least since the 1967 referendum had removed the references to Aboriginal people. Lowitja O'Donoghue, the chairperson of Aboriginal and Torres Strait Islander Commission, observed in 1993: 'A reading of the Australian Constitution...will find no specific reference to Aboriginal people, let alone any reference to any rights or claims we might have as the indigenous peoples of this country'.[7] Throughout the 1990s many Aboriginal leaders made it clear that Australia should not become a republic without ensuring that the Constitution was altered to accommodate their demands for reform. For them, the republic and reconciliation were causes that *had* to be connected to one another.

Several propositions for constitutional change were advanced (see, for example, document 61, pp. 146–7).[8] There were calls for recognition of the prior occupation and ownership of the country by the first peoples, and of their continuing custodianship and/or their dispossession, in the form of a new preamble to the Constitution. This would probably have limited importance legally, though it could be used by the High Court to determine the nature of the Constitution's race power.[9] Its primary significance would be symbolic. The power of this kind of recognition could have substantial outcomes in the long term, it has been argued by those such as Larissa Behrendt:

> Symbolic recognition that could alter the way Australians see their history will also affect their views on the kind of society they

would like to become...It would change the context in which debates about Indigenous issues and rights take place. It would alter the way in which the relationship between Indigenous and non-Indigenous Australians is conceptualised.[10]

More concrete proposals for change have included the repeal of section 25, which relates to the power of the states to disqualify voters on racial grounds; an amendment to section 51 (xxvi) to ensure that the race power can only be used to legislate for the benefit of Aboriginal people; and a new section to outlaw racial discrimination. There were calls for more major change, such as a new section 105b to recognise a treaty with Aboriginal people. Such an agreement would set down a framework in which negotiations regarding the relationship between Aboriginal people and the Australia state could proceed.

Several Aboriginal leaders called for a more fundamental reconsideration of the political relationship between Aboriginal people and the Australian state by pressing the question of sovereignty. For example, Michael Mansell demanded that Aboriginal people be given the opportunity to decide whether they wanted to be party to constitutional reform or even a part of Australia. He suggested another referendum might be held, in which Aboriginal people would have the chance to choose what political arrangements they wanted (see document 62, pp. 147–8).

The Keating Labor Government originally sought to tie together the republic and reconciliation but it soon tried to proceed by separating the two causes. Consequently, Aboriginal demands for constitutional change were sidelined. Many Aboriginal spokespersons held that constitutional reform was central to the work of reconciliation. Noel Pearson, for example, insisted that reconciliation must lead to a document 'guaranteed by our constitution'.[11] A republic without reconciliation with the country's Aboriginal people was not a republic worth having. Australia could only transcend its British colonial framework by making changes to the Constitution which respected Aboriginal people and their rights. The government refused to listen. The cause of constitutional change in respect of Aboriginal matters was set back. Soon it would be crushed by the return to power of the Coalition.

# 10 Race, Rights and the Constitution

The last ten years has been marked by a massive seachange in Aboriginal affairs. Most of the preceding twenty years had been marked by a bi-partisan approach in the area, but this came to an end in the early to mid-1990s. Two factors in particular played a role in this. One was a matter of principle and perspective, the other more pragmatic in nature.

It can be argued that democratic nation–states have been able to accommodate the demand of Indigenous peoples for citizenship rights quite easily, since these have amounted to a call on the nation to be included on the same basis as everyone else. To a limited degree these states have been able to tolerate demands for special rights for Indigenous peoples when these have been calls for special treatment on the basis of need. However, demands for a particular kind of special rights — Indigenous rights — have proven to be much more difficult for such states to accommodate, because (as we have already remarked) they are based on a claim for rights that have a basis that is both permanent and collective in nature rather than temporary or individual. The calls for land rights, but more especially the recognition of sovereignty, pushes democracies to their intellectual limits. In the Australian case, Indigenous rights has posed more of a problem to the Liberal Party and the Country or National Party than to the Labor Party because of the nature of their political principles or perspectives. As the political scientist Judith Brett has noted, liberalism around the world has been a form of political thinking that conjures up and cherishes a historical trajectory in which people abandon their traditional, group-based identities and communities and become individuals who bear certain rights and obligations and enjoy the right to choose and determine their circumstances. Consequently, liberals tend to hold that group-based identities such as those of Aboriginal people, and collective rights such as Indigenous rights, have no place in modernity. (This ignores, of course, the fact that individual rights championed by liberals have been closely associated with the claims of a group, whether it be called British or white, and that it has been long claimed that these can only be protected by ensuring a homogenous nation in which the normative values are those of the dominant group.) As Brett has pointed out, this way of imagining the world has had a peculiarly strong charge in the case of *Australian* liberalism.[1]

In the last fifteen or more years matters of race and nationhood have become more important again in national politics in democracies. In large part this can be attributed to the convergence of the major political parties. As they have come to espouse much the same economic and social policies, they have found it necessary to distinguish themselves from one another in some other terms. To do this, they have turned to the realms of race (or culture), history and nation. During Paul Keating's prime ministership, the Labor Party advanced a 'big picture' which comprised an embrace of Australia's position in the Asia-Pacific region, a celebration of multiculturalism, a demand for Australia to reject its British roots and become a republic, and a championing of Aboriginal culture and history and the cause of reconciliation which included a modicum of support for Indigenous rights and an apology to Aboriginal people who had been separated from their kin as children (the stolen generations). As a consequence, Keating's Labor Party seemed to prosper; at any rate it won the 1993 election, which many thought it could not win. In the wake of this the Liberals were urged to take up an opposing position on matters of race, history and nation, not least by John Howard who returned to the party's leadership shortly afterwards. In the 1996 election he played the race card in order to appeal to those most threatened by social, cultural and economic change. In particular, he claimed that the Keating government had favoured the special rights of groups such as Aboriginal people. His party's election slogan 'For all of us' was a form of dog whistle politics. After thirteen years in the political wilderness, the Liberal Party returned to power.[2]

Once in office, Howard's Coalition government soon made clear it would do its best to overturn the Aboriginal policy that had allegedly been dominant since the 1970s (see document 65, pp. 150–1). It mounted an assault on Indigenous rights, particularly native title, and 'self-determination', particularly the Aboriginal and Torres Strait Islander Commission, and announced a return to a policy which reminded many of the assimilation program of the post-war era, if not the 'protection' of the pre-war one. Howard seemed to condone the attacks that the One Nation Party leader Pauline Hanson made on special rights for Aboriginal people by failing to condemn these. The Coalition abandoned its support for the approach of the Council for Aboriginal Reconciliation to reconciliation, most noticeably by refusing to make an apology to the stolen generations. The government styled its policy on Aboriginal affairs as 'practical reconciliation', spurning what it called 'symbolic reconciliation'. Howard led an assault on so-called black armband history, particularly the work on the history of colonialism and racism in Australia which had helped to create a climate of opinion among settler Australians in support of righting the wrongs of the past. Likewise, he called for a return to a style of celebratory history which had tended to dominate accounts of the national past prior to the 1970s. Howard played on a fear of 'foreigners' (by championing 'border protection'), attacked multiculturalism, and espoused what he called integration.

In the early years of the Howard government, constitutional matters regarding Aboriginal people arose in three contexts. In 1997, on the occasion of the thirtieth anniversary of the referendum, the Prime Minister sought to appropriate its meaning by constructing a particular narrative about it. 'Our approach as a government to the process of

Pat Dodson, chairperson of the Council for Aboriginal Reconciliation, reads the 'Call to the Nation' at the closing ceremony of the Reconciliation Convention in May 1997, which had celebrated the thirtieth anniversary of the referendum and honoured those who had campaigned for it. The Howard government had already begun to undermine the process by attacking Indigenous rights and denying Australians today were responsible for the wrongs of the past. (Courtesy *Age*)

reconciliation is very much guided by and heavily influenced by the spirit of the 1967 referendum', he claimed. 'If the 1967 referendum spoke of anything it spoke of a need to remedy in a practical way the disadvantage of the Aboriginal and Torres Strait Islander people'. In other words, the spirit of the referendum was practical, not symbolic (see document 65, pp. 150–1).

In 1998, Howard made further reference to the referendum. He had belatedly come to feel the need to be critical of Hanson's racist pronouncements on Aboriginal people just as he felt the need to attack the former Labor government's Aboriginal policies. Howard made a number of points. First, he gave Hanson a history lesson by pointing out that she had been mistaken in claiming that the referendum had given Aboriginal people the vote. Hanson was, of course, in good company. Indeed, this included the Prime Minister's own party: two years earlier one of its policy discussion papers had made the same basic claim as Hanson by alleging that the referendum had granted Aboriginal people 'citizenship rights'.[3] Second, in an attempt to distinguish his party's racial policies from those of Hanson's, Howard attacked her allegedly racist claim that the referendum had amounted to a vote for special rights for Aboriginal people (which she thought non-Aboriginal Australians must now regret),[4] by claiming that it was instead an anti-racist gesture on the part of settler Australians. Apart from anything else, Howard's account disguised the fact that the principal constitutional change at stake in the referendum concerned special racial laws. Third, Howard misrepresented the history of the referendum by implying that it had been sponsored by the Coalition government alone and by suggesting it had done so because it wanted to use the new race powers it would provide. As we have demonstrated, neither was true. Fourth, Howard repeated the rhetoric of the principal campaigners for the referendum by claiming that it was a push to treat all Australians the same, thereby disguising once more the fact that these campaigners had pushed for the referendum so that a federal government could enact special racial measures for Aboriginal people. Fifth, Howard contrasted the rightfulness of the referendum's approach to Aboriginal affairs — treating all Australians the same — with that of the Hawke and Keating Labor governments — treating Aboriginal people in a racially divisive manner. We will return to the problematic of this later. Sixth, Howard claimed that the approach embodied by the referendum and its 'yes' vote was a good practical gesture, as distinct from a bad symbolic one. This, of course, overlooked the fact that symbolism had been absolutely critical to the huge 'yes' vote and thus to Commonwealth gaining powers in order to tackle the many areas of Aboriginal people's disadvantage that Howard claimed he wanted to tackle (see documents 58, pp. 141–3; 65, pp. 150–1 and 70, pp. 156–7).

Yet, Howard did not merely deride the importance of this symbolism; he led a government that derogated the most important constitutional change comprised by the referendum, as we will discuss shortly.

Questions about Aboriginal affairs and the Constitution arose in the context of another referendum. In November 1999 a referendum was conducted in which two changes to the Constitution were put to the voters: first, should Australia become a republic (by replacing the British monarch and the governor-general with a president appointed by two-thirds majority of the members of the Commonwealth parliament), and, second, should a new preamble be added to the Constitution. As we have noted, the republic had been sponsored principally by the government's political opponents but they had sought to separate it from constitutional matters regarding the relationship between Aboriginal people and the Australian nation. Howard was opposed to the republican proposal and he used the proposal for a new constitutional preamble in order to promulgate his take on Australia's history, race and identity.

A government-sponsored constitutional convention in 1998 had agreed that there should be a new preamble which acknowledged 'the original occupancy and custodianship of Australia by Aboriginal peoples and Torres Strait Islanders', but it had refused to endorse a recommendation to include an acknowledgement that Aborigines and Torres Strait Islander should have 'continuing rights by virtue of their status as Australia's indigenous peoples'. Most importantly, the convention had stipulated that the preamble be drafted 'in such a way that it does not have implications for the interpretation of the Constitution'.[5] As historian Mark McKenna has observed, 'Aboriginal people were to be given a preamble of gestures and good intentions, but one without legal or political impact'.[6]

One of the convention's working groups, which included the former and then current ATSIC chairpersons Lowitja O'Donoghue and Gatjil Djerrkura, urged that wide consultation and discussions take place with ATSIC and other relevant groups before a new preamble was presented to the voters.[7] In fact, when Howard drafted a preamble early the following year he barely consulted anyone, let alone Aboriginal people and their leaders. In the end, nearly every major Aboriginal figure in the country roundly condemned the preamble that the Howard government proposed to put to the people. Several called for it to be dropped from the referendum.[8] The preamble celebrated racial inclusion and cultural sameness at the cost of any substantive reference to Aboriginal people's distinctive relationship to the nation. At best, it celebrated Aboriginal culture but its representation of this smacked of the way its antiquity had long been appropriated by settler Australians for their own purposes (see document 64, pp. 149–50). The Coalition did little to advocate a 'yes' vote on the preamble until the last week of the referendum campaign. The preamble failed to get a majority of votes in any state or territory, faring even worse that the republic: 39.34 per cent compared to 45.13 per cent of the national vote.[9] Most Aboriginal leaders seem to have welcomed this resounding defeat. This was unremarkable. As Djerrkura commented: 'It did not promote reconciliation or advance our aspirations'.[10]

The failure of the other proposal in this referendum makes even clearer the lessons to be drawn from the 1967 referendum as well as the reasons why it won such an enormous level of approval. The republican movement had adopted a minimalist strategy in its attempt to win support for its call for Australia to become a republic. Consequently, it was difficult for most voters to grasp why the constitutional change being proposed was a significant one for the nation. By contrast, the campaigners for the Aboriginal proposal in the 1967 referendum had set out to convince voters that a 'yes' vote *would* bring significant change, and it was their representation of the constitutional changes at stake which helped to ensure its success.

During this period of the Howard government, another important question regarding Aboriginal people and the Australian Constitution came to the fore: what was the precise nature of the power that 1967 referendum had granted the Commonwealth to make special laws with respect to Aboriginal people? This occurred in the context of the Coalition government's moves to extinguish Indigenous rights in regard to land, first by passing legislation to enable a 'development' project in South Australia that threatened to desecrate sites of cultural significance to the Ngarrindjeri people, and, second, by passing legislation to amend the 1993 Native Title Act (following the High Court's 1996 Wik decision) in order to ensure the interests of capital and the government's racial conception of Australia. The Ngarrindjeri sought to have the government's legislation overturned by taking a case to the High Court regarding the scope of the race power, and this move threatened to foil the government's attempt to extinguish native title rights.

In response, the Howard government claimed that the very power the Commonwealth had gained as a consequence of section 51 (xxvi) being amended in the 1967 referendum was not limited to laws that merely benefited a race such as the Aboriginal people. This provoked considerable debate among lawyers (see document 67, pp. 152–3). Aboriginal leaders voiced their objections (see documents 63, pp. 148–9 and 64, pp. 149–50), and the Labor Party tried to block the government's moves by proposing a motion in the Senate which declared that 'the referendum was passed with the intent that the power conferred on the

Commonwealth only be used for the benefit of the Aboriginal and Torres Strait Islander people'.[11]

The government's claim about the nature of the race power flew in the face of what had been stated at the time the amendment to section 51 (xxvi) was being considered.[12] The Menzies and Holt governments knew that the text of section 51 (xxvi) could be construed as granting the Commonwealth the power to enact legislation to disadvantage as well as advantage Aboriginal people but they had ruled out the former construction because of the context in which amendment of it had been proposed. In August 1965 Attorney-General Billy Snedden had observed in his submission to Cabinet:

> it seems implicit in the arguments put forward that it is accepted generally that, if the Commonwealth were given the power to legislate by the deletion of the words [other than the Aboriginal race], it would not itself discriminate against Aborigines, though it might give them special help.[13]

This construction of the race power was the very reason why the Coalition government had urged voters to endorse the Aboriginal question in the referendum. In May 1967 Prime Minister Harold Holt gave the voters this assurance:

> Nor is it, we believe, acceptable to the Australian people as a whole that the National Parliament should not have power to make special laws for the people of the Aboriginal race, where that is in their best interests...I am confident that acceptance of this referendum proposal by the people will work only for the good of our Aborigines.[14]

The official 'yes' case gave a similar undertaking (see document 43, pp. 126–7). (The historical record here demonstrates, of course, that Howard's representation of the 1967 referendum as merely a vote for Aboriginal people to be treated the same as everyone else cannot be sustained.)

The Howard government rejected the significance of this historical evidence.[15] In 1998 it instructed the Solicitor-General Gavan Griffith to make a case that section 51 (xxvi) gave the Commonwealth unlimited power to make special laws in respect of Aboriginal people. In the High Court Griffith admitted that '[t]here was an expectation that the Commonwealth would pass laws for the benefit of Aborigines', but he argued that 'you can't go from that to say the people narrowed the power to benefit only'.[16] Many conservative lawyers agreed, most liberal lawyers did not (see document 66, pp. 151–2).[17] In the High Court Justice Kirby expressed dismay: '1967 is a great historical event. It can't be ignored'. More importantly, he warned that the interpretation advanced by the Howard government's legal counsel meant the Commonwealth would now have the power to pass laws like South Africa's apartheid laws and Nazi Germany's anti-Jewish laws.[18] In the end, Justices Brennan and McHugh found it unnecessary to address the scope of the race power in reaching their decision (against the Ngarrindjeri), and the remaining four judges hearing the case split into opposing camps on the matter.[19] In other words, the Court failed to resolve the matter of whether the Commonwealth has the power under the Australian Constitution to enact racially discriminatory laws. This was hardly a solid foundation for advancing reconciliation.[20]

Aboriginal leaders reacted to the High Court's ruling by calling for a referendum to clarify whether the Commonwealth had the power to pass discriminatory laws against Aboriginal people (see document 69, pp. 155–6).[21] The Constitutional Convention took place at the same time that the High Court heard the Ngarrindjeri case, and from there Djerrkura called for an alteration to the Constitution to make the race power purely an affirmative one. 'This will guard against detrimental acts by government', he remarked. 'In fact, this should have been done in 1967'.[22] Some critics suggested that those who campaigned for the referendum lacked foresight in 1967, but at the very least this overlooks the fact that few at that time could conceive of a context in which another way of conceiving of rights, namely Indigenous rights, would become very powerful and there could be governments who would want to attack this, in the name of 'racial equality' or the same treatment of all peoples, as an unacceptable form of 'racial privilege' or 'racial divisiveness'. Others called for changes that would prevent any racially specific laws whatsoever (see document 68, p. 154). Among these was the federal president of the National Party, the Coalition's partner in government. Don McDonald made clear that his party's policy required that all Australians be treated 'equally', which is to say they should be treated the same, and he called for the repeal of the race power and its replacement with a guarantee of non-discriminatory treatment of all people.[23]

This vision of racial equality — that everyone, whether they are Aboriginal or settler, should be treated the same — has obviously underpinned the approach of the federal government to Aboriginal policy during the last ten years or so. (It has been suggested that this is the defining quality of contemporary Australian racism, amounting to a bedrock refusal to accept that special measures are required when the specially needy are Aboriginal, and that its motto is 'not for them unless for all of us'.)[24] It can be argued, though, that another, closely related conception of equality has exerted more influence on public policy in Aboriginal affairs under all governments in the last forty years, whether they be Coalition or Labor. This has been called the paradigm of 'formal equality'. This has primarily focused on granting civil rights. It is apparent that this and the repeal of discriminatory laws has led to some improvement in the lives of some Aboriginal people in Australia over the last fifty years, but it is just as clear that this has not wrought dramatic changes in the well being of most. In other words, the paradigm of formal equality, which has traditionally been celebrated in the myth of the 1967 referendum, most recently by the Howard government, has obviously failed to redress the profound disadvantage suffered by Aboriginal people.[25]

This conception of equality can be contrasted to a paradigm of 'substantive equality'. It seeks to achieve equality by bringing about significant social and economic change, and does this through the provision of special assistance. This, as we have demonstrated, was one of the reasons why the principal campaigners for Aboriginal rights fought so hard for the 1967 referendum. Since the early 1970s, at any rate, governments in Australia have undoubtedly acknowledged the need to grant Aboriginal people special rights, including Indigenous rights, but in the end their provision of assistance in accordance with these has been relatively limited. They have been reluctant to move much beyond the paradigm of formal equality in order to use all the avenues that are available to government to devise policies and practices to redress Aboriginal disadvantage. For example, governments have not really tried to use the kind of special measures adopted by comparable countries. Furthermore, contrary to populist myths, the Commonwealth has not allocated significant additional public expenditure and resources to the task. One should not pretend that the profound disadvantage of Aboriginal people in Australia can simply be redressed by the provision of more government funds, but it seems clear that the failure of government to advance much beyond the paradigm of formal equality prevents the implementation of policies that could help achieve this goal.

Governments in Australia are undoubtedly aware that any approach to Aboriginal affairs that recognises the special rights of Aboriginal people and thus provides significantly greater assistance to Aboriginal people than that available to other people is regarded by most Australians with considerable ambivalence. A Newspoll survey conducted for the Council for Aboriginal Reconciliation in 2000 revealed that more than seven in ten people accepted that there was a need for government programs to address the disadvantage of Aboriginal people but that nearly six in ten believed that 'Aborigines should not be entitled to special rights' and claimed that they received too much assistance. This presumably owed much to the fact that only four in ten regarded Aboriginal people as a disadvantaged group and only about three in ten thought they were much worse off than other Australians. As the surveyors concluded, 'there is a significant gap between the facts and what many people believe about the position of Aboriginal people.[26]

Rather than tackle this resistance to special rights for Aboriginal people, the current government has allowed itself to be persuaded by new conservative intellectuals that the task of redressing the profound disadvantage that most Aboriginal people continue to suffer bears no relation to the provision of rights and the protection of those rights. In fact, this government and these intellectuals have mounted an assault on what they have dubbed 'the Aboriginal rights agenda'.[27] They have claimed that this failed because it distracted government from tackling the practical needs of Aboriginal people in the thirty or so years following the 1967 referendum.[28] This assertion cannot be sustained. The most important campaigners for Aboriginal rights in the 1950s and 1960s conceived of rights for Aborigines as a means to a practical end rather than simply a symbolic end in itself, and by the time of the referendum in 1967 these rights included the right of Aboriginal people to resources (or capital) in many forms and the power to determine their own lives. Moreover, as we have made clear in this chapter, this programme for reform has never been properly implemented in this country and so it cannot be said to have failed.

It is apparent that there remains a need to protect the rights of Aboriginal people in Australia. This could be done, for example, by entren-ching these in a bill of rights, taking either a constitutional or a legislative form. Other comparable nations, such as Canada and New Zealand, have all set out the basic rights and freedoms of their people in this way. Each of these nations once relied, as Australia does, on the common law tradition but they have recognised that there is a need to supplement this with a bill of rights. This can provide a cogent statement of rights, and so can help protect the rights of Indigenous peoples from governments that seek to extinguish these.[29]

In the light of this, we can be sure that calls for constitutional change will continue to be made in reference to rights of one kind or another for Aboriginal people. Governments come and governments go. In the future, there will be an opportunity to realise those calls for change by means of another referendum.

# Documents

# Part I

## Written Sources

### 1. 'The Aborigines', *Sydney Morning Herald*, 25 January 1911

The case for the blacks of Australia was admirably put to the Prime Minister yesterday by a deputation of scientific, commercial, religious, and political men...The deputation was introduced by Mr G.B. Edwards...and the speakers were Archdeacon Lefroy, Messrs J.H. Malden (representing the Australian [sic] Association for the Advancement of Science), C. Hedley (president, Linnean Society), G.F. Earp (Newcastle), Senator A. McDougall, T. Brown, MP, and Bishop Stone–Wigg. They gave the views of the various missionary societies, as well as those of ethnologists and patriots.

Briefly, the suggestions made to Mr Fisher covered the following propositions, which were carried at a public conference, held in Sydney a few days ago:

1.  That measures ought to be taken immediately by the Federal Government in order to secure wise and humane treatment of the 18 000 or 20 000 aborigines who inhabit the Northern Territory;

2.  that, recognising the increased native obligations thrown upon the Federal Government by the taking over of the Northern Territory, the Government be urged to appoint forthwith a commission of inquiry, with a view to the drawing up of a comprehensive scheme for dealing with all the native obligations of the Commonwealth;

3.  that the Government be also urged to institute as soon as possible a separate department for native affairs (with oversight of aborigines, Papuan, and other native races), and to appoint a special Minister to be at the head of that department.

4.  that in the meantime the Federal Government should give immediate and earnest attention to the introduction of such legislation as will secure the welfare of the aborigines in the Northern Territory;

5.  that before any existing Crown lands in the Northern Territory are leased or alienated, numerous and ample reserves should be mapped out, sufficient to allow for some increase of the aboriginal race, and also that sufficient money be provided for stocking or otherwise developing these reserves...

## 2. Archdeacon C.E.C. Lefroy, Evidence, Royal Commission on the Constitution, 1927–29, Report of the Royal Commission on the Constitution together with Appendices and Index, Minutes of Evidence, Government Printer, Melbourne, 1929, pp. 478–81

...I propose that all the aborigines in Australia should be made a single national responsibility under a single National Government, namely, the Commonwealth Government. My reasons for that are: That the aborigines, to begin with, are not necessarily a dying race. They could be preserved and increased in number. Everywhere native races, when properly protected and cared for by the white races, show a tendency to increase rather than to diminish...Our natives are not necessarily a dying race, but I think they will not be properly cared for and protected unless they are all treated as one responsibility. Today, there are only from 80 000 to 100 000 of them left. Unless put under one single responsibility they will never bulk large enough to attract much national attention.

My next reason is, this: Not only can they be preserved, but they are well worth preserving. They are not the lowest race on earth. That is a base calumny. The aboriginal has extraordinary human qualities...I have studied a great deal of the early history of our aborigines. All my life I have sympathised with them. My father before me — he was something of an explorer — taught me to be kind to the blacks. I am certain they are worth preserving, and I am certain they could be made a very valuable population and commercial asset... The quickness with which the aborigines pick up European ideas, notions and ways of thinking is extraordinary. Settlement could not possibly have spread as it has done had it not been for the native population. Therefore, as they have rendered good services in the past, why should not the remnant render equally good service to the Commonwealth as a whole...

My next ground is that of humanity. The aborigines should be made a national responsibility because all Australia owes them a debt of reparation. We have certainly dispossessed them of their country; no one will question that. We have certainly to some extent exploited them by using their labour for nothing; no one can dispute that. At times and in places we have treated them very cruelly. The whole of Australia owes a debt of reparation to the aborigines, and the debt is equally distributed. At the present time four States practically wash their hands of the aborigines — South Australia, Victoria, New South Wales, and Tasmania...They should accept the moral responsibility for them, and to a great extent the financial responsibility also. They ought to give time and thought and care to elaborating a policy towards the aborigines worthy of the country. I desire to arouse a national conscience, and it will never be possible to arouse it otherwise.

Another reason is that the Commonwealth is responsible for Papua, and boasts, at the Geneva Conference, of its good administration of Papua and the mandated territories. Quite right, too, but is it not strange that it says nothing of its own aborigines? The Commonwealth cannot speak for them because it does not have the care of them. It seems so inconsistent for the Commonwealth to be spending time and labour and thought upon the natives of Papua, and never be giving thought to the bulk of its own aborigines.

Another reason why I should like them all brought under Federal control is that the churches and all missionary and philanthropic Agencies would be able to do their work much better, or, at any rate, they would be influenced to devote more care and more effort than ever before to this neglected matter...

In the setting up of our colonies and self-governing States, Great Britain has always tacitly admitted that the ultimate responsibility for the native inhabitants rests with the Imperial Government...Whenever a colony was granted self-government, the Imperial Government stipulated that something should be done for the native inhabitants, showing that the Imperial Government realised their responsibility to the native people...The States had not absolute authority over the aborigines. In theory the Imperial Government always reserved a certain amount of responsibility to itself. That shows, I think, that it is in accordance with the British Constitution that the highest Australian authority should hold the responsibility for the Australian aborigines.

Then I suggest that the aborigines could be taken over by the Commonwealth without any prejudice to the general question of enlarging the powers of the Commonwealth...A great many people are opposed to enlarging the powers of the Commonwealth. They fear that if they opened the door a little way to allow the aborigines in, the door might be pushed wider open and other claims for larger powers might be advanced. People are acting wrongly if they sacrifice the aborigines in order to preserve State rights. But if that tendency does exist, the question of handing over control of the aborigines to the Commonwealth should be made a separate issue at any referendum, so that the people of Australia could consider the matter fairly and squarely, and deal with it worthily of our position as a young nation...

I should think [an increase in the number of aborigines is desirable], provided they are raised in the scale of civilisation. Anyhow, they are joint owners of the country with us. It would not compromise the white Australian policy at all...

[T]he Federal authorities would desire to deal with the aborigines in a way worthy of the nation. The State has no such obligation. The State is not recognised in the world, whereas Australia has a position to occupy in the civilised world...

I think in the nature of things it will be easier to get an improved policy from the whole of Australia than from the separate States. National responsibility should be taken up by the supreme national authority...I do not think you can create a national consciousness, unless you put the whole aboriginal responsibility together.

### 3. Secretary, Department of Home Affairs, to Rev. William Morley, Hon. Secretary, Association for the Protection of the Native Races of Australasia and Polynesia, 13 February 1929, APNR Records, University of Sydney Archives, Series MS 55, series 7

With reference to your recent deputation to my Minister on matters affecting Aborigines in the Commonwealth...

*The Commonwealth to control all aboriginals in Australia*

Members of the deputation will probably remember the proposal made by a deputation, which waited upon the Minister for home and Territories some time ago, that a Commission representing the Commonwealth and the

States should be appointed to inquire into aboriginal affairs throughout the whole of Australia.

When negotiations were entered into by the Commonwealth Government with the Governments of the various States in regard to this proposal, the majority of the State Governments expressed the opinion that the aboriginals under their control were adequately cared for, and, apart from the legal difficulties associated with the appointment of such a Commission, the proposal was not viewed with any favour.

In this connection it is pointed out that the control of aboriginals in the various States comes within the jurisdiction of the State Governments...

The proposal put forward by the deputation that the whole of the aboriginals in Australia should come under the control of the Commonwealth Government, could not be given effect to without the concurrence of the various State Governments.

It is highly improbable that the State Governments would agree to transfer their control over aboriginals to the Commonwealth.

### 4. William Morley, Hon. Secretary, Association for the Protection of the Native Races, 2 February 1934, NAA, CRS AI, file 36/6595

This Association like other bodies concerned with our Aboriginal Problems, such as the Australian Aboriginal Association of WA, and the Australian Federation of Women Voters, respectfully urges that full consideration be given at the forthcoming meeting of the Premiers' Conference to the formulation of a Positive Policy for the Aborigines to be administered by one authority, or through the various State Governments concerned, the former for preference.

Recent events have shown that public opinion in Australia is stirred concerning this matter, and further, opinion abroad, especially in England is also being brought to bear on it.

Moreover as a member of the League of Nations we are morally bound to frame and work some policy designed to raise our Aboriginal race, and to solve by a well considered policy the problem of cultural and racial clash in northern and central Australia. To leave this problem to settle itself will continue to bring grave injustice on the natives, and ill repute on ourselves...

We sincerely hope that the Conference of Premiers will give the matter the full time and consideration which is necessary.

On behalf of the Association for the Protection of Native Races.

### 5. Miss AN Brown, Hon. Secretary Victorian Aboriginal Group, to the Rt Hon. the Prime Minister, Joseph Lyons, 10 February 1934, NAA, CRS A431, item 48/ 961

We note with appreciation that the question of a National policy of Federal Control of Aborigines throughout Australia has been placed on the Agenda for the forthcoming Premiers' Conference in Melbourne.

There is constant and widespread dissatisfaction both inside and outside the Commonwealth regarding aboriginal affairs, justified by the condition of natives, particularly...where the small white population cannot possibly provide sustenance...for the relatively large aboriginal population.

We trust that you will use your influence to have the matter fully discussed, and remove the stigma from Australia's good name, by supporting the principle of coordinated control in the interests of the natives under a fully qualified Special Commissioner.

In addition we would like to draw your attention to the fact that the Federal Government has signed Clause 23 of the Covenant of the League of Nations, by which it undertakes as a nation to see that its native people are given just treatment. On that account we are as morally bound to consider the welfare of our own aborigines as we are that of the natives of the Mandated Territory...

The following Societies have authorised us to quote their names as supporting this appeal: The National Council of Women; the Australian Women's National League, The Presbyterian Women's Missionary Union, The Aboriginal Fellowship Group, The Society of Friends.

### 6. William Cooper, Secretary Australian Aborigines' League, to the Rt Hon. The Prime Minister, Joseph Lyons, 22 July 1936, NAA, CRS A461, A300/1, part II

The aborigines are looking forward with deep concern to the forthcoming conference of Premiers in Adelaide next month as they feel that their destinies are somewhat involved.

You have undertaken to bring the matter of aboriginal control and policy to the conference and we do plead that no circumstance be permitted to shelve or delay the matter.

We do plead for one controlling authority, the Commonwealth and request that all aboriginal interests be absolutely federalised. This will enable a continuous common policy of uplift, which we trust will contain provision for the exploitation of all natives' reserves by the natives. By the natives, under able leadership, and for the natives. We submit an aim, which is practicable, and that should be the ultimate self liquidation of the whole problem of uplift. So far from the aboriginal continuing to be a charge on the community, he can be made under sound and capable direction to be an asset to the community. This is a long vision no doubt.

We plead for this, but if the Premiers are not willing to lose a responsibility they do not wish to retain we plead for a common policy under Commonwealth control or influence with a subsidising of the States on the aboriginal per capita basis. We have no hope where the States with large aboriginal populations cannot adequately finance their obligations and the States with small aboriginal populations, or none, as in the case of Tasmania, should not be freed from responsibility.

We would request that the request of this League for parliamentary representation be considered. If the whole control is federalised this should be readily concedable, but if the States retain control, we submit that such representation should be accorded to our people in the States' legislature, at any rate where the aboriginal populations are numerous.

Trusting that you will bring these requests to the notice of the Premiers.

### 7. Bessie Rischbieth, President, Australian Federation of Women Voters, to Rt Hon. The Prime Minister, Joseph Lyons, 19 January 1938, APNR Records, University of Sydney Archives, series 7

In view of the general dissatisfaction felt by representatives of competent bodies actively associated with the welfare of aborigines, the Australian Federation of Women Voters notes with satisfaction that the Federal Government proposes to hold a Conference of responsible Federal and State Ministers for discussion and investigation of the whole position in regard to the aborigines.

Believing this to be a new method of approaching a difficult national problem we urge that at the inauguration of the Sesqui Centenary Celebrations a pronouncement shall be made which will embody an assurance that the investigation shall be of a most comprehensive nature and the findings of the Conference shall be implemented at the earliest possible opportunity. We further believe that anything less than a definite declaration that the Commonwealth's responsibility to Australian natives will be clearly realised and adequately fulfilled would greatly mar the significance of the Sesqui Centenary Celebration.

### 8. 'Our Ten Points: Deputation to the Prime Minister', *Australian Abo Call*, no. 1, 1938, p 1

The following is a full copy of the statement to the Prime Minister at the Deputation of Aborigines on 31st January last...

The Deputation consisted of 20 Aborigines, men and women, and Mr Lyons gave a hearing of two hours to the statement of our case.

Please read these 'ten points' carefully, as this is the only official statement of our aims and objects that has yet been made.

TO THE RIGHT HON. THE PRIME MINISTER OF AUSTRALIA...

In respectfully placing before you the following POLICY FOR ABORIGINES we wish to state that this policy has been endorsed by a Conference of Aborigines, held in Sydney on 26th January of this year. This policy is the only policy which has the support of the Aborigines themselves.

URGENT INTERIM POLICY

Before placing before you a long-range policy for Aborigines, and while the long-range policy is under consideration, we ask as a matter of urgency:

That the Commonwealth Government should make a special financial grant to each of the State Governments, in proportion to the number of Aborigines in each State, to supplement existing grants for Aborigines...

The following 10 points embraces a LONG RANGE POLICY FOR ABORIGINES, endorsed by [the Aborigines Progressive Association].

A LONG RANGE POLICY FOR ABORIGINES
1. We respectfully request that there should be a National Policy for Aborigines. We advocate Commonwealth Government control of all Aboriginal affairs.

2.  We suggest the appointment of a Commonwealth Ministry for Aboriginal Affairs, the Minister to have full Cabinet rank.
3.  We suggest the appointment of an Administrative Head of the proposed Department of Aboriginal Affairs, the Administrator to be advised by an Advisory Board, consisting of six persons, three of whom at least should be of Aboriginal blood, to be nominated by the Aborigines Progressive Association.
4.  The aim of the Department of Aboriginal Affairs should be to raise all Aborigines throughout the Commonwealth to full Citizen Status and civil equality with the whites in Australia...

### 9. APA Burdeu, Hon. Secretary Aborigines' Uplift Society, to Hon. Secretary, APNR, 14 June 1940, APNR Records, University of Sydney, Series S55, series 7

Our Council gave consideration to the matter of the omission on the part of the framers of the Constitution of Australia to provide for matters concerning the care of Aborigines.

It was decided to ask kindred organisations to give consideration to a proposal submitted by one of our foremost members to the effect that the Federal Government should submit the matter to the electorate for decision by referendum when next any matters are being submitted.

It was felt to be improbable that the Government would ever incur the expense of a referendum on this matter unless other matters were being submitted. It might agree to submit the matter at the same time that other matters were the subject of referenda.

### 10. Ruth Swann, Hon. Secretary, APNR, to the Rt Hon. the Attorney-General, Dr HV Evatt, 10 November 1942, APNR Records, University of Sydney Archives, Series S55, series 7

[At a meeting of the executive committee of the APNR] it was unanimously decided to suggest an additional section...to be added to Clause 2 of the proposed amendment of the Constitution. Such a section to run some-what as follows: The administration and advancement of the aborigines of Australia with a view to their being endowed wherever possible with full citizenship rights.

This suggestion was supported by a resolution to the following effect:
1.  The Aboriginal problem being Australian wide in Character should be dealt with as one problem by an authority equally wide in character
2.  Inconsiderate and ill treatment having caused the extinction of the aborigines of some of the States of the Commonwealth, and such conditions persisting in others, though it may be differing in character, and bring upon Australia the opprobrium of the civilised world
3.  In order to preserve as far as is just and reasonably possible the continued existence and peculiar culture of the race it is desirable and expedient that the administration of aboriginal affairs be placed in the hands of the one Australian authority qualified to deal with it as whole viz: the Commonwealth Government.

## 11. AP Elkin, *Citizenship and the Aborigines: A National Aboriginal Policy*, Australasian Publishing, Sydney, 1944, pp. 7–11, 43, 54–9

The decade 1930–39 was characterised in Aboriginal Affairs by an advance from a negative protective policy and outlook to a conviction and demand that a positive and forward looking policy should be framed and put into operation, and that steps should be taken to have a unified system (or at least closely collaborating systems) of Aboriginal administration for the continent. It may be that the present decade will see the working out of some such system of unified or collaborating administration.

The first published draft of the Temporary Post-war Powers Bill made no mention of the Aborigines. But in the belief that the New World and Reconstruction should be theirs as well is ours, representations were made to the Commonwealth Government...to include the welfare of Aborigines in the Bill. In this way the fourteenth point was added, and the Aborigines may at length be recognised under the Commonwealth Constitution.

The referendum may, or may not, be carried. But in any case, willingness to hand over this power was expressed by the Governments of New South Wales, Queensland, South and Western Australia, which States and the Northern Territory include almost all of the *full-blood* and *'half-caste'* Aboriginal population of the Commonwealth. This suggests that at least political opinion is not now opposed to a unified form of Aboriginal Admini-stration. Therefore, irrespective of the fate of the Powers' Bill and the Referen-dum, we should prepare ourselves for some measure of unity and close collaboration in this sphere.

This small book is designed to be a contribution to our thinking and planning on this matter...Considerations is given to...the possible ways in which a unitary policy can be administered by the Commonwealth and the five States concerned...

### Chapter 1. Opinion and Aboriginal Policy in the 1930s

From time to time, especially during the past twenty years, various indivi-duals and organisations have advocated that the Commonwealth should take steps to assume the oversight and control of the Aborigines of Australia – in other words, that there should be one Policy for the Aborigines, administered by the Commonwealth.

The reasons or the suggestion include the following:

1. In the eye of the world at large, Australia as a whole is held responsible for all Aboriginal policies and occurrences, good or bad, irrespective of the State or States concerned, and regardless of the fact that outside the Northern Territory, the Commonwealth has neither say nor power in Aboriginal Affairs.
2. The State boundaries coincide neither with Aboriginal tribal or social sub divisions, nor with the types of region which are differentiated by geographical conditions and degree of white settlement...
3. The six Administrations have worked, and indeed still work, not only under different Acts, but also under differing (as well as separate) definitions and regulations with respect to similar or the same problems...

*Advance in Aboriginal Policies during the 1930s*

The spread of knowledge based on scientific research, the watchfulness and public work of humanitarian and missionary bodies, and the holdings and findings of commissions of enquiry (following on unfortunate occurrences) resulted in an advance of public opinion on Aboriginal affairs during the '1930s'. This, in its turn, was responsible for the advocacy of a unified policy and administration. It seemed to interested citizens an obviously sensible and logical step to take, and one which would ensure that each advance in policy or method would apply all over the Commonwealth and not merely in one State — a line of argument which is still sound...

### Chapter 3. A National Policy for Aborigines, 1944

The following suggested National Policy for Aborigines and Part-Aborigines has been drawn up on the basis of the foregoing principles and of the advance in opinion and attitudes during the past decade...

A. – AIM

The aim must be full citizenship, with all its rights, privileges and responsibilities — for all persons of Aboriginal descent...

### Chapter 4. Administration of a National Policy

...*Forms of Administrative Control*

There are three possible forms of control for the administration of a national policy for Aborigines it Australia.

*Parallelism* — The first may be called parallelism: the five States on the mainland and the Commonwealth (for the Northern Territory) could agree on, and accept, in Conference one policy, to be authorised in similarly worded Acts, sets of definitions and regulations, expressing the one set of aims and principles, to be applied by each administration in the types of regions and circumstances for which the definitions and regulations were framed. Regular conferences of administrative heads would have to be relied on to meet the changing conditions in a uniform manner and so maintain the parallelism. Each administration would meet its own expense...

*Convergence* — In it the parallel lines meet, in that the Commonwealth, in consultation with the States, would determine the policy and be responsible for the total expenditure, while the State Governments would undertake the work of administration within their several territories. Perhaps this form could be called convergence, in that the six administrations converge in the single policy determined by the national Government...

*Unification* — A third form of organisation for implementing a national policy is for the Commonwealth authorities to determine the policy (after consultation with those who have had experience in the States), to frame the Act and all regulations, meet all costs, and appoint and control all staff...This is unification...

Any of these forms of control could be made to work if we set ourselves to the task. If the referendum, 1944, is carried, then the third form, that of unification of control and financial responsibility for Aboriginal affairs will be the logical consequence. This would also follow if the States agreed to hand over to the Commonwealth their authority and responsibility in this matter...

The future will bring a decision. At least this is certain, we would gain much by getting away from our present form (or lack of form) of six completely separate, and almost separatist, Aboriginal Administrations. We are all Australians dealing with Australian Aborigines...

## 12. 'The Welfare of Native Races', Newspaper clipping, 11 August 1944, Elkin Papers, University of Sydney Archives, Series 1/12/193

No conflict arises in respect of the proposal to give the Commonwealth power to control aborigines.

### Dr H.V. Evatt, Attorney–General and Minister for External Affairs.

Including half-castes, there are now fewer than 100 000 people of the aboriginal race in Australia. The bill makes their welfare and protection a national responsibility.

The part they have played during the war has given them a special claim to consideration in the postwar years. Neither the Commonwealth nor the States can feel satisfied with their care of the aborigines in the past.

When the present Constitution was drafted, the Commonwealth was given power to make special laws, if it thought necessary, with respect to the people of other races. However, our own aborigines were expressly excluded.

Since then, the Commonwealth has become responsible for the welfare of native populations both in the Northern Territory and in New Guinea. In the postwar years it will play a much larger part in protecting native peoples in the South–West Pacific.

The exclusion of the Commonwealth from the protection of the Australian aborigines was always an anomaly. Postwar responsibilities will make this exclusion an absurdity.

Vote 'YES' for Reconstruction and the protection of our own racial minority...

### R.G. Menzies, Federal Opposition Leader.

...If this amendment could be voted on separately, we would support it. But we would do so with a warning that while there should be a sense of national responsibility toward the descendants of the original inhabitants of Australia, there should also be a clear recognition of the fact that what the aborigines need is not a centralised administration in Canberra, but a wise local administration by specially qualified people of sympathy and understanding.

On most of the amendments we have considered there would be a far greater readiness on the part of people to increase central power if they could feel more certain that we were really going to study the art of decentralising administration.

## 13. Chairman and Secretary, National Missionary Council, and President and Secretary APNR, to the Rt Hon. the Acting Prime Minister, JB Chifley, 21 June 1945, NAA, CRS A461, item A300/1

### Commonwealth Control of Aboriginal Welfare

For more than a decade the National Missionary Council and its constituent members, also the Association for the Protection of Native Races and other bodies concerned in the welfare of the Aboriginal peoples of Australia have been urging the adoption of a National Policy for Aboriginal Welfare under the control of the Commonwealth Government, and you will recall that such a proposal was included in the matters submitted to the Nation in the Referendum last August.

Although the Referendum as a whole was not carried we have reason to believe that there is a large measure of support for this matter concerning Aboriginal Welfare, and we understand that the Governments of New South Wales, Queensland, South Australia and Western Australia have expressed willingness to hand over Aboriginal Welfare to the Commonwealth.

We therefore beg to request that you will take the necessary steps to have the matter brought up for consideration at the next Premiers' Conference in order that ways and means may be found for giving effect to this very necessary advance in placing our Age responsibility towards these Aboriginal people upon a truly national basis.

Some reasons for the adoption of a uniform Policy are:

1.  In the eyes of the world at large Australia as a whole is held responsible for all aboriginal policies and occurrences, good or bad, irrespective of the State or States concerned.
2.  State boundaries coincide neither with Aboriginal tribal or social sub-divisions nor with the different types of country differentiated by geographical conditions and degree of white settlement.
3.  The six Administrations work not only under different Acts but under differing definitions as to what is an Aborigine, and differing regulations with respect to similar or the same problems...

There has been a definite advance in public opinion during the last decade and in the advocacy of a unified policy and administration. It seems to interested citizens an obviously sensible and logical step to take, and one which would ensure that each advance in policy and method would apply all over the Commonwealth and not merely in one State. The desirability of such collaboration between the authorities concerned appears to have been definitely recognised by the Conference of Commonwealth and State Ministers held in Adelaide in August 1936 and the meeting of Government Officers controlling Aborigines held in Canberra in April 1937.

We therefore request your assurance that this important national question will be brought up for consideration at the next Premiers' Conference as this appears to be the most practicable way of effecting this necessary reform.

### 14. Henry Wardlaw, Secretary, Council for Aboriginal Rights, to Rt Hon. Paul Hasluck, Minister for Territories, 28 August 1951, CAR Papers, State Library of Victoria, MS 12913/1/2

Members of my Council have read with pleasure of the convening by the Federal Government of a Conference of Ministers responsible for the administration of native affairs within the various States...

As you are no doubt aware from your personal experience in the United Nations Organisation, the treatment of the aborigines in Australia has laid the Australian Government open to justifiable charges of hypocrisy when its representatives have charged the Governments of other countries with depriving their subjects of elementary human rights. We would therefore urge upon you that the Universal Declaration of Human Rights, to which the Australian representative at the United Nations has set his name, should be taken as the basis for the necessary reforms in the treatment of the aborigines.

In particular, I would be grateful if you would bring to the notice of the Conference the following Articles of the Universal Declaration; it should not be necessary to draw attention to the specific portions of the legislation of the Commonwealth and the various States which directly contravene these Articles ...

I think that a perusal of the Universal Declaration will show that the above list could be considerably expanded without injustice to any of the States or to the Commonwealth Government.

May I, on behalf of my Council, express the hope that this Conference will go far towards achieving uniformity of policy towards the aborigines, and the speedy improvement of conditions under which they now live. May I also hope that its decisions, unlike those of the Conference of Commonwealth and State Welfare Authorities of 1948, will be rapidly put into effect.

### 15. Jessie Street to Ada Bromham, c. 15 March 1957, Jessie Street Papers, National Library of Australia, MS 2683/10/165a

...I did not do anything about the aborigines while I was there [in Brisbane]. I thought it better to wait until you returned and could make some arrangements for me.

I had an interview with Paul Hasluck last week and on his suggestion I am going up to Canberra to see him and departmental officials within the new few days. I discussed with him the possibility of a referendum to amend the Constitution to vest powers over the aborigines in the Commonwealth Parliament and to extend all legal rights as enjoyed by the white population to the aborigines. He appeared to be quite favourably disposed to this suggestion. I hope he is going to arrange for me to visit various places in the Northern Territory.

I have had a nice letter from Brian Fitzpatrick in which he says that the Australian Council for Civil Liberties will be prepared to organise a conference of bodies dealing with aborigines which might be interested to form a federal organisation to sponsor the report that I am doing for the Anti-Slavery Society.

I am sending him all the answers to the various questionnaires I receive and any other information I get. I hope very much that you will see him on your way through Melbourne so that he can discuss with you the information you supplied...

### 16. Aboriginal-Australian Fellowship, Petition, 1957, Brian Fitzpatrick Papers, National Library of Australia, MS 4965/1/5273

THE HUMBLE PETITION of the Electors of the State of New South Wales respectfully sheweth — The Aboriginal Residents of Australia suffer under disabilities political, social and economic, and that these in important respects are not remediable without Amendment of the Constitution of the Commonwealth, and that Aborigines are entitled to human rights equally with other Australians

OUR PETITIONERS THEREFORE HUMBLY PRAY

THAT the Government of the Commonwealth bring down a Constitution Alteration Bill in the Parliament of the Commonwealth, and submit the Bill when passed to a Referendum of the people, each at the earliest practicable date, so as to:

Delete the words underlined in Section 51 (xxvi) of the Constitution of the Commonwealth (other than 'the aboriginal race in any State') which gives power to the Parliament of the Commonwealth to make laws with respect to 'the people of any race *other than the aboriginal race in any State* for whom it is deemed necessary to make special laws', and

Delete Section 127 of the Constitution of the Commonwealth which reads, 'In reckoning the numbers of the people of the Commonwealth, or of a State or other part of the Commonwealth, aboriginal natives shall not be counted'.

AND your Petitioners, as in duty bound, will ever pray.

### 17. Aboriginal-Australian Fellowship, Leaflet, 1957, CAR Papers, State Library of Victoria, MS12913/2/7

THE ABORIGINAL-AUSTRALIAN FELLOWSHIP IS PRESENTING THE FOLLOWING PETITION TO THE COMMONWEALTH GOVERNMENT

1. That the Commonwealth Government hold a referendum or take other appropriate action to take over all the powers of the States regarding Aborigines and to amend the Constitution in so far as to delete Section 51 (xxvi) and Section 127 on which the discrimination against Aborigines is based.

2. That the Commonwealth Government extend to Aboriginal Australians in all States of the Commonwealth the same political, social and civil rights and opportunities as enjoyed by European Australians.

IF THESE SECTIONS ARE DELETED: —

1. The Commonwealth Government would be responsible for the welfare of all Aborigines.
2. A uniform policy for the whole Commonwealth would apply to Aborigines.
3. All Aborigines would receive the same social benefits as white Australians, i.e. — Old Age and Invalid Pensions, Widows Pension, Baby Bonus and Child Endowment.
4. Aborigines would receive the same pay for the same work and the same industrial protection as white Australians.
5. As far as Aborigines living in tribal state are concerned, land would be provided for suitable co-operative development, Pastoral, Agricultural or Mining, for those Aborigines who have been driven from their tribal land...All co-operative schemes, where Aborigines are concerned, would be controlled by Aborigines and grants obtained from the Commonwealth Government for their development.

### 18. The Rt Hon. the Minister for Territories, Paul Hasluck, to Mr Joske, 2 May 1957, Brian Fitzpatrick Papers, National Library of Australia, MS 4965/1/5275

Following our discussion yesterday regarding the suggestion that responsibility in respect of aborigines should be transferred from States to Commonwealth, I would like to take the opportunity of mentioning some matters which would have to be considered. I shall not comment on the constitutional aspects of the proposal but only on the administrative aspects.

Most of the practical work which can be done to advance the welfare of the native people has to be done in the States by State Departments, such as the Department of Education, Department of Lands, Department of Agriculture, Department of Health, the Housing Commission, the Department of Justice, the Child Welfare Department, and so on. Even if the powers were transferred to the Commonwealth, it would still be necessary for the Commonwealth to use the State instrumentalities in any practical efforts it made to assist the aborigines. I am personally convinced that the welfare of the aborigines depends far more in the present generation on practical steps to improve their health, hygiene, education, housing and chances of getting a job than amendments of legislation and all these practical steps could be taken at once by the existing governments of Australia under their existing powers, if they chose to do so.

I feel, too, that I must express my own personal disagreement with the views that have been expressed regarding the meaning of Section 127 of the Constitution. This Section does not appear to me to have the significance which has been attached to it. Earlier in the Constitution, provision is made regarding the way in which the House of Representatives shall be elected and the number of members to be chosen in each State is determined by dividing the number of people of the State by a quota which is fixed in relation to the number of people of the whole Commonwealth (See Section 24). To my mind, Section 127 says little more than that, in doing the piece of arithmetic required by Section 24, the population figure taken shall be, in fact, the population who at present or in due course will qualify for a vote. By all means let us do everything possible to aid the advancement of aboriginal people towards full citizenship but, recognising the fact that at the present time there are still some thousands of them whose lack of education and manner of living mean that they cannot exercise responsibilities, do not let us fill into the error of saying that, in spite of the fact that they are not yet citizens, they have to be counted as citizens. I feel that the practical task of advancing their welfare and aiding their assimilation is of far more importance at the present time than taking fine points regarding the meaning or intention of an obscure section of the Constitution.

In my constant work for the advancement of native welfare, I am finding that some of the biggest obstacles are being set by people who think they have done something when they have changed words, whereas what we want is to change lives.

### 19. Federal Council for Aboriginal Advancement, Petition, 1958, CAR Papers, State Library of Victoria, MS 12913/11/5

To the Honourable the Speaker and Members of the House of Representatives assembled:

The humble citizens of the Commonwealth respectfully showeth that while the aboriginal people of Australia suffer under disabilities social, economic and political, your petitioners are concerned and anxious on their behalf, requiring that they be adequately fed, clothed and housed and given such securities as are the people of all races who have come to live in this country. These disabilities in important respects are not remediable without the Commonwealth Government accepting responsibility for the care of the aboriginal people throughout Australia.

Your petitioners therefore humbly pray that the Commonwealth Government make provision for an alteration of the Federal Constitution by means of a Referendum to be held at an early date, in order to:

1. Delete the words in Section 51 (xxvi) of the Constitution of the Commonwealth ('OTHER THAN THE ABORIGINAL RACE IN ANY STATE') which now gives power to the Parliament of the Commonwealth to make laws for the peace, order and good government of 'the people of any race', OTHER THAN THE ABORIGINAL RACE IN ANY STATE for whom it is deemed necessary to make laws, and

2. Delete Section 127 of the Constitution of the Commonwealth which reads 'In reckoning the numbers of the people of the Commonwealth or of a State or other part of the Commonwealth aboriginal natives shall not be counted'.

And your Petitioners, as in duty bound, will ever pray.

## 20. The Rt Hon. the Minister for the Territories, Paul Hasluck, to Jessie Street, 3 September 1959, Brian Fitzpatrick Papers, National Library of Australia, MS 4965/1/5305

...I had not previously known of the South Australian interpretation which you quote. The Commonwealth viewpoint in this connection is, however, that aborigines born in Australia are Australian citizens by virtue of the Nationality and Citizenship Act 1948–1958. This citizenship is the only national status which people have in relation to Australia although by dint of our relationship to the Queen and to the British Commonwealth of Nations Australian citizens are also British subjects.

The rights and disabilities of Australian citizens, that which they may and that which they may not do within Australia, are not to be found in the Nationality and Citizenship Act. Those rights and disabilities are to be found in the general laws of Australia which is made up of the common law and Federal and State statutory law. Thus people born in Australia are subject to many disabilities by reason of the general law. Further, their rights and [the] disabilities to which they are subject are not necessarily the same throughout Australia. This condition results from the element of State statutory law in the general law.

The status of aborigines in relation to nationality and citizenship is determined by the Federal Statute. Being born in Australia, and not within any of the groups which the Act excepts, aborigines are Australian citizens. But to ascertain what rights Australian citizens, including aborigines, have and to what disabilities they are subject, it is necessary to look at the general law.

### 21. Shirley Andrews, Federal Council for Aboriginal Advancement Petition Campaign Organiser, Circular Letter to Members of Executive, State Secretaries, Affiliated Organisations, undated, c. July 1962, Gordon Bryant Papers, National Library of Australia, MS 8256, box 174

The last Annual Meeting of the Federal Council for Aboriginal Advancement decided on an Australia wide petition calling for a referendum to amend the Federal Constitution so as to delete the clauses which discriminate against Aborigines.

During the discussion many suggestions were made concerning other urgent questions which could also be the subject of petitions. The executive considered, therefore, that some of these matters should be mentioned in the preamble of the petition. Considerable thought has been given to including these without making the preamble too long. Our draft is enclosed herewith. Please indicate whether it would be acceptable to you in this form, before 10th of August.

As the handling of an Australia wide petition will require a considerable amount of organisation, we would suggest that steps be taken as soon as possible to set up a committee in each state to deal with the petition. The subject of this petition is one which should command the widest possible support and it should be possible to get many organisations, trade unions, etc to take part in a campaign built around this petition.

Affiliated organisations are asked to give the FCAA state secretaries all possible assistance in setting up these committees.

### 22. The Rt Hon. Kim Beazley snr, Speech during Question Time, Commonwealth of Australia, House of Representatives, 24th Parliament, First Session, 1962, pp. 878–9

...Everything which reasonably can be construed as discrimination should be eliminated from the Constitution of the Commonwealth. Section 127 reasonably can be construed as discrimination. The practical difficulties of reckoning the numbers of aborigines, which would have been very great in 1897, would not be insuperable to-day. Section 127 is now operating unjustly to the States which have the largest aboriginal populations. Now that aborigines have voting rights, an indefensible anomaly has arisen. Unnaturalised people who may not vote and are not citizens count in a State's quota. Aborigines who may vote and are citizens do not count in a State's quota. The removal of section 127 does not involve us in any dispute over the distribution of power between the Commonwealth and the States.

Section 51, paragraph (xxvi), is another provision which can be construed as discrimination. It is a mention of aborigines which has had in the past — unnecessarily it is true — the serious effect of depriving them of social services. This was a misconstruction of the section, remedied comparatively recently by the present Government, but there is no reason why aborigines should be mentioned. If, as the conferences of State and Federal Ministers recently declared, aborigines are fully Australian citizens, then their constitutional position should be that they are subject to State and Federal law in the same way as are other citizens. This would be the effect of not mentioning them at all in the Constitution of the Commonwealth. The truth is that they are not citizens in the same sense as are other Australians while this section exists. The Commonwealth can confer full citizenship rights on an aboriginal in the Northern Territory. He loses them on entering Western Australia or Queensland. The Commonwealth is powerless to insist that citizenship rights have Australia-wide force. Section 51, paragraph (xxvi), has a different effect from section 127. It means that the aborigines in the States are a body of citizens to whom the Commonwealth is denied access.

I realize that the deletion of the words "other than the aboriginal race in any State" may not reach voting rights in State parliamentary elections, but other features of citizenship — the right of movement to seek employment, for instance — might be reached by the elimination of these words. Special laws might be necessary to meet the special needs of aborigines, but those special laws are forbidden by the presence of the words we propose to delete from this paragraph.

At international conferences the Commonwealth bears the odium of any discrimination against aborigines. Absence of any discrimination would be a significant part of the ideological defences of the nation. Aborigines facing the problems of citizenship are facing senseless anomalies. They are subjects of the Queen; they are people of the Commonwealth; they are people of a State. But their whole status is called into question by these two sections.

We do not doubt that a referendum to delete these provisions would have the support of the great majority of the people of Australia, and of the press. A liability on Australian diplomacy would be removed and reality could be given to aboriginal citizenship. Barriers to tackling their special needs would be removed. This is not a party question. It is not the wielding of a governmental economic power at the expense of private enterprise. It is not the removal of something that inherently should be an exclusive power of a State. It is a removal of a barrier to effective Commonwealth power to confer a meaningful nationality and citizenship on the people of the aboriginal race.

## 23. Federal Council for Aboriginal Advancement Petition Leaflet, 1962, CAR Papers, State Library of Victoria, MS 12913/11/5

PETITION FOR A REFERENDUM TO REMOVE DISCRIMINATION AGAINST ABORIGINES FROM THE FEDERAL CONSTITUTION

THE AUSTRALIAN CONSTITUTION AT PRESENT PROVIDES:

The Council maintains that these examples of racial discrimination should be removed.

Aborigines are people, despite Section 127, and they have the right to peace, order and good government under the Commonwealth Parliament.

*Section 51, Clause XXVI*

Means that laws with respect to Aborigines are the responsibility of the States apart from those living in the Northern Territory.

The effect of this clause is that there is little uniformity in the laws governing Aborigines in the States and Territory...

Such variations and inconsistencies can hardly be justified and must cause a great deal of confusion. Consider, for example, the case of an Aboriginal transferring from a settlement in NSW to one in the neighbouring State of Queensland.

The types of benefits should depend on the degree of education and integration enjoyed by the Aborigine and not on the State or Territory in which he resides.

The Federal Government has no power to make laws with respect to Aborigines and yet must try to defend in the United Nations and other International bodies the varied assortment of Rights and Restrictions practised by the States.

This clause has been used to justify the practice of not paying Federal Award Wages to Aborigines. These awards should apply to all workers in the relevant industries.

The only practical way in which these variations can be removed is for the Commonwealth to Possess and Exercise the power to make laws with respect to Aborigines.

*Section 127 — Census:*

Implies that Aborigines are not people or at least not people of any account. Apart from its institutionalised insult to Aborigines, this section has some practical implications.

I. Reimbursements to the States of money collected as Income Tax are based on their populations as obtained in the Census. The States thus receive no reimbursements for the Aborigines in their communities but are expected to provide basic services such as Education, Housing and Hospitals. On the other hand, the Commonwealth collects Income Tax from Aborigines in the States, but has no power (under Section 51) to make laws to assist them and cannot under Section 127, reimburse the States with this money.

This anomaly can be corrected by deletion of Section 127.

II. Aborigines may now vote at Federal Elections, but are not counted in the Census, which is used to fix electoral boundaries. The exercising of this right will increase the size of the electorate and so decrease the effectiveness of their vote. Both Queensland and Western Australia probably lost a seat in the House of Representatives because of this section.

III. Australia has a responsibility to educate Aborigines and integrate them into the economic life of the community. This responsibility is recognised by both the Commonwealth and the States. It is difficult to see how this responsibility can be met if accurate information is not obtained as to how many Aborigines are living in each locality.

FOR BOTH MORAL AND PRACTICAL REASONS, SECTION 127 MUST BE REMOVED FROM THE CONSTITUTION

## 24. Gordon Bryant, 'A Referendum', *Smoke Signals*, vol. 2, no. 1, 1962, pp. 2–3

No aborigine can feel absolutely free and equal to other Australians whilst the Commonwealth Constitution contains the two clauses which exclude him from the Census...and from Commonwealth laws ...

This placitum of section 51 was for a long time the excuse given by the Commonwealth for the exclusion of aborigines from Social Service benefits.

It was not until a number of members of the Commonwealth Parliament challenged the logic of this in the House, that a new look was given to the old question, and this discrimination removed. It is, of course, a question of language. A law which excludes aborigines from a benefit is just as much a law about Aborigines as one which includes them.

The demand for the removal of these clauses from the Constitution is not just an academic one — it rests on two grounds. The first — that the implied discrimination is a reflection[,] in fact an insult to the aboriginal people; the second — that the specific exclusion of the Commonwealth from the right to make special laws about the aboriginal race means that the Commonwealth denies any responsibility (outside the Territories) and the State Governments therefore claim it. And in so claiming, they exercise rights and powers over the aboriginal people, which they would not dare to exercise over the last arrived migrant.

A great deal of the energies and thinking of organisations...outside Victoria is devoted to trying to have State acts altered.

So we find our friends in NSW mounting campaigns to have the restricted clauses of the State act amended.

In Queensland, Western Australia and South Australia, the position is much the same. In Western Australia and Queensland, for instance, despite the grant of votes for aborigines at Federal Elections, aborigines are still excluded from State elections.

**ABORIGINES STILL HAVE NO VOTE** for State elections in Queensland and Western Australia.

So all over Australia — outside Victoria — the Aborigine is beset with a more complicated set of laws than any other Australian.

**The quickest and the most logical way to amend this position is to change the Constitution by Referendum.**

Remove from the States the right to make special laws for the aboriginal people, and the State acts which deprive Aborigines of fundamental rights and freedom must surely be invalid.

This does not mean, of course, that the Commonwealth has been full of sweetness and light on the Aboriginal question, but the Commonwealth carries out its activities under much closer public national scrutiny than any State Government or the totality of them.

At present, those of us concerned with the plight of the Aboriginal people have to fight six State Governments and the Commonwealth — seven legislatures and seven administrations — an enormous organisational task ...

Transfer the responsibilities to the Commonwealth and immediately every Federal parliamentarian and every Federal department has to accept its share of responsibility. And this must be said, 'that whether one agrees with i[t]s politics or not, when the Commonwealth acts — it acts in [a] grand manner'.

Compared with the resources at the disposal of the States, when applied to a particular field, the resources of the Commonwealth are relatively limitless ...

[T]he Federal Council...[has] adopted such an amendment of ·the Constitution as urgent policy...

We should therefore commence campaigning immediately — the task is in two stages: To convince the Commonwealth to conduct the Referendum, and Secure a majority of votes in a majority of the States when the Referendum is submitted to the people...

No stone must be left unturned — a vote approaching national unanimity on this question would give notice to all Governments that the conscience of Australia is stirred, and the public will brook no delay in tackling the other disabilities of the aboriginal people.

Come then, let us to the task.

### 25. Shirley Andrews, 'Could Legislation Help Instead of Hindering the Aborigines?', *Smoke Signals*, vol. 2, no. 3, 1963, pp. 19, 21–2

Now that the National Petition for the amendment of the Commonwealth Constitution is circulating, people often ask what sort of legislation the Federal Government should be asked to introduce when it has the power to do so.

The amendment of Sections 51 and 127 will not immediately remove all legislation discriminating against Aborigines. But the way would then be clear for the passing of uniform Federal legislation which would take precedence over existing States legislation.

Doubts have been expressed as to whether legislation that is uniform throughout Australia could provide adequately for Aboriginal people living at different levels of development, from tribal life to modern industrial society.

Many Aborigines who have suffered bitterly from the present discriminatory legislation feel that no Australian Parliament can be trusted to introduce legislation that is really in the interests of the Aboriginal people, and that the only safe procedure would be for them to come under only the same laws as the rest of the community. The proposition has been put forward that any special needs, such as the ownership of reserves...could be dealt with by new sections introduced into existing Acts such as the Lands Act, Social Services and other social welfare legislation and Education Acts.

It is not surprising that the Aborigines feel so strongly that legislators cannot be trusted when dealing with laws intended only for Aboriginal people. It has happened again and again that laws brought in supposedly to protect Aborigines have been turned into instruments of oppression...

Despite this previous experience, it could be that special legislation does offer the Aborigines a better chance of ensuring that their special needs are properly provided for. Any procedure that requires the amendment of several important Acts is likely to defeat its own purpose by getting hopelessly bogged down. As the Aborigines constitute only one per cent of the Australian population, their special needs may not be given the importance and degree of urgency that is desirable if they are just fitted into general laws already in existence. The main objections raised by Aborigines to special Aboriginal laws could be overcome by drawing up laws which would apply only to those Aborigines who wished to take advantage of the special facilities provided by them, and to ensure that Aborigines who took advantage of the special facilities available for them would not suffer any restriction of their rights as they do under existing legislation...

Many Australians feel that proper compensation has not been given to the Aborigines to make up for their unjust treatment in the past...The present restrictive laws must be completely abolished and the Aborigines themselves consulted as to their special needs...Participation in the provisions of these new laws is to be entirely voluntary, and it is essential that Aborigines must be given the opportunity to take part in the control of their own affairs. The time has come for Aborigines to take their proper place as the indigenous people of Australia, entitled to respect and consideration as such.

Australia's past policies towards the Aborigines have been based on out-moded ideas belonging to the era of colonialism. We are not sufficiently aware of the more advanced policies being adopted in many other parts of the world...A great deal of useful information is contained in the International Labour Organisation's 'Indigenous and Tribal Populations Convention 107', drawn up in 1957. The Federal Council for Aboriginal Advancement fully endorsed the articles of this Convention at its conference in 1959, and adopted it as a basis for policies to be followed in obtaining social justice for the Aboriginal people of Australia...

The particular importance of the ILO Convention is that it advocates integration as a people rather than the assimilation of individuals...

Another important aspect is that the Convention advocates a completely equal status with other sections of the population, and at the same time, such special measures as are required for 'promoting the social, economic and cultural development of these populations and raising their standard of living'...Article 3, Section 3 emphasises that these two principles must operate simultaneously 'Enjoyment of the general rights of citizenship without discrimination, shall not be prejudiced in any way by such special means of protection'...

Unfortunately we are still only approaching the very first stages of this legislative reform, namely, the primary necessity of amending the Federal Constitution. But having a clear idea of how legislation could function in the true interests of the Aborigines can help us all to work with greater enthusiasm for our National Petition as the first step in this program of urgently needed legislative reform.

## 26. Submission to Cabinet by Attorney-General the Rt Hon. BM Snedden, 22 February 1965, NAA, A5827/1, item 660

...Section 127...

25. It would, in my view, be politically inexpedient, in the present climate of public opinion, to put any proposals for Constitutional amendments to a referendum without including in those proposals the repeal of section 127. Moreover, the inclusion of this proposal would, I think, tend to create a favourable atmosphere for the launching of the proposal regarding section 24.

26. Cabinet considered the question of the repeal of this section in considering the Report of the inter Departmental Committee on Racial Discrimination in September, 1964. It felt then that there might be a case for its repeal, but thought that it was not clear that all the practical considerations

surrounding the taking of a referendum would justify, or even permit, action to initiate a referendum on this subject alone. It therefore held over a final decision on section 127.

27. The Constitutional Review Committee considered that section 127 should be repealed and so recommended in its [1959] Report...

28. One of the reasons for the inclusion of section 127 seems to have been the practical difficulties that would be encountered in satisfactorily enumerating the aboriginal population. There were no doubt real difficulties in 1900 in ensuring that a census of aborigines could be effectively taken. In modern times, however, this would be by no means impracticable and any argument in favour of retention of section 127 based on difficulty in ascertaining the numbers of aborigines has little force. Moreover, whatever was the original position, the existence of section 127 is hardly related to the qualification of aborigines as voters...

29. As aborigines are...now entitled to enrol and vote, they should, I think, undoubtedly be recognised as forming part of the population of their State for the purposes of the Commonwealth Constitution.

30. There would assuredly be international approbation of any move to repeal section 127, as it savours of racial discrimination. Its repeal could remove a possible source of misconstruction in the international field.

31. I accordingly recommend that a Bill to amend the Constitution by repealing section 127 be introduced as soon as the Parliament meets in March and that the Bill be submitted as soon as possible to a referendum.

32. I have referred in paragraph 20 of this Submission to my proposal that section 25 be repealed as part of the bill to provide for a new section 24. Section 25 has been criticised as being of a discriminatory nature and it appears to me that its repeal is a natural concomitant of the proposal to repeal section 127.

*Section 51 (xxvi)*

...

34. When Cabinet considered the Report of the inter–Departmental Committee on Racial Discrimination in September, 1964, it stated that it did not support the proposal to amend section 51 (xxvi) by omitting the underlined words [i.e. 'other than the aboriginal race in any State'].

35. I wish to raise this matter again for Cabinet's consideration...

37. I think that the public believes that the underlined words in section 51 (xxvi) amount to a discrimination. I do not personally accept that in truth they are: indeed, I think that their inclusion in the section constitutes a protection rather than a discrimination. But I think we must have regard to the electors' view of the matter. The deletion of the words would have the consequence that the Commonwealth would have concurrent legislative power to make laws with respect to people of the aboriginal race as such and in this I see no harm.

38. ...I believe that failure to include a proposal to delete the underlined words might well prejudice the success of a referendum that sought the repeal of section 127...

39. I might mention that the Darwin Conference of Commonwealth and State Ministers on aboriginal welfare held in July, 1963, resolved that 'in view of the widely varying conditions in different States and the fact that

so many aspects of Aboriginal welfare are in the State lawmaking field, it would not be in the best interests of the Aboriginal people to have uniform Commonwealth legislation or uniform administration. The whole tendency in Australia is to eliminate laws that apply specially to the aboriginal people'. However, if the Commonwealth were given the power to legislate it would not follow that it would exercise its powers and so long as the State — and Territory — laws were operating satisfactorily, the Commonwealth Parliament need not intervene.

40. I therefore recommend that a Bill be drafted forthwith to omit from section 51 (xxvi) the words 'other than the aboriginal race in any State' and that the Bill be introduced as soon as possible after Parliament resumes and be submitted to a referendum as soon as possible after it has been passed by both Houses...

### 27. GM Bryant, Vice-President, FCAA, The Case for Changing Section 51 (section 26), leaflet, 18 April 1965, CAR Papers, State Library of Victoria, MS12913

The Parliament shall, subject to this Constitution, have power to make laws for the peace, order, and good government of the Commonwealth with respect to the people of any race, other than the Aboriginal race in any state, for whom it is deemed necessary to make special laws.

The Prime Minister stated in the House of Representatives that he was not persuaded that this was desirable as it may introduce a new element of discrimination into Commonwealth Law but was still considering the matter and implied that he was open to conviction.

At present, the Commonwealth may make laws for the Aborigines in the NT and ACT and WHEN OUT OF AUSTRALIA — that is an Australian Aboriginie in NZ or Britain is a full Australian subject to all the benefits of Commonwealth law — for instance, full social service benefits under our reciprocate Social Service Agreement but not necessarily for example, in Queensland.

Nor may the Commonwealth make laws for the Aborigines in any state, that is any Aborigine in Vic, NSW, Qld, WA, SA, Tas — approximately 84% of Australian area and 80% of the Australian Aborigines.

The Commonwealth acts in favour of many separate groups in the community, for instance it has established schools for migrants in many parts of Australia under its immigration power where it teaches English but does not and in strict fact, would not have the constitutional power to do so, teach Aborigines.

The Commonwealth has an extensive Repat. Act for service men and women established under the Defence Power but while a similar system is desirable even essential, for Aborigines, the Commonwealth has no power to establish such a system, especially for Aborigines.

The Commonwealth has offered the Nauruan people a home on Curtis Island with substantial cash advances for housing, etc. and special rights there. It has not done so for any group of Australian Aborigines displaced by mining or other developments in a state and in fact would have no power to do so.

The Commonwealth has established secondary and tertiary scholarships for a wide variety of Australian students including, of course, Aborigines, but because of Section 51 (Section xxvi) could not make a special case of the Aborigines although one doubts whether it would be challenged if it decided to do so. THEREFORE: 1% of Australia's citizens (100,000) have not the full benefit of Commonwealth law or the fundamental protection available to any other person in Australia whether Australian born, migrant or even illegal entry.

Great legal battles, over illegal entrants, and the Government's power to deport them are frequent. They have access to the courts in a way denied to some Aborigines because of the absolute paramountcy of state laws.

The Queensland State Government denies votes for Aborigines of that state for state elections. Can you imagine them excluding naturalized Italians as a group? While they possibly have the legal right to do so, the moment they did this, they would come into collision with the Commonwealth. Is there any doubt which would prevail?

The Aborigines of Australia are discriminated against without any benefits being available in lieu of thereof. We ask that Section 51 (Section xxvi) be submitted to a referendum to remove this limitation on Commonwealth action in the belief that all Australian laws ought to apply equally to all Australians and that no one should be excluded from Commonwealth benefits on account of race. For the foreseeable future, the Commonwealth would be expected to DISCRIMINATE IN FAVOUR of the Aborigines by special beneficial legislation. Only the Commonwealth has the resources to do this but a change would not remove the states from the right to act any more than the Social Services Legislation prevents the states having Child Welfare Services, etc.

## 28. Kath Walker (later Oodgeroo Noonuccal), Hon. Secretary, Queensland Council for the Advancement of Aborigines and Torres Islanders, Circular letter to Members of the Commonwealth Parliament, 9 June 1965, NAA, A432/70, 67/3321 Pt 1

This organisation wishes to bring to your attention the fact that the proposed Referendum to alter the Constitution with regard to its legislative power over Aborigines, fails to include Section 51(Placitum XXVI).

This is, in our opinion, a most serious omission. Our Organisation believes that Aborigines should enjoy equality as Australian Citizens.

To delete Section 127, will certainly represent a welcome removal of an existing discrimination. However, in failing to seek the people's removal of Section 51 from our Constitution, the Federal Government is vastly diminishing the value of the proposed Referendum.

The real question at issue will still remain unsolved: Are Australian Aboriginals Citizens of the Commonwealth of Australia, or not? Until all legal and executive discrimination is removed, this country stands in danger of being stigmatised, as is South Africa, in failing to observe the Universal Declaration of Human Rights.

We hope, Sir, that you will use your voice to present these points in the Parliament of Australia.

**29. The Rt Hon. Sir Robert Menzies, Speech introducing the Second Reading of the Constitution Alteration (Repeal of Section 127) Bill 1965, Commonwealth of Australia, House of Representatives, 25th Parliament, First Session, 1965, pp. 2638–9**

The purpose of this Bill is to alter the Constitution by repealing section 127... The Government believes that the first opportunity should be taken to have it repealed and proposes to submit the Bill to referendum at the same time as the referendum on altering the method of determining the number of members of the House of Representatives. The Joint Committee on Constitutional Review recommended repeal in its report — that is the 1959 report...

I think I should at this point make reference to the Government's decision not to put forward any amendment of section 51 (xxvi). I mention this because the Deputy Leader of the Opposition (Mr Whitlam) had a question on the notice paper about it and I am now, in effect, answering that question...

Some people wish — and indeed the wish has made been made clear in a number of petitions presented to this House — to associate with the repeal of section 127 the removal of what has been called, curiously to my mind, the 'discriminatory provisions' of section 51 (xxvi). They want — and I understand their view — to eliminate the words 'other than the Aboriginal race in any State', on the ground that these words amount to discrimination against Aborigines. In truth, the contrary is the fact. The words are a protection against discrimination by the Commonwealth Parliament in respect of Aborigines. The power granted is one which enables the Parliament to make special laws, that is, discriminatory laws in relation to other races — special laws that would relate to them and not to other people. The people of the Aboriginal race are specifically excluded from this power. There can be in relation to them no valid laws which would treat them as people outside the normal scope of the law, as people who do not enjoy benefits and sustain burdens in common with other citizens of Australia.

What should be aimed at, in the view of the Government, is the integration of the Aboriginal in the general community, not a state of affairs in which he would be treated as being of a race apart. The mere use of the words, 'Aboriginal race' is not discriminatory. On the contrary...If the words were removed, as some people suggest — and there is quite an attractive argument in favour of that — it would change dramatically the scope of the plenary power conferred on the Commonwealth. That must be borne in mind. If the Parliament had, as one of its heads of power, the power to make special laws with respect to the Aboriginal race, that power would very likely extend to enable the Parliament to set up for example a separate body of industrial, social, criminal and other laws relating exclusively to Aborigines...Conferring such a new power could have most undesirable results...

Returning to the Bill before the House, the matter can be simply put by saying that section 127 is completely out of harmony with our national attitudes and with the elevation of the Aborigines into the ranks of citizenship which we all wish to see ... [T]o omit from section 51 (xxvi) the words 'other than the Aboriginal race in any State'...would give the Commonwealth Parliament...a plenary power, to make laws...with respect to Aborigines — for example, industrial laws, social service laws, health laws, and so forth. Is this desirable? I have endeavoured to point out that we do not think it is. Should not our overall objective be to treat the Aboriginal as on the same footing as all the rest, with similar duties and similar rights?...

### 30. WC Wentworth, 'Does Referendum Go Far Enough?', *Sydney Morning Herald*, 17 November 1965

The present Federal Government has done more for the advancement of our Aborigines than has any of its predecessors — perhaps more than all its predecessors combined.

In the last decade it has given them rights as electors; it has made them eligible for social services; it has removed most of the discriminations against them; and it has moved steadily towards the elimination of their economic disabilities. In the establishment of the Institute of Aboriginal Studies it has recognised the value of their culture and thus helped them to regain something of their inherent dignity.

At first glance, therefore, it may seem somewhat strange that the Government's present referendum proposals are not more far-reaching. The present bill before Parliament...merely repeals Section 127 of the Constitution...

This modest proposal will, of course, receive overwhelming support — but does it go far enough? Even when carried, it will still leave the Commonwealth Government without any direct responsibility for Aboriginal advancement outside the Northern Territory, and it will leave power of 'discrimination' against Aborigines in the hands of the various States.

The Aboriginal problem should be looked upon as a national problem, even though the States may continue to administer Aboriginal welfare. It will involve a good deal of expense, and it would seem unfair to place the overwhelming burden of that expense on the States of Queensland, Western Australia and South Australia, where the problem is greatest...

Can the situation be cured, as some people advocate, by simply removing the words 'other than the Aboriginal race' [from Section 51 (xxvi)]?

Probably sure a cure would be worse than the disease. As the Prime Minister has rightly pointed out, the Commonwealth now has power to make special laws on a racial basis for everybody except Aborigines, and to remove these words would subject Aborigines to potential discrimination rather than protect them from it. The removal of these words might, perhaps, imply some Commonwealth responsibility, but would not necessarily mean the end of discrimination under State laws, since the Commonwealth powers under Section 51 are concurrent rather than exclusive.

There is, however, another approach. Would it not be possible to remove the whole of paragraph XXVI from Section 51? This would mean that the Commonwealth would have no power to make laws on a racial basis in regard to Aborigines or anyone else...

With our ideal of a homogenous Australian people, it has no place in our Constitution today, and indeed it could be argued with some reason that the power to discriminate among Australians on racial grounds is exactly the kind of power which no Government should have...

It is true that the excision of the whole of paragraph XXVI...would not prevent the States from making [racial] laws, and it would be desirable to guard against this by inserting into the Constitution a positive prohibition against racial discrimination inside Australia, binding upon both Commonwealth and States [a new Section 117A — 'Neither the Commonwealth nor any State shall make or maintain any law which subjects any person who has been born or naturalised within the Commonwealth of Australia to any discrimination or disability within the Commonwealth by reason of his racial origin. Provided that this Section shall not operate so as to preclude the making of laws for the special benefit of the Aboriginal natives of the Commonwealth of Australia'].

Such a provision would surely be in line with our national thinking and it would be very helpful to our representatives overseas in some of the difficult discussions which they must conduct in the United Nations and elsewhere.

The gap left in Section 51 of the Constitution could be appropriately filled with a new paragraph XXVI, giving the Commonwealth power to make laws for 'The advancement of the Aboriginal natives of the Commonwealth of Australia'. This would be a concurrent and not an exclusive power, so that welfare administration could still be left in State hands; but the new provision would publicly declare the responsibility of the Commonwealth to assist the States with finance and encouragement in this work.

The course outlined is fairly straightforward. It seems to offer many advantages and to be free from any foreseeable disadvantages...Why then has this course not been taken by the Government?

The explanation is probably a fairly simple one. The Prime Minister is naturally and very properly anxious to get his constitutional proposals approved at the referendum next year. He does not want to include too much, in the fear that the electors may become confused and thus inclined to vote against everything proposed.

This attitude is quite understandable and can only be changed if there is evidence of some popular demand for a more far-reaching measure *before the Parliament finally decides upon the form of referendum.*

If, therefore, there is any indication of widespread popular feeling in favour of specific measures to outlaw racial discrimination inside Australia and to give the Commonwealth some direct responsibility for Aboriginal advancement, then there would be some prospect of getting an amplification of the bill at present before the House, or the acceptance of an additional proposal for inclusion in next year's referendum.

In default of any such indication of popular feeling, the Government might well feel disinclined to take the matter any further.

More than Government support is needed. No referendum on this kind of issue can have much prospect of success unless it has backing from both sides of the House and without evidence of such bipartisan support there would be no purpose in proceeding.

A constitutional change can only take place if duly approved at a referendum and in this case there is no prospect of getting the extra proposals even submitted to a referendum unless there is an indication of popular support, sufficient to impress both Government and Opposition, before the matter is crystallised in Parliament and the necessary legislation is finalised.

### 31. Federal Council for the Advancement of Aborigines and Torres Strait Islanders, Petition, 1966, Barrie Pittock Papers, personal collection

TO THE HONORABLE THE SPEAKER AND MEMBERS OF THE HOUSE OF REPRESENTATIVES IN PARLIAMENT ASSEMBLED:—

The Humble Petition of citizens of the Commonwealth respectfully sheweth —

1. That paragraph (xxvi) of section 51 of the Constitution empowering the Parliament to make laws with respect to "the people of any race, other than the aboriginal race in any State, for whom it is deemed necessary to make special laws" implies a discrimination against the Aboriginal people and is, in any case, unjustifiable at the present day.
2. That specific provision should be made in the Constitution for the advancement of the Aboriginal people.

Your petitioners therefore humbly pray that your honorable House will act to enable the submission at a referendum of Constitution Alteration proposals to give the Commonwealth power to make laws for the advancement of the Aboriginal people and prevent the making of racial laws by the Commonwealth and any State which would discriminate against any person born or naturalised in Australia.

And your petitioners, as in duty bound, will every pray.

### 32. FCAATSI, Operation Referendum, Recommendations on Campaign Structure, 25 March 1967, FCAATSI Papers, Mitchell Library, MSS 2999, box Y600

OBJECTIVES OF THE CAMPAIGN

To ensure that the proposed change is supported by a majority of people in a majority of States. (We need the support of four States and approximately 21/2 million voters.)

To take the opportunity to establish the identity of the Federal Council and its aims.

To make as many people as possible aware of the work of Aboriginal advancement, and to solicit their participation.

The success of the referendum campaign will depend, in a large measure, on the whole–hearted participation of the Aboriginal community in the campaign.

The Australian people are sure to respond to a demand for equal recognition from the Aboriginal people themselves. To this end every opportunity must be created for Aboriginal bodies to be seen and heard in their own cause.

METHOD OF OPERATION

It is suggested that maximum use be made of the existing Federal Council machinery.

It is suggested that a National Directorate be set up comprising members of the Executive, with the Melbourne-based members acting as the central bureau...

It is suggested that State Committees be set up, with State Secretaries acting as convenors...

DIRECTORS OF THE CAMPAIGN

The President (Mr Joe McGinness) and Senior Vice President (Mr Gordon Bryant) are suggested as co-directors...

SECTIONS OF THE COMMUNITY TO BE APPROACHED TO TAKE ACTION

Aboriginal communities

Service clubs (Apex, Jaycees, etc.)

Local governments

Tertiary students

Unions and Churches

Miscellaneous organisations: RSL, Housewives' Associations, Country Women, etc...and affiliates

MISCELLANEOUS

A press committee to be formed in Canberra.

Seek co operation of the Australian Association of National Advertisers who [will] nominate an agency to give — free of charge — advice to community services. One request will be to national advertisers, whose image is 'Australian', to include in their advertising a brief statement (or slogan) on the campaign.

Ask Gary Shearston to compose a 'vote yes' song; a singing commercial. Produce 'vote yes' badges.

*Slogan Suggestions ...*

Towards an Australia free and equal Vote yes Vote 'Yes' for Aborigines

Let's be counted — Vote 'yes'

Remove discrimination — Vote 'yes'

Vote 'yes' for equality

The Federal Council cast the referendum as a means of overthrowing racial discrimination. This was the front cover of a special issue of *Smoke Signals*, the journal of the Victorian Aborigines Advancement League, one of the Council's affiliates. (Courtesy VAAL)

END DISCRIMINATION — VOTE "YES" ON MAY 27

### 33. Referendum on Aborigines (Background Notes), prepared by the National Directorate, Vote Yes Campaign, 31 March 1967, Gordon Bryant Papers, National Library of Australia, MS 8256, box 175

On 27 May all enrolled voters in the six States of Australia (but not in the Australian Capital Territory and the Northern Territory) must answer 'YES' or 'NO' to each of two questions. These questions are 'Do you approve the proposed law for the alteration of the Constitution entitled "An act to alter the Constitution so that the number of Members of the House of Representatives may be increased without necessarily increasing the number of Senators"', and 'Do you approve the proposed law for the alteration of the Constitution entitled "An Act to alter the Constitution so as to omit the words relating to the people of the Aboriginal Race in any State and so that Aboriginals are to be counted in reckoning the population"'.

The questions will be in the above order and must be answered separately by 'YES' or 'NO' in the appropriate boxes. An informal vote on one question will not invalidate a formal vote on the other.

Our concern here is with the second question which concerns Aborigines. The relevant Act would omit from paragraph (xxvi) of Section 51 of the Constitution the words 'other than the Aboriginal race in each State', and would repeal Section 127. It was passed unanimously by both Houses of the Commonwealth Parliament.

Section 127 reads, 'In reckoning the numbers of the people in the Commonwealth, or of a State or other part of the Commonwealth, Aboriginal natives shall not be counted'. This section was originally included in the Constitution for two reasons, both of which are no longer valid. Firstly, some sixty or seventy years ago there was genuine difficulty in counting Aborigines because many were nomadic, which is not the case today. Secondly, Aborigines were at that time not considered worthy of a vote, and therefore were not to be counted in the numbers determining electoral boundaries. Today Aborigines are entitled to vote in all States and Territories of the Commonwealth and therefore ought to be counted in the census which determines the size of the electorates. There is no reason for the retention of this Section of the Constitution and...all parties are agreed on the desirability of its repeal.

Section 51 reads 'The Parliament shall, subject to this Constitution, have power to make laws for the peace, order and good government of the Commonwealth with respect to (xxvi); the people of any race other than the Aboriginal race in any State, for whom it is deemed necessary to make special laws'. The proposed deletion of the words 'other than the Aboriginal race in any State', will thus have the effect of enabling the Commonwealth to make special laws in relation to Aborigines anywhere in Australia.

The Commonwealth power to legislate on Aboriginal affairs would be a power held concurrently with the States, and need not conflict in any way with State powers. Indeed Commonwealth power ought to complement the State Powers, facilitating, for instance, Commonwealth financial assistance for State projects such as Aboriginal housing or vocational training. This would particularly benefit those States, such as Western Australia and Queensland which have large Aboriginal populations.

In addition, Commonwealth power would enable the Commonwealth to take the initiative in setting up such bodies as an Aboriginal Education Foundation (along the lines of the very successful Maori Education Foundation in New Zealand and an Aboriginal Arts and Crafts Board (similar to the Indian Arts and Crafts Board in the United States) which would be most effective on a nationwide basis.

In its original form, Section 51 (xxvi) was apparently designed to protect Aborigines from Commonwealth laws discriminating against them. However, with the change of Australian (and world) opinion on the rights of racial minorities it is now apparent that any Commonwealth laws in relation to Aborigines would be favourable to Aborigines. In view of the special disadvantages of lack of capital, education and 'know-how' suffered by the Aborigines, the well known principle of justice that 'it is as unjust to treat unequals equally as to treat equals unequally' is a strong argument for special legislation to enable Aborigines to overcome their disadvantages.

This principle is widely applied to other classes of peoples, for instance, ex-Servicemen under the Repatriation Act. Something similar is needed for Aborigines.

Australians are held collectively responsible for the treatment and conditions of the Aboriginal people by world opinion. Proper race relations is a national and international issue which therefore ought to be dealt with by Australia at a national level as well as at the State and local levels. Australia ought, for instance, to be able, at a national level, to ratify Convention 107 of the International Labor Organisation which deals with the right[s] of indigenous minorities such as the Aboriginal people. At present there are six different Aboriginal administrations with six different policies, and only one (South Australia) is endeavouring to satisfy Convention 107.

Aborigines are a national responsibility. We must see to it that the National Parliament is able to accept that responsibility. We can make this possible by voting 'YES' for Aborigines on 27 May.

### 34. Gary Shearston, 'Vote Yes for Freedom', ABC Television, *The Day of the Aboriginal*, broadcast 19 May 1967

We are going
We are going
We are going
To Freedom
We are going
We are going
We are going
To Freedom

Equal Rights
Equal Rights
Together Unite
For Freedom

Children run
Children run

The time has come
For Freedom

We are going
We are going
We are going
To Freedom
We are going
We are going
We are going
To Freedom

27th of May
Each one say
YES YES YES
For Freedom

We need your vote
We want your vote
Vote YES YES YES
For Freedom

We are going
We are going
We are going
To Freedom
We are going
We are going
We are going
To Freedom

## 35. Charles Perkins, Letter to the Editor, *Australian*, 3 April 1967.

An article in the *Australian* on March 27 implied certain points which I feel need some clarification...

The Federal Council [for the Advancement of Aborigines and Torres Strait Islanders] has my trust and confidence. It has organised to support the Yes vote for the coming referendum, which in my opinion is of vital importance to the Australian society — apart from Aboriginal people.

This coming referendum is an opportunity for white people to demonstrate in a positive way their desire to help in the emancipation of the Aboriginals of Australia.

For myself as an Aboriginal, it is a moment of truth — whether the white people really are interested in our welfare or rights.

It will be an historic moment in Australia's social history.

## 36. '"No Vote Fear on Rights Issue"', *Age*, 11 April 1967.

'I am not at all confident Australians will vote Yes in the coming referendum on Aborigines' rights,' the president of the Aborigines Advancement League (Mr Bill Onus) said last night.

Mr Onus...was officially opening the league's campaign for the May 27 referendum.

'Australians in general are apathetic towards the Aborigines' problems', he said. 'Although they agree on the morality of full rights for the Aborigines, they do not feel inclined to do anything about it.'

Mr Onus said it had been suggested that the Aborigines' referendum was strictly a political issue...

'But this is not a question of politics. It is a fundamental question of human rights, the case of one man being equal to the other'...

'It is essential that the public be told clearly of the moral and social consequences of the referendum where it affects the Aborigines,' he said.

Mr Onus said Australians must vote to give the Aborigine full citizenship rights. It was a basic question of human rights.

'The referendum must be passed,' he said. 'The image of Australia throughout the world is at stake. If it is not passed, Australia will be held up to ridicule.'

### 37. Aboriginal Rights and the Referendum, Publicity for the media authorised by Bill Onus, Director, Victorian Vote 'Yes' Campaign Committee, Gordon Bryant Papers, NLA, MS 8256, box 175

Mr Bill Onus, Aboriginal President of the Aborigines Advancement League of Victoria, says that Australians should vote yes to give the Aborigines full citizenship rights. It is a question of human rights. Mr Onus believes that the image of Australia throughout the world is at stake.

Aboriginal leader Charles Perkins has stated that the coming referendum is an opportunity for white people to demonstrate in a positive way their desire to help in the emancipation of the Aboriginal of Australia...

Until now Aborigines haven't been counted with Australian citizens in a National Census. You can change this. On May 27 vote *yes* in the lower square.

100 000 Aborigines need your help to be governed under one Federal law. So be sure to vote yes for Aboriginal Legislation on May 27.

As a nation we have a chance to show our willingness to really help the Aboriginal people. Vote yes for Aboriginal Legislation on May 27.

On Referendum Day a Yes Vote for Aboriginal Legislation will prove to the world our determination to help the Aboriginal people. Be sure you vote yes in the lower square.

If you really want to help the Aboriginal people, now is your chance. A yes vote on Referendum Day will give them Federal Government rights...so vote yes in the lower square.

### 38. 'Yes for the Aborigines', *Sydney Morning Herald*, editorial, 10 May 1967

The appeals by distinguished Anglican Churchmen for a Yes vote on the Aboriginal sections of the referendum on May 27 will be supported by thinking people of all creeds. There is, however, a danger that these sections could be defeated through sheer carelessness and apathy. Many people who are against the constitutional amendment to break the nexus between the sizes of the Senate and the House of Representatives might fail to distinguish between the two separate issues and vote No right down the paper. And inevitably there will be another, perhaps not inconsiderable, section of voters who do not understand either proposal, and do not want to, and who will vote No with some vague idea of being on the safe side.

If the combined votes of these two sections should prove strong enough to frustrate the good intentions of the Government and the Opposition, and dash the hopes of the Aborigines, it will be sad indeed. Whatever divisions of opinion there may be over the need for breaking the nexus, there can surely be none over the proposals affecting the Aborigines provided they are thoroughly understood. They are designed to do two things: first, to repeal the hopelessly outdated Section 127 of the Constitution which discriminates against Aborigines by excluding them from the census, and secondly to amend Section 51 which gives the Commonwealth power to legislate for the people of any race 'other than the Aboriginal race' in any State.

In simple terms the object of these constitutional changes is to provide the Commonwealth with more definite power to give positive and practical aid to the Aboriginal people whose plight, in some places, has been rightly described by Bishop Leslie as "disgusting and inhuman". It is true that the referendum proposals do not go as far as was wanted by crusaders for Aboriginal welfare but they do go most of the way, and if carried they should, at the very least, dispose of any excuse by the Commonwealth for not helping the Aborigines on the ground of constitutional difficulties. As the Anglican Primate, Archbishop Strong, said: 'The proposal can only advance the Aborigines and make them completely Australian.'

**'YES'**
for
Aborigines

**THERE'S NO ARGUMENT ON ABORIGINES**

All Parties want you to vote 'YES' for Aborigines on Referendum Day so that Aborigines can be counted as Australians in the Census and so that they can benefit from Commonwealth Legislation

Apprehensive that opposition to the other question on the referendum ballot paper would result in the defeat of the Aboriginal question, the Federal Council tried to emphasise the unanimity of support for voting '"Yes" for Aborigines'. (Courtesy Gordon Bryant Papers, National Library of Australia)

## 39. Kay Keavney, 'Let's tell the World...', *Australian Women's Weekly*, 10 May 1967, p. 7

SAYS A FRIEND OF THE ABORIGINES: 'Let's tell the world there's only one Australian, and his color doesn't matter at all'.

'I wanted to understand', said Faith Bandler. 'I wanted to know why a man should be an outcast in his own country just because his skin is black.'

Faith had just been elected at a packed meeting of Aborigines and whites to direct the NSW campaign for a Yes vote in the Aboriginal rights referendum on May 27.

She has fought all her life for what she sees as a question of human dignity. Her own skin is deep cafe-au-lait. She has not one drop of Aboriginal blood. Her father was Melanesian, from the New Hebrides. Her mother was part-Scots, part-Indian.

But she is colored, she knows what prejudice and poverty mean...

Time till the referendum is very short, the job is enormous, even if Faith could work at it full-time. Funds are almost nil, unless a sympathetic public rallies to help.

Substantially, the [NSW] campaign is being run from the living room of the house in the Sydney suburb of French's Forest where Faith lives with her Viennese-born engineer husband, Hans, her daughter, Lilon, 12, and [Aboriginal] foster-son, Peter, 10.

The telephone begins ringing at about 8 a.m. and goes on till past midnight.

'If I want to snatch a shower or a cup of coffee', said Faith, 'I have to put cushions over the phone'.

Meanwhile, she cares for her family and deals with the household chores, along with her other honorary jobs as executive [member] of the Aboriginal-Australian Fellowship and the Council for the Advancement of Aborigines and Torres Strait Islanders.

She also speaks to innumerable groups on the cause for which she fights.

There is nothing of the battle-axe about Faith. She is small and very attractive, with lively eyes, musical voice, and ready smile.

And she is singularly free from bitterness...

'I just don't believe one kind of person is inferior to another. All that is needed is opportunity, and above all a sense of dignity.

'And a Yes vote on May 27 can open new doors for all the Australians who happen to be black.

'A Yes vote will mean that the Aboriginal people can come under Commonwealth law and derive all those benefits which only the Federal Government can give them.

'At the moment, for census purposes, they're not even counted as existing. A Yes vote will change that.

'Aborigines are the only Australians who live under six separate laws, one for each State...

'The eyes of the world are on Australia and her handling of black Australians. Not only Asia is watching but Africa and the whole Western world.

'That one word 'Yes' on May 27 will open the door for real reform. It will tell the world at large that there is only one Australian, and his color doesn't matter at all.'

### 40. 'Appeal for Yes Vote to Realise Dream', *Sydney Morning Herald*, 13 May 1967

A senior executive of the Foundation for Aboriginal Affairs said last night a Yes vote for Aborigines in the referendum on May 27 would realise a 'long cherished dream' of his people.

He is Mr Bert Groves, who was a guest speaker at a 'Yes-for-Aborigines' meeting at Paddington organised by the Liberal Reform Youth Group.

Mr Groves...said, 'We want to be part and parcel of the community'.

'But we want to do this without losing our identity as Australian Aborigines.'

He said Aborigines wanted integration, not assimilation — a word that reflected 'a failure to accept a minority race on a basis of equality'.

Mr Groves called assimilation 'a modified method of extermination over a long time'.

Once assimilation was complete the Aboriginal race would cease to exist, and the Aboriginal problem would cease with it.

Mr Groves said the present situation with different laws in each State, was an embarrassment to his people, who had to change their status if they changed States.

In the referendum on May 27 voters will be asked to vote on the inclusion of Aborigines in the Census, and to give the Commonwealth Government power to make laws for the improvement of their living and working conditions.

### 41. The Rt Hon. the Prime Minister, Harold Holt, radio and television address launching the referendum campaign, *Age*, 16 May 1967

...This referendum is necessary because your Federal Parliament proposes — and this is subject to your decision — to make certain alterations to the Commonwealth Constitution which the Parliament considers desirable...

Now let me say something about the second referendum question — the one concerning our Aboriginal people.

There was no opposition to it in Parliament in either House and I would anticipate overwhelming support for it by the electors.

The Aboriginal people of Australia are mentioned explicitly in the Constitution twice only...

At the turn of the century, when the Constitution was framed, the principal reason for including Section 127 was the practical difficulty of counting the Aboriginal population at the time. It is, however, no longer a serious difficulty. The basis for the existence of the section consequently no longer remains.

It is completely out of harmony with our national attitudes and modern thinking. It has no place in our Constitution in this Australian.

The second alteration Federal Parliament wants to make is the deletion of the words 'other than the Aboriginal race in any State' from Section 51 (xxvi).

We have been influenced by the widespread impression which exists that [these] words...are discriminatory.

Unanimously, Federal Parliament wants to remove these two references to the Aborigines, because one of the provisions is out of date and because the other is widely believed to discriminate against Aborigines...

## 42. Mr EG Whitlam puts the YES case on behalf of the Australian Labor Party Broadcast, 16 May 1967, Whitlam Institute, University of Western Sydney, <www.whitlam.org/collection/1967/19670516_Referendum/19670516_Referendum_TV.rtf>

On Saturday the 27th, you will be voting on two proposals to modernize the Australian Constitution which was passed by the British Parliament back in 1900. There is only one method of changing this constitution: that is for the Federal Parliament to pass a Bill and for the Australian electorate to approve it at a referendum. These proposals concern the structure of the Parliament and the rights of aborigines. It is sixteen years since there was last a referendum, so perhaps I should remind you that voting is compulsory, that you will each receive a single ballot paper, and that on that ballot paper there will be two questions.

The Australian Labor Party asks you to write the word YES in each of the squares opposite those two questions. We are supporting the Liberal Party and the Country Party on this occasion. The Labor Party has sought these amendments to the Constitution for many years past. The Constitution Review Committee, which sat from 1956 to 1959, recommended these amendments. Dr Evatt, the Leader of the Labor Party at that time, supported them. Every year for the last six years the Labor Party has sought a referendum on these two proposals. Now that the Government has decided to put the proposals to the people, we are whole-heartedly supporting them. In fact, everybody in the House of Representatives supported the proposals. I remind you that it is only in the House of Representatives that governments can be formed. In the Senate, every Labor member, every Country Party member, and all but four Liberal members supported them.

Let me deal first with the proposal concerning the structure of the Parliament ...

The other proposal concerns aborigines. At present, the Constitution makes two references to aborigines. One section prevents the aborigines from being counted when the number of House of Representatives seats for each State are allocated. Because of this provision, Western Australia and Queensland, where most of the aborigines live, have been in danger of losing one of their House of Representatives seats.

The other provision concerning aborigines prevents the Commonwealth Parliament passing special laws for their benefit. The Commonwealth can pass laws for the people of any other race, but not for the aboriginal race. Yet the aboriginal race in many respects is more deprived than any other identifiable racial group in the world. They have the greatest incidence of infant mortality, leprosy and tuberculosis. The Commonwealth alone has the finances and, in many cases, alone has the facilities to permit aborigines to have an equal opportunity in education, housing, health, employment, and all the social capital that Australians enjoy and expect.

There is another feature too. Australia has promised the International Labour Organisation and the United Nations Educational, Social and Cultural Organisation to give certain benefits to aborigines. We have not yet been able to do so because the Commonwealth has not got the constitutional power to pass laws to carry out these international obligations. The consequence is that, if Australia fails to write YES to the proposal on aborigines, the rest of the world will believe that we have neither comprehension nor compassion.

I would ask you to vote YES for both questions...For a contemporary structure, a comparable structure, for Australia's national Parliament; for equal opportunities for our aboriginal fellow citizens, I ask you to write YES against each of the two questions which the Parliament has put to you, in its quest for amendment of our 1900 Constitution.

### 43. Constitution Alteration (Aboriginals) 1967: Argument in favour of the proposed law, in Commonwealth of Australia, *Referendums to be held on Saturday, 27th May, 1967...*, Commonwealth Government Printer, Canberra, 1967, pp. 11–12

The Case for YES

The purposes of these proposed amendments to the Commonwealth Constitution are to remove any ground for the belief that, as at present worded, the Constitution discriminates in some ways against people of the Aboriginal race, and, at the same time, to make it possible for the Commonwealth Parliament to make special laws for the people of the Aboriginal race, wherever they may live, if the Commonwealth Parliament considers this desirable or necessary.

To achieve this purpose, we propose that two provisions of the Constitution be altered which make explicit references to people of the Aboriginal race.

The first proposed alteration is to remove the words 'other than the Aboriginal race in any State from paragraph (xxvi) of Section 51. Section 51 (xxvi) reads:

'The parliament shall, subject to this Constitution, have power to make laws for the peace, order, and good government of the Commonwealth with respect to:

(xxvi) The people of any race, other than the aboriginal race in any State, for whom it is deemed necessary to make special laws.'

The proposed alteration of this section will do two things. First, it will remove words from our Constitution that many people think are discriminatory against the Aboriginal people.

Second, it will make it possible for the Commonwealth Parliament to make special laws for the people of the Aboriginal race wherever they may live, if the Parliament considers it necessary.

This cannot be done at present because, as the Constitution stands, the Commonwealth Parliament has no power, except in the Territories, to make laws with respect to people of the Aboriginal race as such.

This would not mean that the States would automatically lose their existing powers. What is intended is that the National Parliament could make laws, if it thought fit, relating to Aboriginals — as it can about many other matters on which the States also have power to legislate. The Commonwealth's object will be to cooperate with the States to ensure that together we act in the best interests of the Aboriginal people of Australia.

The second proposed alteration is the repeal of Section 127 of the Constitution. That section reads:

In reckoning the numbers of the people of the Commonwealth, or of a State or other part of the Commonwealth, aboriginal natives shall not be counted.

Why was this provision included in the Constitution in 1900? Well, there were serious practical difficulties in counting the Aboriginals in those days. They were dispersed, and nomadic. Communications in inland Australia were poor, and frequently non-existent. Today the situation is very different and counting is practicable.

Our personal sense of justice, our commonsense, and our international reputation in a world in which racial issues are being highlighted every day, require that we get rid of this out-moded provision.

Its modern absurdity is made clear when we point out that for some years now Aboriginals have been entitled to enrol for, and vote at, Federal Elections. Yet Section 127 prevents them from being reckoned as 'people' for the purpose of calculating our population, even for electoral purposes!

The simple truth is that Section 127 is completely out of harmony with our national attitudes and modern thinking. It has no place in our Constitution in this Australian.

All political parties represented in the Commonwealth Parliament support these proposals. The legislation proposing these Constitutional amendments was, in fact, adopted unanimously in both the House of Representatives and the Senate. We have yet to learn of any opposition being voiced to them from any quarter.

Just as every available Member of the Commonwealth Parliament voted for the proposals outlined above, we believe that the Australian electorate as a whole will give strong support and endorsement to them.

We urge you to vote YES to both our proposals as to Aboriginals by writing the word YES in the square on the ballot paper, thus:

YES

This case has been authorised by the majority of those Members of both Houses of the Parliament who voted for the proposed law and was prepared by the Prime Minister, the Rt Hon. Harold Holt, Leader of the Federal Parliamentary Liberal Party; by the Deputy Prime Minister, the Rt Hon. John McEwen, Leader of the Australian Country Party; and by the Leader of the Opposition, Mr. Gough Whitlam, Leader of the Australian Labor Party.

### 44. 'Aboriginal Rights and the Referendum', publicity for the media authorised by the National Directorate, Vote Yes Campaign, Gordon Bryant Papers, box 175

On May 27th you will be asked to amend two clauses of the Constitution that exclude Aborigines from being counted in the Census as Australian citizens, and that prevent Federal Parliament from passing laws in respect of Aborigines. Give Aborigines a fair go. Vote yes for Aboriginal rights at the referendum.

Aborigines all over Australia ask for a *yes* vote for Aboriginal rights on May 27th. Give the Aborigines a fair go — Vote Yes for Aborigines.

May 27th is referendum day. One of the questions you will be asked concerns Aboriginal rights. You will be asked to agree to Constitutional changes which will ensure that Aborigines will be counted in the census of the population. You will also be asked to give the Commonwealth Parliament authority to pass laws to benefit Aborigines. For example, this would enable the Commonwealth to set up an Aboriginal Education Foundation. Aboriginal organisations all over Australia ask you to vote yes for Aboriginal rights. The eyes of the world will be on Australia on May 27th. *100 words*

Aborigines all over the country are looking upon the forthcoming referendum as the acid test for white Australians. The eyes of the world — particularly African and Asian eyes — will be on Australia on May 27th. A 'no' vote to the Aboriginal rights question will brand this country racist and put it in the same category as South Africa. *50 words*

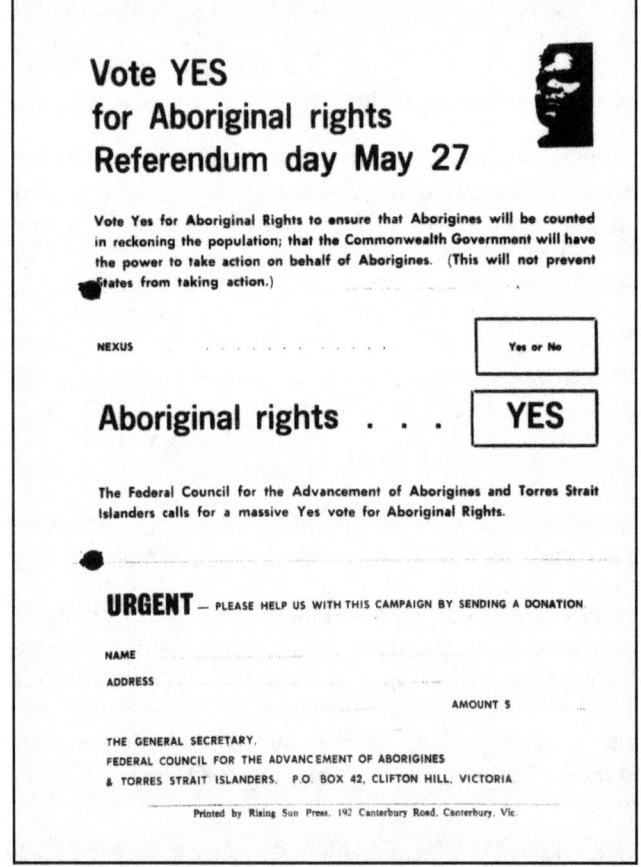

The Federal Council campaign wanted to suggest the federal government would have more power to intervene in Aboriginal affairs but was fearful of upsetting the supporters of state rights. (Courtesy Mitchell Library)

## 45. AP Elkin, 'A Yes Vote for Aborigines', *Sydney Morning Herald*, 16 May 1967

Having been closely associated with Aboriginal policies and welfare for about 40 years, I am often asked for advice on the Aboriginal clauses in the referendum to be held on May 27. I shall vote Yes, though not for some of the reasons given by campaigners.

I shall do so because the two clauses are out of date, and are misinterpreted both in Australia and abroad. Being unaware of the historical circumstances to which they applied, most persons quite understandably think they discriminate against Aborigines. Therefore, the words should be deleted.

On the other hand, such deletion does not mean that Aborigines have not been counted hitherto (they have been), or that they will receive the franchise (they have it), or that the Federal Government will henceforth be free to legislate for Aboriginal welfare to a degree not possible up to date. Let us consider the two proposals.

(1) Clause 127 of the Constitution reads...

Three points should be noted:

(a) The census and other Commonwealth authorities have only regarded as Aboriginal persons who are either *full-bloods* or in whom Aboriginal ancestry predominates. Half and lighter castes have not been so regarded for census, electoral, social service benefits or any other purpose. Accordingly, the tables in the population chapter of the Commonwealth Year Book are marked 'Excluding Full-blood Aboriginals'. Half and lighter castes are included.

(b) The reason for the exclusion was obvious at the time of Federation in 1902 [sic]. Only occasional, if any, contact had been made with the majority of full-bloods in the central and northern parts of the continent. Moreover, the view was firmly held that they would die out.

In spite of this, attempts have been made at census times to enumerate where possible and to estimate elsewhere the number of full-blood Aborigines. Although the results were unreliable, they have been recorded in Commonwealth Year Books. Now, however, as hardly any Aborigines are living in the old-time nomadic way, a reliable enumeration can be made with the help of patrol and welfare officers and missionaries.

Therefore, when reckoning the Commonwealth population, the inclusion of the number of full-bloods, so obtained, makes demographic sense. Moreover, it makes social sense: the full-bloods, who now number around 45 000, are increasing, and they possess the franchise.

(c) This last point needs emphasis because some campaigners for a yes vote give the impression that the referendum will give voting rights to Aborigines. Rather, we should, as I have just implied, include them in the total reckoning of the Australian population, because they have the vote...

(2) The other clause, on which we are asked to vote Yes or No, is number XXVI of Section 51 of the Constitution...

In 1902, the Commonwealth Government had no special responsibility for the Aborigines as such...It was not until 1911 [sic]...that [it] became responsible for any Aborigines, namely those in [the Northern] Territory. Clause XXVI of Section 51 did not prevent it legislating through ordinances for the protection and welfare of these Aborigines.

Likewise, although the Federal Parliament has no power to make special laws in regard to Aborigines, yet the latter, being Australian citizens, come within the ambit of particular lawmaking powers which that Parliament possesses under the Constitution.

Thus, it has brought them within the range of the benefits which flow from the Social Services Act. It has extended the Commonwealth franchise to them; and indirectly, through its allocations of loan money to the States for housing, assists materially in the provision of houses for Aborigines (and part-Aborigines).

In other words, the Commonwealth does legislate for the welfare and progress of Aborigines in the States as well as in the Northern Territory, but it does so in their status as citizens, not through enacting special laws with regard to them.

Moreover, we cannot take for granted that the mere deletion of the words 'other than the Aboriginal race' will enable the Commonwealth to enact such special laws. To do this might require a referendum to confer a specific power to legislate for the welfare of Aborigines...

Further, the States as a whole have not been prepared to hand over to the Commonwealth the administration of Aboriginal affairs, nor are they willing to do so now. However, through the Ministers' Welfare Council, policies are converging and the Commonwealth is cooperating with the States in their work for the progress of Aborigines and part-Aborigines. The deletion of Clause XXVI (Section 51) from the Constitution will at least give an impetus to this co operation, as well as getting rid of apparent discrimination in the Constitution against the Aborigines.

### 46. Chicka Dixon, 'I Want to be a Human Being', *Sun-Herald* [the Sunday edition of the *Sydney Morning Herald*], 21 May 1967

There's a simple reason why I want a huge 'Yes' vote on the Aboriginal question at next Saturday's referendum: *I want to be accepted by white Australians as a person.*

There are scores of other reasons why the vote should be yes.

But for most Aborigines it is basically and most importantly a matter of seeing white Australians finally, after 179 years, affirming at last that they believe we are human beings.

I have not thought through what would be my reaction — and the reaction of my people — to a No vote.

It would be a crushing rejection. It would create disastrous bitterness.

And it could mean bad blood between black and white for the foreseeable future. But I find it difficult to believe that Australians would do this. Yet we fear this result.

We fear that apathy, ignorance, a complicated ballot paper and racial hatred — in that order — could defeat us.

We particularly fear that many who will vote No on the question of politicians and the nexus will also believe they must vote No on Aborigines.

This is not so...

What is this referendum about?

A Yes vote will mean the rubbing out of two sections of the Australian constitution concerning Aborigines.

One section excludes Aborigines from the census; the other prevents the Federal Government from making laws specially for Aborigines.

Neither section, if and when they go, will make much difference to these old bones.

It's too late to heal the scars of years of discrimination.

I doubt even that the change will have much effect on my two daughters, who are 16 and 19. It could even be too late for them.

For at first a Yes vote will mean to grown-ups merely a change of mood by white Australians: acceptance instead of rejection.

But for the youngsters still at school this vote will be vital.

For once the Government gets the right to make special laws for Aborigines, we will believe that it will.

For too long the Constitution has been a handy excuse for the Commonwealth Government neatly to sidestep its responsibilities to Aborigines.

Once this excuse is removed we expect the Commonwealth will finally make a man of itself and accept its responsibilities.

We want a clear national policy towards Aborigines — and an undivided one. At present we are subject to different laws in every State.

Few white people realise that I, as an Aboriginal, would break the law somewhere by merely moving around the country as an ordinary citizen.

Somewhere I would come under restrictive laws which demand that I get approval — from a magistrate, policeman or Public servant — just to exist on that very spot.

Here is another example: I may legally enter a hotel in NSW, yet doing the same thing in Queensland could mean trouble with the police because technically I am breaking the law.

Here in Sydney I can go where I like. If I go into Queensland I become the subject of a Government Department which can order me around, confine me to a certain area of the State or even separate me from my family.

There is another important point about Commonwealth responsibility for Aborigines. Responsibility in Canberra means responsibility where the money bags are.

We would hope for Commonwealth funds for trained personnel to make a new-look policy work.

We would hope for the establishment of an Aborigines' Bureau — eventually staffed, at least in part, by Aborigines.

Commonwealth power to legislate for Aborigines, I should point out, would be power held concurrently with States — as in other fields.

But it could mean Federal assistance for State projects such as Aboriginal housing and job training.

This would be important for States with large Aboriginal populations such as Queensland and Western Australia.

Commonwealth responsibility, we hope, would also mean the establishment of an Australian authority similar to New Zealand's Maori Education Foundation.

This would make certain that bright young Aborigines received the education they deserved.

Its main task would be to raise the level of education of all Aborigines in the country.

Aborigines regard education as vital. They know that through it lies equality...The census issue is different. A yes vote will finally end a long-standing insult to the Aboriginal people in the census.

Dogs, horses, cattle and sheep get counted in the census. So do TV sets and motor cars. But not Aborigines.

We don't even rate as high as the goggle box.

A woman rang me the other day and asked me: 'How many Aborigines are there in NSW?'

'Madam', I replied, 'how would I know? We are invisible citizens. Until we are counted in the census we will never know'.

We don't exist officially — yet we pay taxes.

We don't exist — yet we are subject to a net of restrictive laws.

We don't exist — yet we have to serve in the Army and accept the other responsibilities of citizenship.

We don't mind accepting our responsibilities, but in return we want White Australia to recognise officially that we exist.

We want to be human like everyone else.

Representations such as this Herbert McClintock drawing, published in a trade union newspaper in May 1967, reinforced the impression that Aborigines would win citizenship rights if the referendum was passed.

## 47. 'Public Confusion Evident on Aboriginal Issue', *Sydney Morning Herald*, 2 May 1967

With only three days to go before voting, the public is in a state of confusion about the referendum on Aborigines.

A Yes vote at the referendum on Saturday will allow the Commonwealth Government to make laws for Aborigines and allow Aborigines to be counted in the Census.

At present only the State Governments can legislate for Aborigines.

If the referendum is carried it will permit the Constitution to be amended and the Commonwealth Government will have the power to enact uniform legislation for Aborigines throughout Australia.

The referendum does not give Aborigines the right to vote. They already have it. It does not deal with equal rights for Aborigines.

Mrs Faith Bandler, the campaign director in NSW for the Federal Council for the Advancement of Aborigines and Torres Strait Islanders, emphasised these points yesterday.

She blamed the Commonwealth Government and the political parties for the public's confusion...

'The Government has not gone out of its way to explain the issues properly'...

## 48. 'The case should have been put!', Letter to the editor, *Australian*, 26 May 1967.

I have always felt that the Australian referendum was the most democratic of institutions, particularly in the provision to all voters of statements for and against the proposals, which do much to offset political domination of the Press and other media of communication.

This cherished belief has been shattered by the fact that the official pamphlet this time gives the case for only one side concerning the proposal on the Aboriginals; and, so far as I can observe, scarcely a word for No has been published in the press.

I should have thought that liberal-minded people could have been found to propound the point of view that the amendment is highly discriminatory (one law for the whites, another for the blacks); and that it opens the door to discriminatory legislation of the South African kind.

Contrary to Mr Whitlam's statement on television, the wording is not 'special laws for their benefit', and while there is no doubt that the present Government will apply it in a benevolent manner, there is no guarantee that all future governments will have the same attitude.

Personally, I shall vote Yes, because I think the Yes case leads on points and because I do not share the world wide revulsion against paternalism in racial relations.

But in all fairness I think the case for No should have been put.

# Vote 'YES' for Aborigines

ON May 27, a Referendum will be held at which all enrolled voters in the six States of Australia must answer "YES" or "NO" to each of two questions.

## These questions are:

"Do you approve the proposed law for the alteration of the Constitution entitled 'An Act to alter the Constitution so that the number of Members of the House of Representatives may be increased without necessarily increasing the number of Senators'," and

"Do you approve the proposed law for the alteration of the Constitution so as to omit the words relating to the people of the Aboriginal Race in any State and so that Aboriginals are to be counted in reckoning the population."

The questions will be in the above order and must be answered separately by writing in "YES" or "NO" in the appropriate boxes. An informal vote on one question will not invalidate a formal vote on the other.

## Unanimously Approved

The proposed Act on Aborigines would amend Section 51 of the Constitution and repeal Section 127. This has been approved unanimously by both Houses of the Commonwealth Parliament.

**Section 127 reads: "In reckoning the numbers of the people in the Commonwealth, or of a State or other part of the Commonwealth, Aboriginal natives shall not be counted."**

This section was originally included in the Constitution for two reasons. Sixty or seventy years ago there was genuine difficulty in counting Aborigines because many were nomadic. This is not the case today. Also, Aborigines were at that time not considered worthy of a vote. Today they are entitled to vote in all States and Territories of the Commonwealth, and therefore ought to be counted in the census which determines the size of the electorates. All Parties are agreed on the desirability of repealing this Section of the Constitution.

Will THEY have equal opportunities?
WRITE "YES" ON MAY 27.

**P.T.O.**

---

**Section 51 reads: "The Parliament shall, subject to this Constitution, have power to make laws for the peace, order and good government of the Commonwealth with respect to (xxvi); the people of any race OTHER THAN THE ABORIGINAL RACE in any State, for whom it is deemed necessary to make special laws."**

It is proposed to delete the words, "other than the Aboriginal race in any State." This will enable the Commonwealth to make special laws in relation to Aborigines anywhere in Australia.

## Would Help States

This need not conflict in any way with State powers. Rather, it should result in the Commonwealth helping the States—for instance, with financial assistance for Aboriginal housing, vocational training, etc. This would particularly benefit Western Australia and Queensland, which have large Aboriginal populations.

In view of the special disadvantages of lack of capital, education and "know-how" suffered by the Aborigines, there is a strong argument for special Commonwealth legislation to enable Aborigines to overcome their disadvantages.

This principle is widely applied to other classes of peoples, for instance, ex-servicemen under the Repatriation Act.

World opinion holds Australians collectively responsible for the treatment and conditions of the Aboriginal people. Proper race relations is a national and international issue which therefore ought to be dealt with by Australia at a national level as well as at the State and local levels. At present there are six different Aboriginal administrations with six different policies.

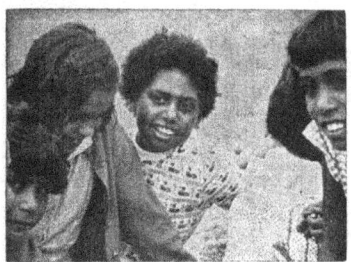

*Aborigines are a national responsibility. We must see to it that the National Parliament is able to accept that responsibility. We can make this possible by writing "YES" for Aborigines on May 27.*

Authorised by Mrs. Kath Walker, Qld. Secretary, Federal Council for Advancement of Aborigines and Torres Strait Islanders (FCAA) and Secretary, Qld. Council for the Advancement of Aborigines and Torres Islanders (QCAATI). Address: P.O. Box 212, North Quay, Brisbane.

ARTCRAFT PRINT

A leaflet, authorised by the Queensland Council for the Advancement of Aborigines and Torres Strait Islanders, cast the referendum as a matter of equality for Aborigines. (Courtesy Gordon Bryant Papers, National Library of Australia)

## 49. Bruce Grant, 'Shoulder to the Wheel', *Age*, 26 May 1967

The reasons for voting Yes on both questions in tomorrow's referendum are compelling...

A vote against the proposal on Aborigines...will not register one's disapproval of its half-heartedness or publicise the problems it does not solve or accept the guilt of the past it does not remove.

The vote would merely go to swell the numbers of those who are opposed for more substantial reasons, such as racial prejudice or cultural superiority or a belief, which the evidence suggests is mistaken, that the States are better equipped than the Commonwealth to legislate on Aboriginal welfare.

A vote for the proposal is a vote for changes which are intended to improve the prospect of the Aborigine in Australia. We cannot be sure that this will be the result. The history of constitutions here and abroad is the history of intentions later reinterpreted in the light of experience. All we can say is that in 1967, this is the intention.

It has been pointed out that the issue of the referendum is not 'civil rights' or 'freedom now', but whether the Commonwealth, as well as the States, should have power to discriminate — for or against — in respect of Aborigines.

The question is asked: 'Are we not really perpetuating the separation of the Aborigine from Australian society by giving to Canberra the authority to make the separation more uniform and more effective? Is this not subtle apartheid?'

While it is true that the referendum does not deal with policy and therefore avoids a commitment to assimilation or integration, I think the fears underlying the question are misplaced.

The referendum does propose, in fact, that a constitutional discrimination, by which Aborigines are not included in population counts, should be removed. This establishes intention clearly.

Moreover, the Aboriginal people themselves are fully supporting the proposals. They assume that this is the beginning of a move toward equality and that progress will be more rapid with Commonwealth assistance.

They already have a Federal vote and they would be justified in thinking that, as a pressure group, they could exercise more influence on one key power centre than, as their influence is at present, dispersed throughout the States.

In addition, the Commonwealth, because of foreign policy considerations, is more sensitive than the States to the kind of international opinion which is favourable to Aboriginal advancement.

There has been no organised No campaign on this part of the referendum. But we have a reputation for being niggardly about referendums, not so much, I suspect, because we revere the constitution, which is not an awesome document, but because we do not like giving power to anyone. The Commonwealth, which has the specified powers, is always the beggar.

Only four out of 40 proposed constitutional amendments since 1903 have been approved. This time the wheel is rolling but every push helps...

## 50. 'Natives: A Yes Vote', *West Australian*, editorial, 26 May 1967

It is difficult to give unqualified support to the double-barrel referendum question on Aborigines.

The proposition that they should be counted in the census is straight forward and should be universally acceptable. But to delete the few words of the Constitution which prohibit the Federal Government from making laws about Aborigines does not mean that the natives will be any better off. Canberra has given no guidance on how it would exercise its new power or how it would react to a no vote.

Support for the question might bring more Federal money for Aboriginal advancement; it might also bring interference in State affairs. Opposition to the question might give Canberra an excuse to wash its hands of Aboriginal matters altogether, outside the Northern Territory.

The voter has no evidence that the Federal Government has evolved a policy at all, though Federal influence has helped to promote policy reforms in the States. Money is the key to the problem, but Canberra does not need to change the Constitution to give financial or other help if it really wants to. It should not weaken local administration in such a matter.

In this vague situation we feel drawn to vote yes to end discrimination against Aborigines in the census and to hope for a constructive approach by Canberra to Australia's most urgent social problem. Having thus exposed the voter to the coercion of his own conscience, it is implicit that the Prime Minister should interpret a yes vote to this question as a demand that Canberra should give a strong impetus to Federal–State co operation.

## 51. 'Yes, yes', *Sydney Morning Herald*, editorial, 27 May 1967

The yes case on both questions in the referendum should be carried today...

Today's vote will be a measure of the responsibility of our attitude towards Aborigines. Unfortunately, few of us are likely to do something ourselves for Aborigines. By voting Yes to the question affecting them, we are at least taking this opportunity of supporting their cause. And it IS their cause. Aboriginal leaders have made it plain that they want a referendum carried. It would be an intolerable act of paternalism to ignore their wishes. In the non-debate on this question during the campaign, the politicians have given little encouragement to feel strongly about the issue. The Prime Minister has not undertaken to use the additional legislative power he is seeking. Yet it is still vital that he should have it. The Commonwealth will then have no excuse for failing to do more for Aborigines. There have been warnings of the damage a No vote would do to Australia's image abroad, but it is as well to think first that the image would be a shamefully true reflection.

## 52. 'Vote is Only a Start', *Age*, 29 May 1967

The triumph of the 'Yes' vote in Saturday's referendum was seen by Aboriginal leaders yesterday as only the start on the long road to a new deal for their people.

The Federal Council for the Advancement of Aborigines immediately called on the Federal Government to establish a national policy on aborigines based on the needs and desires of Aborigines and Torres Strait Islanders.

In a statement welcoming the 'Yes' vote, the council said it would assure both the Aboriginal people and the Commonwealth Government of the desire of Australians to end all forms of discrimination and to further the advancement of the Aboriginal people.

Pastor Doug Nicholls, Field Officer for the Aborigines Advancement League in Victoria, said the Aborigines welcomed the 'Yes' vote with joy.

'It is evidence that Australians recognise Aborigines are part of the nation and not another people', he added.

## 5–POINT PLAN

In the wake of the 'Yes' vote the Federal Council for the Advancement of Aborigines has put a five point proposal before the Federal Government.

It calls on the Federal Government:

To establish a national policy on Aboriginal affairs based on the needs and desires of Aborigines and Torres Strait Islanders.

To provide immediately for an expert survey of all matters relevant to Aboriginal affairs throughout the Commonwealth.

To make provision for the establishment of a national secretariat involving all State Aboriginal authorities.

To establish a National Education Foundation similar to that provided by the New Zealand Government for Maoris.

To establish a National Aboriginal Arts and Crafts Board to encourage and protect the work of Aboriginal artists and craftsmen.

The MHR for Wills (Mr Gordon Bryant) said last night that the mammoth 'Yes' vote majority was not accidental. The Australian people had to be won over.

It was essential now that the Commonwealth Government took action immediately in a number of fields — particularly housing.

## 53. 'Were the Voters Cheated?', *Australian*, editorial, 29 May 1967

...The result of the first referendum proposal must raise doubts about the motivation behind the huge majority for Yes on the second. If there was such an unrealistic 'no more politicians' approach to one, there may well have been a euphoric 'give them a go' attitude to the Aboriginal question.

Fortunately, the rules are the same for both. The right result is on record, whatever the reasons, and it is a huge mandate for the Government.

By itself, the vote is a statement of intent rather than a solution to any problems. Its very size, however, will be a valuable weapon for the proponents of reform in Aboriginal welfare.

The Commonwealth Government should make a clear statement as soon as feasible, setting out its view of its new constitutional position in this field.

Presumably, the various State instrumentalities concerned with Aboriginal welfare will continue on their present basis, but even if it is on a most modest scale initially, there must now be some comparable authority in Commonwealth jurisdiction.

It should be made very plain to the Government from the outset that the Department of Territories would be totally inappropriate for this role.

Most of all at this stage, however, there is need for an assurance that the matter does not rest at mere changes in the constitution — valuable and significant as they may be.

### 54. John Jost, 'Taking the Responsibility', *Age*, 15 June 1967

When more than 4 million Australians voted at last month's referendum to give the Federal Government power to legislate for Aborigines, most thought the Government had legislation in mind.

But at the present time the only plans the Government has for Aborigines is to count them in the next census.

Despite the fact the Government has been given the most overwhelming mandate yet given in Australia, it already is apparent that the present division of Aboriginal responsibility which exists between the Commonwealth and the States will be perpetuated.

The Government is not likely, however, to escape entirely from the Aboriginal responsibility.

Already there are moves afoot among Liberal and ALP backbenchers for a parliamentary select committee inquiry into Aboriginal affairs.

Should they succeed — and its supporters hope to know the outcome of their moves within two months — the Government might be forced to consider seriously the question of Aborigines...

The Commonwealth could, if it wanted to, create a new department and take full responsibility for Aborigines but this is most unlikely for several reasons.

There already exists, in some of the States at any rate, legislation which, when fully implemented, will go a fair distance in helping old Australians ...

The other reason is that the Federal Government is unwilling to assume Aboriginal responsibility.

At a stretch it might be willing to assume some responsibility, but although Mr Holt is sympathetic to the Aboriginal cause he will not want to trespass on what always has been the States' administrative territory...

Mr Holt could make a start towards the Federal assumption of Aboriginal responsibility if he grouped all the Commonwealth Government's Aboriginal affairs under one head.

How he does this is not important. A new department, a possibility in the future, is not likely at the moment.

Many parliamentarians feel a new department would only add to the mass of bureaucracy which already exists.

But a fair number do feel that Aboriginal affairs should be given a new break under a new and streamlined system. If all Aboriginal responsibilities were amalgamated much discrepancy would be avoided. This would also be the first step taken by a Federal Government towards a firm Aboriginal rehabilitation policy.

No doubt a select parliamentary committee, if formed, would investigate along these lines.

### 55. 'Post Referendum', *Smoke Signals*, vol. 6, no. 3, 1967, p. 28

Australians on 27th May gave a clear directive to the Federal Government to stop messing about and get on with it when 5,183,113 voters — 90.77 per cent — marked their Constitutional Referendum ballot papers 'Yes' to the Aboriginal question. So the Federal Government now has the power to make laws governing Aborigines, and a clear instruction to use it...

Having had this greatness thrust upon them, the Federal Government soon showed itself to be singularly unprepared to use its new powers...On 31st May — four days after the Referendum — the *Canberra Times* reported 'The Federal Government is unlikely to begin in the near future any program to assist Aborigines following the success of the Referendum. The Minister for Social Services, Mr Sinclair had made this clear when he said he believed the Aborigines were best served through State Welfare Boards. "I can't see that, in the immediate future, the Commonwealth is likely in any way to replace the boards"'.

The widespread criticism which followed Commonwealth Government hints of its intention to do little had their effect, and at the end of September it was announced a new Office of Aboriginal Affairs would be established in the Prime Minister's Department. This was good, even if nobody seemed too clear as to what the office would do...

## 56. Kath Walker, 'Black–White Coalition Can Work', *Origin*, vol. 1, no. 4, 1969, p. 6

When the Federal Council for the Advancement of Aborigines and Torres Strait Islanders was formed in 1958, it was expected to be a fighting organisation, consisting of Aborigines and white Australians who would work together with such allies as they could influence on the national scene.

It was to be a coalition in the interest of Aborigines' and Torres Strait Islanders' advancement.

Unfortunately, the coalition today is seen as 'patting on the backs' of selected Aborigines (selected by whites) whom they call leaders.

Aborigines have never recognised all the top black Australians as their leaders. White people in the movement have always dictated to the black Australians.

Looking back, the only major improvement has been the 93 per cent 'Yes' vote of the referendum of May 1967; but this improvement did not benefit the black Australians though it eased the guilty conscience of white Australians in this country and overseas.

It can be regarded therefore as a victory for white Australians who formed the coalition with black Australians. Black Australians must be seen as stooges of the white Australians working in the interest of white Australians.

If black Australians are to become masters of their own destiny, white Australians must recognise them as being capable of formulating their own policy of advancement ...

White Australians must understand that what is good for them does not necessarily follow as being good for black Australians...

Most white Australians, even those who attempt to communicate and cooperate with black Australians, do not see racial inequality in the same way as black Australians do...

The political and social rights of black Australians have been and always will be negotiable and expendable wherever they conflict with the interests of the white Australians...

As long as black Australians remain politically dependent upon white political machines, their interests will be secondary to those machines.

White Australians establish their own goals and demand that black Australians identify with them. When black reformers begin to expound theories and goals in the interest of their people, whites decry them as being ambitious...

These reformers are classed as being unacceptable by the white Australians and they define them as being of no use to their own people. White Australians feel they are better judges than the black Australians in selecting black leaders.

### 57. '20 Years of Lost Opportunities', *Age*, editorial, 27 May 1987

Twenty years ago today Australians voted overwhelmingly to give the Federal Government the power to legislate for the advancement of the nation's Aborigines. The size of the referendum vote — slightly more than 89 per cent — was a measure of popular feeling on the subject. Australians felt ashamed of the fact that, almost 180 years after the arrival of the First Fleet, Aborigines were still regarded for most practical purposes as non-citizens. If ever a government had a mandate to act on behalf of a particular group, here it was. Yet to the dismay of Australians, both white and black, there was no concerted follow up. The McMahon Government, which was in power at the time [sic], promised that it would give 'careful consideration' to Aboriginal advancement. It was a polite way of saying that the nation's blacks were low in priority, and that nothing much by way of action could be expected.

Logically, the 1967 referendum should have been followed by a symbolic act, such as the granting of limited land rights or a concerted health and welfare program, which would have convinced the nation's blacks that they were indeed citizens with the same rights and status as the white population. The government's failure to act at the time helps explain the cynicism and the disenchantment which many blacks feel about government today. For them the history of the past 20 years is a history of failure: failure to honour promises, failure to show concern and, above all, a failure to deliver. Some progress has been made in the area of land rights, although it is no longer a popular cause with politicians. But in the basic areas of health, education, welfare, housing and employment, Australia's blacks are not much better off than they were 20 years ago.

On average, they live 20 years less than other Australians, and are particularly prone to diseases such as trachoma. The infant mortality rate, while it has improved substantially, is still more than three times the national rate. Unemployment among Aborigines is rife. Their housing remains for the most part sub standard. They drop out of school earlier than white students, and only four per cent of them have post school qualifications, compared with 24 per cent of non Aborigines. Ministers regularly issue statements designed to convince the electorate that progress is being made and that the Government is alert and sensitive to their needs. But the blacks, marooned in their world of disadvantage, know better. What is desperately needed is what they were denied 20 years ago — a concerted and large-scale program of assistance aimed at improving their health, welfare and living standards. The Hawke Government should make this a high-priority Bicentenary project.

### 58. Lowitja O'Donoghue, Chairperson of Aboriginal and Torres Strait Islander Commission, 'One Nation: Promise or Paradox', in ATSIC, *Twenty Five Years On: Marking the Anniversary of the Aboriginal Referendum of 27 May 1967*, ATSIC, Canberra, 1992, pp. 5–9, 13–16

We are here to mark the occasion of the 25th anniversary of the Constitutional Referendum which took place on 27 May 1967.

Anniversaries are always very important.

They link us with our past; they remind us of how far we have come; they provide an opportunity to think about the future.

In 1988 Australia celebrated the bicentenary of European settlement.

In the year 2001 Australia will celebrate the centenary of its Federation.

Twenty-five years ago Australians voted overwhelmingly to change that product of Federation — the Australian Constitution — to do two things: to enable Aboriginal people to be counted in reckoning Australia's population; and to give the Commonwealth Government the power to make laws for Aboriginal people in the States, concurrently with State Governments.

This referendum is often represented as having finally given Australia's Aboriginal and Torres Strait Islander people full citizenship rights.

The most basic rights — among them the right to vote — we had before 1967.

And a great many of the evils of the old system — including paternalism on the reserves or the breaking up of Aboriginal families by 'welfare' authorities — continued after 1967...

I myself grew up in the pre 1967 world, the world of protectors and restrictive laws. As a child of two, I was taken away from my mother and placed in [a home] for 'half-caste' children...

Along the way I joined the Aboriginal Advancement League, and became part of that political movement — which really began in the 1930s — whereby Aboriginal people from all around Australia agitated for what was called 'citizen rights'. This was our own Civil Rights movement...

These events also show that I am from a generation of Aboriginal people for whom those experiences — to which so many Australians today react with disbelief — are part of living memory. They occurred, for me, in the last 50 or so years. They have occurred for some much more recently. They, too, have come to live with those memories not because they accept what was done to them, but because if you are not resolute about those things they will kill you...

Many Aboriginal people campaigned for the two amendments to the Constitution, and saw the passing of the 1967 Referendum as powerfully symbolic.

The Referendum was — in a small way and at no real cost — an act of redress on behalf of Australia's majority population to a people who were largely dispossessed and marginalised. Voting 'Yes' — which 92 per cent of

Australian people did — was presented as an urgent issue of social justice; it was a righting of the wrongs.

If then 1967 heralded a new era, I'm sure that most of you are here today to hear my opinion of what has happened to that promise, that idealism ...

The most important consequences of the Referendum were at the governmental level: 1967 ushered in a national approach to Aboriginal advancement. Over the last 25 years the Commonwealth Government has effectively assumed a special responsibility in Aboriginal affairs, one that has had bipartisan support.

The Liberal-Country Party Government of the late 60s was fairly slow to exercise its new powers to legislate for Aboriginal people...

1972...saw a major policy shift, from assimilation for Aboriginal and Torres Strait Islander people to self-determination. Self-determination was defined as 'Aboriginal communities deciding the pace and nature of their future development as significant components within a diverse Australia'.

Since then self-determination has been the cornerstone of government policy, the central word.

However, for most of the last 25 years Aboriginal affairs was administered by a bureaucracy, in tandem with a Minister...

Over the past 25 years all Aboriginal affairs programs have been aimed at what has turned out to be a vast and difficult task: trying to achieve social justice for indigenous Australians, including the right to similar employment prospects and educational opportunities, to adequate shelter and basic municipal facilities, to the same life-expectancy, as other Australians.

All of these conditions are basic to our enjoying our 'full citizenship rights'. The aims of self-determination can be summed up in one word: wellbeing.

For many Aboriginal people, however, a sense of wellbeing has proved elusive.

It has also evaded the good intentions of policy makers.

In Aboriginal Australia today the positives and negatives exist side by side...Which is not to say that what the Referendum promised has come to nothing.

It does say, however, that there are very complex processes at work — that improvements in one area may have been undermined by other factors...

In at least one fundamental respect Australia cannot be called 'One Nation'. There remains a great divide between indigenous Australians and other Australians...

This year...we appear to be reaching a high-water mark in Commonwealth funding of Aboriginal affairs, and funding committed to grapple with some of the more difficult and intangible problems in indigenous Australia.

I can only hope that this commitment will be long-term, as it must be, and not just a case of modern Australia — and by extension the now triumphant liberal democratic world — having reached such a pitch of civilisation that it can afford, momentarily, to indulge a comparatively powerless minority, and its own conscience.

In a sense our political strength lies in our weakness; our 1.5 per cent of the national population. We present no threat to mainstream Australia...

As in 1967, our influence is largely based on an appeal to abstract matters — social justice, equality, righting the wrongs of history.

We remain very much dependent on the patronage and goodwill of governments...

Though the ultimate aim of self-determination is an end to this situation, Aboriginal people clearly have a long way to go.

Today, we certainly have the illusion of progress in Aboriginal affairs, of once again living through a ground-breaking era. This era will ultimately be judged, however, on how it affects individual Aboriginal lives out there.

I do not disparage the symbolic, however. As the 1967 Referendum shows, the larger gestures may have to underpin other forms of progress.

Here I should recognise yet another recent Government initiative — the Council for Aboriginal Reconciliation...

I have described it before as an attempt to change the invisibles, the larger context in which Aboriginal people live, and which...[has] such a devastating effect on individual lives...

Reconciliation will be based on mutual understanding...

The reconciliation process — which will ideally conclude for the year 2001, the centenary of Australia's Federation — may culminate in the completion of a document, an instrument of reconciliation...

These issues fit into, and should play a part in, Australia's current debate about national identity.

There is also a whole new environment of debate about constitutional reform in Australia which could and should work to the advantage of Aboriginal people...

It has already been suggested that the position of Aboriginals and Torres Strait Islanders be considered as part of this process.

What we seek is appropriate recognition of our status as the First Australians...As with the Constitution of the United States of America, it is the people from whom our Constitution derives its authority.

In the process of redefining the basis of this constitutional authority in terms of popular sovereignty, specific recognition could be given to indigenous Australians as a constituent source of this authority, because of our historical experience in this continent.

This recognition would not threaten the wider population; it would be based on partnership and reconciliation.

I think that this is the task of the 1990s.

The 1890s, the decade before Federation, was a period of great artistic and political activity, as Australians — white Australians — laid the foundations for a new democracy, a working man's paradise...

But Federation barely recognised Australia's indigenous people. In 1901 the prevailing tendency was towards isolation and exclusion: it was a White Australia.

It is now within our hands to make the nineties of this century stand out. Australia has an opportunity rarely given twice to redefine itself as a nation.

### 59. 'When Aboriginal Liberation Began', *Australian*, editorial, 27 May 1992

The 25th anniversary of the referendum that recognised Aboriginal rights in their own country is worth remembering today. The achievement of a 92 per cent majority in favour of empowering the Commonwealth to legislate for

Aborigines was a watershed in our history. It began officially the liberation of the Aborigines. They could now vote and be numbered in the Census.

Until 1967, Aborigines were assumed to have no right to self–determination. Their image was degraded, their position in Australian society servile and their abilities recognised in few vocations...[G]enerally they were neglected and many were torn from their families and brought up in foster homes. Their education was as impoverished as their status and many gave themselves over to despair. Accused of laziness, drunkenness and welfare dependence, the 'manly' appearance which the first colonial Governor, Captain Phillip, so much admired was mostly destroyed by disease, malnutrition and the depredations which attended European settlement.

This national disgrace, for such it was, gave Australia itself an image of insensitivity at best, and incipient racism at worst. The long-term imposition of the White Australia policy seemed only too well substantiated by the attitude of government — federal, State and local — when dealing with Australia's indigenous people. That it was as much due to the general separation between the two races, and European ignorance of the Aborigines themselves, was not really an excuse. Where contact did take place, however, there was often mutual respect, and some notable white figures stood up for Aboriginal culture and Aboriginal rights. The patronage [sic] and condescension to which most Aborigines had been subjected started to change.

The referendum itself disclosed a tide of general goodwill towards the Aboriginal race that was unexpected. It gave hope that the racist image of Australians need not persist. Aboriginal awareness became a living issue. Their own leaders emerged who both articulated their needs and took responsibility for their own decisions. Even though there is much left to do to redress the imbalance between black and white in our country, the process is inevitable. The respect in which the Aboriginal and Torres Strait Islanders Council [sic] is held is evidence of the ability of our indigenous people to determine their own affairs...

**60. Kevin Gilbert: The following is a transcription of a speech made by the late Kevin Gilbert, recorded on Wednesday 27 May 1992 at the Aboriginal Tent Embassy in Canberra. The occasion was a day of protest and mourning for the 25th anniversary of the 1967 Referendum; copyright Kevin Gilbert Memorial Trust**

It's twenty-five years since we Aboriginal People have had Australian citizenship imposed upon us, very much against the will of the Aboriginal People, for we have always been Australian Aborigines, not Aboriginal Australians.

We have never joined the company. We have never claimed citizenship of the oppressor, the people who have invaded our country.

Twenty-five years after this citizenship, which was supposed to give us some sort of rights and equality, we see that instead of lifting us to any sort of degree of place or right it has only given us the highest infant mortality rate, the highest number of Aboriginal people in prison, the highest mortality rate, the highest unemployment rate.

And after twenty–five years we still have Aboriginal children and people dying from lack of clean drinking water, lack of medication, lack of shelter.

We have still had twenty-five years of economic, political and medical human rights apartheid in Australia. And it hasn't worked for Aboriginal People.

At the end of the twenty-five years, we have seen the Australian Government and the Australian people try and get off the hook of responsibility by saying, ten years down the track, we'll have Reconciliation.

And Reconciliation doesn't promise us human rights, it doesn't promise us our Sovereign rights or the platform from which to negotiate, and it doesn't promise us a viable land base, an economical base, a political base, or a base in which we can again heal our people, where we can carry out our cultural practices.

It is ten more years of death! There must be something better.

Australia is calling for a Republic and a new flag, a new vision. It cannot have a vision. It cannot have a new flag. It cannot have a Sovereign nation until it addresses the right of Aboriginal People, the Sovereign Land Rights of Aboriginal people.

You cannot build a vision, you cannot build a land, you cannot build a people, on land theft, on massacre, on continuing apartheid and the denial of the one group of Aboriginal people.

We have committed no crime, we have done no wrong except own the land which the churches and white society want to take from us.

It must change.

And we can never become, and we never will become, Australian citizens. For we are Aboriginal People. We are Sovereign Aboriginal People.

We fly the flag at half mast, in respect for Alice Dixon, the mother of the boy who died in custody, Kingsley Dixon; and for all the Aboriginal people who have died in custody and been murdered in custody. And for all the Aboriginal people in gaol. And for all the children who are dying. A mark of respect and mourning for those who have died in the struggle. Because Australia still has not had the maturity, or the vision, or the guts, or the will, or the humanity, to come to justice, to come to terms, with our rights, as Sovereign Indigenous People.

Today is not a day of rejoicing, not a day of pride for Australia. It's a day when we hold our flags at half mast, in respect for Alice Dixon, and all the people who have died in custody, all the children who continue to die, even as we talk, through economic and political apartheid in this country

We are still dying. Nothing has changed.

And white Australia and the politicians, are trying to avoid the responsibility, by pushing it off ten years in the future, where it promises nothing.

It has to change.

The Aboriginal vision for this country Aboriginal Land Rights, is right for everyone. It means you cannot build any nation without integrity. You cannot build it without justice. You cannot build it without humanity. You cannot build it without compassion.

These are things that have to be addressed. We have to go forward with a vision. We have to go forward with a justice for everyone. That vision, that justice, that integrity, must address Aboriginal Sovereign rights, reparation, so we can have an economic and a political voice.

We can't be done anymore. Australia is not going to get away with killing us anymore. This type of apartheid has to be addressed.

If the Referendum hadn't been passed, we would have been further advanced, because white Australia would not have fooled the world into thinking that something positive was being done.

The international world would have looked much more closely at us, much sooner. They are now, but it would have advanced our cause by at least fifteen years.

We are now going to light our international distress flares...and we are going to signify with these distress flares the position Aboriginal People are in, and we want to signify to the world, that we need international aid, that our arms and legs have been taken from us, and we ask the International World to help restore our legs...and we need our arms.

**61. Pat Dodson, Chairperson, Council for Aboriginal Conciliation, Welcoming speech to conference on the position of Indigenous people in national constitutions, 4 June 1993, in Council for Aboriginal Reconciliation and Constitutional Centenary Foundation, *The Position of Indigenous People in National Constitutions*, AGPS, Canberra, [1993], pp. 6–8**

...A century ago, the Australian people engaged in a debate about creating a nation. They held meetings...They wrote articles and letters in newspapers. Many views were canvassed and voices were heard. The separate colonies, having divided up the land between them, discussed ways of sharing powers in order to achieve a vision of a united Australia. The result was the Australian Constitution, establishing the Commonwealth of Australia in 1901.

A century later we are beginning a new debate on that Constitution and are considering a republican path. The old links to the crown and the British Empire, once so central, are not so relevant or meaningful to the nation we have today. The old allegiances no longer seem so appropriate. The old anthems and coats of arms no longer seem to fit our sense of ourselves as Australians in this place at this time.

A century ago our Constitution was drafted in the spirit of *terra nullius*. Land was divided, power was shared, structures were established, on the illusion of vacant possession. When Aboriginal people showed up — which they inevitably did — they had to be subjugated, incarcerated or eradicated: to keep the myth of *terra nullius* alive.

The High Court decision on native title shatters this illusion and Aboriginal and Torres Strait Islander people have survived to make their contribution to the shape of the nation's political and legal future.

The nation has now woken from two centuries of sleep to become aware that Aboriginal and Torres Strait Islander people were owners of the land and were managers of the country long before the Union Jack was raised and rum drunk, here or elsewhere. While it may seem to be a new dawn for Australia's indigenous people, it has been a rude awakening for others. A moment of truth has arrived. The deeds of the past and present require those who have benefited most to take the steps towards those who have suffered most in the last 204 years. They must reconcile themselves with a new reality and then find the path of restitution that will lead to reconciliation.

No longer can Aboriginal property rights be ignored. No longer can indigenous customary laws and traditions be disregarded. The decision brings the wider Australian community closer to a true reconciliation on honest, negotiated terms with Aboriginal and Torres Strait Islander Australians.

A century after the original constitutional debate we have an opportunity to remake our Constitution to recognise and accommodate the prior ownership of the continent by Aboriginal and Torres Strait Islander people. But in this new debate there is a danger of history repeating itself. There is a danger of Aboriginal and Torres Strait Islander rights to land and cultural identity being ignored in the rush to establish a republic with minimal change to the Constitution. There is a danger of new arrangements to share power being developed without seeing and somehow meeting the Aboriginal and Torres Strait Islander peoples' yearning to escape the powerlessness of exclusion and dispossession. There is a danger of a new Constitution being drafted that tries to capture the spirit of a modern Australia, but that denies the spirit of indigenous Australia.

Terra nullius may be gone but the old habits of constitutional drafters die hard. The silences and omissions of the past echo loudly in the present...

[T]he Council for Aboriginal Reconciliation and the Constitutional Centenary Foundation share an aim of encouraging education and promoting public discussion, understanding and review of these issues. We both encourage the kind of debate of a century ago. We encourage the meetings, the letters, the articles, the arguments if a new vision of Australia is to emerge that is in keeping with our sense of ourselves as Australians, as belonging to this place, as being a part of this time...

### 62. Michael Mansell, National Secretary, Aboriginal Provisional Government, 'Issues and Options for Australia', in Council for Aboriginal Reconciliation and Constitutional Centenary Foundation, *The Position of Indigenous People in National Constitutions*, AGPS, Canberra, [1993], pp. 88–9

I think it is important that the debate that has been going on here in the last two days is continued because it has connections with debates in other forums. For example, we are here talking about constitutional reform as it affects Aborigines. We are also discussing, both here and in the broad community, the implications of the Mabo decision and, with the Prime Minister kicking on the issue of the republican debate, I am sure that the issues of Aborigines will also come up in that debate as well. In my view, all three different forums will have to consider the same fundamental question and that is: what is the political relationship between Aborigines and Australia. A question that flows from that is: who is it that decides, ultimately, what that political relationship is?

They are very important questions because to date the prevailing view has been that the relationship that Aborigines have to Australia and Australians is that of citizens. That is, that their rights are those accorded to Australian citizens, no more, no less. It is a convenient argument and one which has prevailed, not only since this country was invaded but also since the Constitution was drafted in 1901. The most serious consequence of that attitude continuing unchallenged is that the rights of Aboriginal people to the rights that are accorded other indigenous people, are necessarily taken away because how could it be consistent for Aborigines, if we are to be Australians, to advocate the right to self-determination?

The emphasis on Aboriginal rights as Australian citizens is necessarily an emphasis on the rights as individuals and not on a collective [basis]. If this important question is going to determine finally what rights are going to be accorded Aboriginal people, then another question arises and that is: if Aborigines are deemed to be Australians, or if it is accepted that a choice has been made, when was the decision taken by Aborigines to accept that we are Australians and that our rights are necessarily limited to being those of Australians? I would defy anybody in this country...to name the date at which Aborigines were asked the question or expressed a view on that...

Let us assume that Aborigines at some stage have an informed discussion about the issue of the political relationship we are to have with Australia and let us assume that Aboriginal people make a decision...

There are a number of options that are going to have different consequences for the debate on constitutional reform. We have boiled it down to essentially four options. They are, first, that Aborigines may decide to be fully integrated into the Australian political system as Australians. A second alternative is a form of autonomy or local government powers at the local community level; nevertheless, we would still be Australians. A third option is one that seems to flow from the Norfolk Island debate; that Aborigines ought to have some broader recognition of their collective community right and that is the right of self–government within the context of the Australian political structure... All [these] options are based on the notion that Aborigines must necessarily be confined within the life of the Australian nation. This notion is based on the notion of white supremacy...

It really raises the question of an Aboriginal choice. Now the Aboriginal Provisional Government has put up a model which is based on the notion of Aboriginal sovereignty and the basis of our view is that, if Aboriginal people wish to consider it, we will provide the basic outline for it, because we believe that the right of all other people in the world — that is, a right to decide their own future — should also be accorded to Aborigines...

### 63. Patrick Dodson, 'Wrongs Mars Rights Issues', *Sydney Morning Herald*, 23 May 1997

Two years ago, when the Council for Aboriginal Reconciliation began planning for a major convention to coincide with the 30th anniversary of the 1967 referendum on indigenous rights, it had little idea of the heated context in which the event would ultimately take place.

We could not have anticipated that the same powers that were vested in the Commonwealth as a result of the referendum could be seen by some, at the time of the reconciliation convention, as a potential tool to legislate against indigenous interests.

Our elected representatives in the national Parliament are now faced with the decision of whether or not to destroy a real opportunity for Aboriginal people and the wider Australian community to extend to each other a genuine hand of trust through co-existence.

If the Government proceeds down the road of extinguishing native title, or effectively extinguishing it, none of the stakeholders will end up feeling better. Australians, in general, will not be comfortable with the plan because they will know in their hearts that it's wrong...

Strong support has been expressed for the acknowledgment of the unique place of indigenous citizens in the Australian Constitution and for some kind of national document which promotes respect for indigenous culture and law ...

It is not only indigenous people who have something to lose if the formal reconciliation process fails to lay the necessary groundwork for the future. Many Australians already know that.

But it must be said that indigenous people's commitment to reconciliation is being sorely tested by the Wik debate. It is our duty, as a council, to point out that further dispossession will gravely jeopardise the prospects of achieving meaningful reconciliation. Indigenous Australians will view extinguishment or a version of extinguishment as an indication that they are still to be treated as second-class citizens in their own country; that their rights are not respected and that reconciliation is an empty, tokenistic concept, based on other people's terms.

The foundation of Aboriginal and Torres Strait Islander culture is our relationship with the land and waters. Dispossession has occurred over many areas of this country. Further dispossession will be strongly resisted, now and forever.

Co-existence is the foundation of reconciliation.

Next week's convention will consider a range of questions, ideas and propositions aimed at charting the process of reconciliation through the council's final term and beyond.

It is an opportunity for Australians to take a closer look at the issues behind co-existence, and to tap back into the compassion and the goodwill that led them to support the landmark referendum 30 years ago.

### 64. Geraldine O'Brien, '1967 Vote "Crucial" To Black Rights', *Sydney Morning Herald*, 26 May 1997

Australians needed to debate whether the 1967 referendum giving the Commonwealth power to legislate for Aboriginal welfare included the power to legislate adversely, the lawyer and Aboriginal spokesman Mr Noel Pearson said yesterday. Speaking at a constitutional forum to mark the opening of National Law Week, Mr Pearson said that although some constitutional lawyers argued the referendum did not give such powers, the matter would be debated over the coming months.

If the answer was yes, then the Commonwealth would indeed be able to "wind back the Wik powers" on the basis of that referendum, he said.

He believed that the Australian Constitution should, in its preamble, recognise the special place of Aborigines in the Australian system, guarantee "the collective right of internal self-determination for Aboriginal communities within the life of the nation" (as was the case for indigenous people in Canada), and state a "general guarantee" of the equality of all Australian citizens.

"It is not sufficient to turn to the High Court to see if an implied equality already exists (in legislation)", he said.

Human rights in Australia needed to be safeguarded in common law, by international treaty and specifically in the Constitution, he argued. "But we now have reached the stage of sufficient awareness, and controversy, that we need apolitical and social consensus of what those rights should be".

### 65. Rt Hon. the Prime Minister John Howard, 'Reconciled To Look Forward', *Australian Financial Review*, 28 May 1997

*John Howard's remarks to Parliament yesterday on the 30th anniversary of the referendum to recognise Commonwealth power over Aboriginal affairs.*

Our approach as a government to the process of reconciliation is very much guided by and heavily influenced by the spirit of the 1967 referendum. If the 1967 referendum spoke of anything it spoke of a need to remedy in a practical way the disadvantage of the Aboriginal and Torres Strait Islander people.

If you want unanimity of view within the Australian community, or near unanimity of view within the Australian community, on issues relating to the indigenous people, then you must look at areas of disadvantage and issues such as health, housing, employment and education.

In the remarks that I made to the Reconciliation Conference yesterday, I deliberately said, and I repeat it today, that we believe that the essence of reconciliation lies not in symbolic gestures — although some of them are important. This motion in a sense is a symbolic gesture. It is important on these issues that the Parliament do, as far as possible, speak with one voice, not in overblown rhetoric but in a practical determination to address the areas of disadvantage that indigenous people suffer.

I have said repeatedly that anybody who argues that Aboriginal and Torres Strait Islander people are not as a group more profoundly disadvantaged than other sections of the Australian community are flying in the face of reality. That does not mean to say that every Aboriginal and Torres Strait Islander in Australia is disadvantaged. It does not mean to say that some of the programs over recent years that have been directed to curing their disadvantage have not involved substantial elements of waste and fraud. That does not alter the fact that they remain a very disadvantaged group.

We are not obsessed with symbolism. We are concerned though with practical outcomes. That is why we have put such an enormous focus in recent months since we came to office on addressing areas of disadvantage. It is why, despite the necessities of the time, we have quarantined from any expenditure restraint some of the critical areas in relation to indigenous education. We have in fact expanded expenditure in a number of areas. I am very happy to say that in the last Budget we announced a significant expansion of programs which are designed to help Aboriginal and Torres Strait Islander people succeed in their own businesses and generate a greater sense of economic independence and a greater sense of self-empowerment.

There continues to be within the community, not least within the indigenous community itself, significant debate about the value of the ATSIC system. When coming to power, the Government decided to retain it. In conformity with our election undertakings, there were changes made and increased levels of accountability imposed, but the structure was retained.

I know that the Government's response to the Wik decision has generated considerable opposition, not only within some sections — I stress some sections — of the rural community of Australia, but also within the indigenous community of Australia. Can I say to the indigenous people of Australia that I understand why they are opposed to the amendments that we have put forward, but can I put to them and can I put through this Parliament to the Australian people that the plan that we have devised to deal with the consequences of the Wik decision and also to deal with the unsatisfactory features of the Native Title Act is a fair and balanced plan...

I do not believe that, as a community, we can ignore history. We must openly acknowledge the injustice of the past. As an intensely proud Australian along, I am sure, with all other Australians who have a balanced view of the history of this country, I am immensely proud of what we have achieved over the last 200 years. It has been a heroic achievement in the face of immense difficulties.

That does not gainsay the fact that there have been significant blemishes. Undoubtedly, the most significant blemish of all in the history of this country over the last 200 years has been the treatment of our indigenous people. I would have thought that was an unarguable fact. I would have though it was a concept that all of us could embrace, but I would have thought that we could have embraced it without developing an approach to reconciliation that looks backwards rather than forward.

### 66. Margo Kingston, 'Libs Enlist Nazi Race Laws For Court Fight', *Sydney Morning Herald*, 10 February 1998

The Federal Government yesterday endorsed its lawyers' claim to the High Court last week that the Constitution's 'race power' permitted Nuremberg laws and apartheid, and that the court had no right under the power to strike down extremist race laws.

A spokesman for the Attorney-General, Mr Williams, QC, said the claim was "theoretically right".

"It's the Attorney-General's view that the court was testing the theoretical limit of the powers and not the present situation...The Government would not seek to introduce any such extreme laws".

He said that "the democratic checks and balances that restrain the executive and legislature" would protect Australians from such laws.

Justice Michael Kirby said last week that "it seems unthinkable that a law such as the Nazi race laws could be enacted under the race power and that this court could do nothing about it".

The Government argument that the race power allowed untrammelled racial discrimination came during the hearing of the Hindmarsh appeal.

The Government's Hindmarsh law — which assists a South Australian developer by excluding the Ngarrindjeri people from using heritage protection laws — is the first since Federation to use the "race power" to take away rights on the grounds of race.

The Hindmarsh judgment, to be handed down by May, is considered important to the fate of the Prime Minister's Wik bill, which relies on the race power to wind back native title rights.

The Government also argued that although voters in the 1967 referendum giving the Commonwealth power to make laws for Aborigines expected it to be used for their benefit, it also allowed laws detrimental to indigenous Australians.

The shadow attorney-general, Senator Nick Bolkus, said the Government's views "are morally repugnant — they put the Government in the same boat as Pauline Hanson".

"If they can't distinguish between a decent constitutional framework in a democracy and a dictatorship or oppressive regime, then they're in the same category as Pauline Hanson in the eyes of the world", he said.

The president of the Executive Council of Australian Jewry, Mrs Diane Shteinman, said it was "incomprehensible to think that this is the case in Australia — I just hope it is not the correct interpretation of the Constitution".

She said the council hoped the republic convention would "consider changes to the Constitution to endorse the rights of minorities".

The chairman of the Aboriginal and Torres Strait Islander Commission (ATSIC), Mr Gatjil Djerrkura, said the Government's view "certainly does not accord with community standards".

"Whatever the situation was in 1901 [when the Constitution came into force], the circumstances of the 1967 referendum and our international human rights obligations lead us to believe that the race power cannot now be used for a detrimental purpose".

### 67. Bernard Lane, 'Race Power Play', *Australian*, 4 April 1998

Australia stands on the threshold of a new century, with a Constitution that permits a democratic parliament to make laws discriminating between people on the basis of their race. This power, the race power, is a relic of the 1890s and the White Australia Policy. There may not be a great deal the High Court can do to make the race power safe for the age of anti-racism. This week's Hindmarsh decision is inconclusive.

Should a referendum be held to ask the Australian people to do away with the race power entirely? Former chief justice Sir Harry Gibbs says: "There's a lot to be said for taking the race power out of the Constitution altogether". He does not say this because of the Hindmarsh decision but because of "general principles". "No government should aim to pass legislation that is racially biased, whether favourable or unfavourable", Gibbs says. Adverse discrimination is not a tautology.

But other people who deplore racism oppose the outright repeal of the race power. They do so because, despite its racist origins, the power has been used by recent governments as a force for Aboriginal affirmative action. Well-known examples are the 1993 Native Title Act, which the Howard Government wants to change significantly with its Wik Bill, and the heritage law central to the Hindmarsh Island bridge affair.

If the race power were repealed, it would also undo the work of the 1967 referendum, which brought Aborigines back within the federal parliament's lawmaking power. "There is merit in continuing to treat the plight of Aboriginal people as a national issue, not a State issue", says George Williams, senior law lecturer at the Australian National University and a barrister in the Hindmarsh case. He is not alone in judging the State record as a poor one.

But Williams also sees the inherent dangers in the federal power. Nor does he think the Constitution allows the judges to provide adequate safeguards. "Even if the court did impose limits on the race power in subsequent cases, and even if they were applied to invalidate discriminatory legislation, such as the Wik Bill, that would still not be enough", he says.

Williams proposes a constitutional amendment that would guarantee freedom from adverse racial discrimination.

For now, Aboriginal affirmative action remains heavily dependent upon a legislative power that was devised for the White Australia Policy. How did this happen?

In 1901, the race power allowed parliament to make laws affecting "the people of any race, *other than the Aboriginal race in any State*, for whom it is deemed necessary to make special laws". In 1967, those eight words in italics disappeared because the people overwhelmingly approved the Aboriginals referendum.

What did the referendum mean? "What was in the public mind was simply this view that Aborigines should have the same rights and obligations as other Australians", says Bill Wentworth, who became the first federal minister for Aboriginal affairs in 1968.

But did the people of 1967 transform the racist power into an affirmative action only power, at least for Aborigines?

The Constitution framers of the 1890s would not have described the power as racist; they saw nothing wrong in white men exerting strict control over people, such as "Chinese miners, laundrymen, market gardeners, and furniture manufacturers; the Japanese settlers and Kanaka plantation labourers". The founding fathers did not exclude Aborigines to protect them from what was to be the primary use of the power: adverse discrimination. It just seems to have been assumed that blacks were a State affair.

Race and imperfectly examined assumptions go together. By the end of the Menzies era, sponsors of indigenous advancement had generated enough support for the belief that Aborigines' exclusion from the race power denied them the benefits of federal legislation. This belief carried the day in 1967.

But not everyone was convinced. The year before, Geoffrey Sawer, doyen of constitutional law, wrote an article discussing the unsavoury nature of the race power and its apparent pointlessness. "Having regard to the dubious origins of the section, and the dangerous potentialities of adverse discriminatory treatment which it contains, the complete repeal of the section would seem preferable to any amendment intended to extend its possible benefits to the Aborigines", he said.

Twice during the Hindmarsh hearing in February this year, Justice Michael McHugh drew attention to Sawer's opinion that complete repeal would have been better than returning the Aborigines to the race power.

## 68. Bob Hogg, Letter to the editor, *Australian*, 7 April 1998

It was sad to read of the ATSIC commissioner, Geoff Clark, apropos the Hindmarsh Island Bridge decision, calling on the Prime Minister to "put a referendum to the people to protect the rights of its indigenous people as citizens of this country with full and equal rights". Sad, not because I disagree with Mr Clark in this — I support him 100 per cent — but sad because the wheel has finally come full circle on the most misguided piece of constitutional engineering that Australia has ever seen: the 1967 constitutional amendment which cancelled the exclusion of Australian Aborigines from the power of the Commonwealth government to make racially specific legislation.

Last year, at the 30th anniversary of this event, we were treated to a skilfully orchestrated show of enthusiasm for the benefits which it was claimed to have conferred on Aborigines. We were told that it had given them citizenship, given them the vote, given them equal civil rights, placed them for the first time under Commonwealth jurisdiction, and even protected them from racially discriminatory legislation passed by the States.

These claims are totally without foundation. What that amendment did was to take away the protection which Australian Aborigines previously had from being included in any racially specific legislation the Commonwealth might contemplate. And that kind of legislation was seen, by the founders of our Federation, as unashamedly racist. The provision was designed to enable the Commonwealth pass the sort of laws the States had previously passed, controlling and protecting Indian, Afghan and Syrian hawkers, Chinese workers, Japanese and Kanakas, restricting them to certain trades and localities, and allowing their easy deportation.

[Sir Samuel] Griffith's own words to the 1891 Convention, in his (unsuccessful) appeal to have this power as an exclusively Commonwealth one, show beyond doubt the feeling of the times: 'The introduction of an alien race in considerable numbers into any part of the Commonwealth is a danger to the whole of the Commonwealth, and upon that matter the Commonwealth should speak, and the Commonwealth alone'. There was never any argument at the time of Federation that the Aboriginal population should be included in such legislation. Their exclusion, it should noted however, was not based on any racially benign sentiment. It was because it was readily accepted that any specifically Aboriginal issues always had been, and clearly should be, decided at State level.

A personal confession. I voted 'Yes' in 1967 because, having taken the trouble to read the Constitution, I knew there was nothing there which prevented the States from being as racist as their own Constitutions allowed in respect of Aborigines, and felt (perhaps with hindsight, naively) that their best protection and prospects for advancement lay in giving the Commonwealth the power to override the States. I still don't know whether I did the right thing or not.

What I do know, however, is that I will pledge my support to any movement dedicated to restoring the exemption of Australian Aborigines from racially specific Commonwealth legislation, and introducing a prohibition in the Commonwealth Constitution against States making any racially specific laws, whether in respect of Aborigines or not.

## 69. Patrick Dodson, 'Laws Detrimental to Aborigines will Diminish the Nation', *Australian*, 7 April 1998

Aboriginal people need certainty about their status, not to be at the mercy of a race power IN 1967, the Australian people voted overwhelmingly to rewrite the race power in the Constitution so that Aboriginal people be treated in a fair, just and honourable way in this country. At least this has been the assumption for the past 31 years.

Now this head of power and what it means, and the will of the people in 1967, are under question. It also means that, as a nation, we are entering a new era of uncertainty.

The High Court decision in the Hindmarsh Island bridge matter last week has thrown open the question of whether, under the race power, the Commonwealth can make laws to the detriment or benefit of Aboriginal people.

The race power was originally inserted into the Constitution to give the Commonwealth the power to enable parliament to discriminate against certain groups.

At that time it was intended to be used to discriminate against Chinese people and South Sea Islanders in Australia in favour of the majority of white Australians. Ironically, the Australian Constitution at that time also explicitly excluded the possibility of the Commonwealth making laws about Aboriginal people - beneficial or detrimental. It was as if we didn't exist.

In 1967, it was put to the Australian people, in a bipartisan manner, that the Commonwealth should have the capacity to make and administer laws to address and advance the interests of Aboriginal people. This was agreed to by more than 80 per cent of the Australian public.

Since that time — maybe not at the speed we would like — Australian governments have used this power to progress our interests, to recognise and protect our rights and our culture.

Now there is a view within Government and the High Court that laws can be made that are detrimental to our indigenous interests, laws that take away or diminish our rights. It will be a tragic day if that ever happens. Indigenous people belong to a culture and have traditions that are distinct and different from those of Western society.

Central to this is our attachment to land, which has continued but only recently has been recognised in the native title judgment of the High Court in the Mabo decision.

We are different. We do have a distinct and unique culture. Many Australians enjoy and appreciate the expression of our culture in art, dance and song.

We simply want Australian political and legal institutions to accept and respect the rights of indigenous people to be the people that we are. But difference does not mean that we cannot co-exist.

Aboriginal people have tried to be dignified in asserting our rights, in trying to share and in trying to accommodate the many interests of non-Aboriginal people.

But enough is enough — there can be no more whittling away of the rights of indigenous people. No more taking away of our right to express authority over our own lands. The right to have a say over the things that matter to us as we work our way into the next century. This can all take place with accommodation of other interests in the lands. We believe that it can be worked out.

But it does come back to the interpretation of the race power and the 1967 referendum. Our view and hope is that the Commonwealth, in the spirit of the 1967 referendum, should only have the power to make laws that are beneficial to our interests. That is to recognise and respect our rights.

The Government confidently asserts that its Native Title Amendment Bill is beneficial to Aboriginal people and, therefore, is not inconsistent with the race power of 1967. The indigenous view, and that of many fine legal brains in this country, is quite different.

While indigenous groups agree that the workability of some of the existing provisions in the current Act needs to be addressed, this doesn't require the total rewrite that is taking place under the Government's amending Bill.

The Native Title Amendment Bill, if passed, will be exposed to a challenge on the basis that it does not benefit Aboriginal people. It will end up in yet another High Court case specifically aimed at this question of whether the race power can be used beneficially or not. The question is always going to be the substantive aspect - is it a benefit or not?

Significantly, the Hindmarsh decision indicates that the Government, if it passes a law, can then legitimately repeal that law. Consequently, it means laws such as the Aboriginal and Torres Strait Islander Commission Act, including the provisions for the Indigenous Land Corporation, the Heritage Protection Act and the Northern Territory Aboriginal Land Rights Act can be changed or repealed, almost at whim.

This is a serious concern for indigenous people because these Acts may be changed to our detriment. If this is the case, the protection of indigenous rights will be harder to maintain, and the principles of social justice and equity will be given cursory acknowledgment.

This is why I say we should not be the playthings of our community any longer. Australia will be a diminished nation until indigenous rights are entrenched in our political and legal system, and guaranteed forevermore.

## 70. Prime Minister John Howard, The 1967 Referendum, media release, 15 July 1998, <www.pm.gov.au/News/media_releases/1998/1967.htm>

Last night's comments by the leader of One Nation [Pauline Hanson] about the 1967 Referendum on aboriginal issues were factually wrong in two important respects.

She was wrong to say that the 1967 Referendum gave Aboriginal and Torres Strait Islanders the vote. Their right to vote already existed, including under State laws. The Referendum gave the Commonwealth concurrent powers with the States in relation to aboriginal people and put beyond doubt that indigenous people were finally counted in the census along with all other Australians.

In other words, the 1967 Referendum was about treating all Australians equally.

It was not the 1967 Referendum which produced bad indigenous affairs policies.

Those bad policies came from the Hawke and Keating governments. Not only did their policies permit mal-administration but they also included a tendency to brand any Coalition critic of their aboriginal affairs policies as a racist or a bigot.

The present Government has restored proper accountability and credibility in the area of aboriginal affairs.

It has ensured that funding is used to meet areas of disadvantage in health, housing, employment and education and not for purposes of political advocacy.

It was a Coalition Government led by the late Harold Holt and John McEwen who sponsored the 1967 Referendum which secured the votes of more than 90% of the Australian people. It represented a proper and practical gesture towards ensuring that all Australians, irrespective of their racial background, are treated equally under the laws of Australia.

## 71. Question submitted for approval in constitutional referendum, 6 November 1999, in reference to a new preamble to the Constitution of Australia, *Parliamentary Handbook of the Commonwealth of Australia*, <www. aph.gov.au/library/handbook/referendums/r1999.htm>

With hope in God, the Commonwealth of Australia is constituted as a democracy with a federal system of government to serve the common good. We the Australian people commit ourselves to this Constitution: proud that a unity has been forged by Australians from many ancestries; never forgetting the sacrifices of all who defended our country and our liberty in time of war; upholding freedom, tolerance, individual dignity and the rule of law; honouring Aborigines and Torres Strait Islanders, the nation's first people, for their deep kinship with their lands and for their ancient and continuing cultures which enrich the life of our country; recognising the nation-building contribution of generations of immigrants; mindful of our responsibility to protect our unique natural environment; supportive of achievement as well as equality of opportunity for all; and valuing independence as dearly as the national spirit which binds us together in both adversity and success.

# Part II

## Aboriginal Oral Sources

Documents 72–93 is oral testimony collected by Dale Edwards and Kath Schilling in January–February 1997.

### 72. Chicka Dixon, 39-years-old in 1967, was managing the Foundation for Aboriginal Affairs in Sydney

The 1967 Referendum ended seven years of frustration of trying to force the Feds into changing the Federal Constitution and with it ended one campaign for justice for Kooris. When it did happen we became citizens in our own country and it gave the feds the power to override the States and take full responsibility for Kooris.

### 73. Kaye Price, 26-years-old in 1967, was living in Hobart, and attending Hobart Teachers' College

I remember the debates leading up to the Referendum, particularly post–Referendum, when it was realised that almost all the 'No' votes were in the Top End. I feel that the Referendum marked a turning point in attitudes to Aboriginal rights. At last we were to be counted in the census, which gave us more 'status' as human beings. The Referendum also showed that Aboriginal people had been denied human rights and this was now brought to the attention of voters, the majority of whom were non-Aboriginal.

1967 was a landmark in that we would never get 92 per cent of the population voting in our favour these days. As a teacher and writer, it is very important to me that Indigenous people themselves do not confuse 'counted as citizens' with 'citizens'.

1967 will always be a recognised milestone in Australian history!

### 74. Burnum Burnum, 31-years-old in 1967, was at the Wagga Agricultural College and working in the New South Wales public service

I participated in the ten year campaign with Gordon Bryant and FCAATSI prior to the Referendum. When it finally did happen we thought that it was about time.

The 1967 Referendum changed certain discrimination realities in the Constitution against Aboriginals – Section 127 allowed us to be counted and all States and Territories voted in favour of this. For the first time we were counted, along with the cattle and sheep.

The Referendum also ushered in basic anti-discrimination and human rights laws as well as *Heralding* the land rights era. It was a definite turning point in modern Australian political history and the conscience of the nation was expressed by the people.

At the time I definitely thought that the Referendum achieved something — personally, it made me lose my inferiority complex. Also, Aboriginal people started getting into tertiary institutions. It also made me prouder to proclaim my Aboriginality.

It gave me the impetus to attend Land Rights handovers such as Uluru, Kakadu, Pitjantjarra (Ernabella), Wallaga Lake and Jervis Bay National Park.

For Australia, it was a conscience 'yes' vote of a nation — overwhelmingly so. But I think that the change to decimal currency a year earlier helped, as well as what I perceived as the emerging cosmopolitan nature of Australian society.

I also knew that I could vote in the Referendum and I definitely did.

Between my birth and now (1997) I can honestly say that my emotional high of the Referendum in '67 is still with me today — a real highlight of my whole life and today I honour the Australian people for their vote.

The Referendum spelt the end of ABSCHOL and FCAATSI and the beginnings of a new flag, Land Rights, a decent burial for Truganinni, culminating in the very honourable return of our 'First Lady' to Lake Mungo. The Gove Case dictum 'the people don't own the land — the land owns the people' was seen as 'bad' law.

Exploitation of subsurface estate in minerals on Aboriginal lands began in earnest for the benefit of overseas stakeholders White Australia's 'black history' continued.

But the Referendum meant the emergence of white champions from scholars and lawyers at this major eventful turning point in black memory.

The ten year FCAATSI campaign should never be erased but highlighted in our history.

## 75. John Maynard, 13-years-old in 1967, was attending high school in Newcastle

Sadly, I don't remember anything about the 1967 Referendum. At the time I was obviously politically unaware and naive to the nature of the Referendum or its relevance. At the time the Referendum made no apparent difference to my life; however in light of where I am today, I feel, as with most Aboriginal people, the '67 Referendum was a very significant point.

I also now believe that the Referendum meant that the volume and numbers of Aboriginal voices was beginning to unite, grow louder and begin to be heard by mainstream Australian society.

For good or ill the '67 Referendum will remain an important point in our history. Many Aboriginal people lobbied and campaigned long and hard before that Referendum and the landslide 'Yes' vote can be attributed in no small way to the work they put in.

However, whether the result was a first step in equality or just another, maybe more subversive means of dismantling our culture and society is yet to be determined. Certainly, the right to enter hotels has had a major influence on the state of Aboriginal family life.

### 76. Leisha May Eatts, 27-years-old in 1967, was living in Narrogin, Western Australia

In 1967 I was just living and that's all: fighting for my rights, which I did a lot of in towns such as Narrogin, Kellerberrin, Northam, Beverley and Cunderdin. These sorts of towns were full of Nyungah people.

The hotels were full of our people. The thing I remember about the Referendum is that Nyungahs celebrated going into hotels to have a drink, and for the first time they felt happy the alcohol drowned the frustrations that were kept since white invaders. The sad thing was, they kept it up and they turned into compulsive drinkers.

The Referendum also meant throwing away our dog tags, citizenship rights and exemption. It meant Aboriginal people need not be afraid of having a drink with their family and not being caught by the police and sent to jail for six months for supplying alcohol.

At the time I really didn't think that the Referendum had achieved anything: for some it did, for some it never achieved anything, only disaster. I saw many parents going into hotels with their money and staying there until broke and drunk and fights started to break out among our people. Meanwhile the children were hungry at home, running around dirty. And their poor old grandmas trying to feed them with what little food they had.

It did make some difference to my life: we were allowed to go to some places that we never went before, such as pictures, swimming pools, and have glass soft drink in shops. But basically we were still looked down upon. Racial prejudice was and still is very strong. Kellerberrin Shire took the toilet down that said 'Native Women Only', and next to it a toilet that said 'Ladies Only'.

I didn't know that I could vote in the Referendum and believed that the Referendum had to pass for us to vote. But I started to vote after the 1967 Referendum. I believed that we were nothing before that the Referendum]: we did not have a vote or a say in anything — we were a non people.

Now the Referendum means to me that we can vote. It also gave us a step closer to being counted worthy in the Community. It was a start in this country of ours to have a say in voting.

### 77. Bev Elphick, in her 20s in 1967, was living in Sydney

At the time my husband was facing armed combat in Vietnam and the war was my main concern.

It has only been in later years that I have had a chance to reflect on issues like the Referendum. Being one of the victims of the separation and assimilation policies of Australia's recent past, I now feel cheated and angry over not being allowed the feelings I could have had for my heritage.

I can only now begin to understand why I felt displaced for so many years.

In reflection, I see the Referendum as having only created more politicians. I see very little else having changed for the people I now have the right to call my people.

### 78. Tjuki Pumpjack, 41-years-old in 1967, was doing station work at Angus Downs Station, Imanpa, and Mt Ebenezer, Erldunda, South Australia

The 1967 Referendum questions were not relevant at the time for me. But now it means a lot to me to be able to vote. I now understand how important it is to vote. Before we didn't know anything about voting.

### 79. Dr Bill Jonas, 25-years-old in 1967, was teaching at Maitland Boys High School in Newcastle

I clearly remember the 1967 Referendum, specifically because there were a number of things going on with teaching and classroom activities. Current affairs was a very popular part of the curriculum at that time and so we were dealing with all sorts of issues surrounding the Vietnam War. In my classroom I always tried to provide a very balanced view of everything that was going on. I did this in the case of the Vietnam war and so I was also most acutely aware of doing this in regards to the 1967 Referendum. I tried to put across a balanced viewpoint, which of course was influenced by my own views, especially in terms of the injustices happening to Aboriginal people.

During this period I became very outspoken about the Vietnam War and the Referendum, and because Maitland Boys High School was a military type of school, there were a lot of conservative attitudes throughout the place. As a result, I had quite a few arguments with other teachers about toning down my views.

At the time the Referendum didn't make any difference to my life. However, I did know that I could vote in it and of course I did — I was acutely conscious of it. It was a moral issue even though I was not that politically active at the time. I definitely thought that we would be better off without the States and much better off getting out from under their control.

In terms of what the Referendum means to me now, I believe that it was important. I believe that Aboriginal people are better off (as opposed to it not having happened at all).

### 80. Elizabeth Hoffman was married and living on the Murray River at Moama in New South Wales in 1967

I was involved with the Victorian Women's Council at the time, which later became the National Women's Council of which I was Chairperson. I later became administrator of the Aborigines Advancement League in Victoria.

Anyway, we were always trying to organise transport so that we could attend FCAATSI meetings.

The '67 Referendum didn't really affect everyday life – you still now have to fight for things. We had to fight for anything we ever got and are still doing it.

### 81. Greg Norria, 14-years-old in 1967, was living in Moora, north of Perth, and attending high school

I don't really remember anything about the Referendum, and don't recall ever being taught anything about it at school. I only really found out about it when I went to college. So, at the time, it didn't really make any difference to my life: it didn't make any difference that I realised at the time. Now, though, I realise that there were restrictions, barriers and racism.

On reflection, it hasn't achieved much in regards to reconciliation – Aboriginal people can have their own culture but people's attitudes haven't really changed. Equality is still a long way off.

The Referendum is more significant to me now because of my continually learning about Aboriginal history and of our continuous struggle. My learning about my own history also opened my eyes.

It seems that the Referendum was like only the opening of one door and there are still many other doors to open.

### 82. Susan O'Neil, 17-years-old in 1967, was a student and living in Darwin

I don't specifically remember knowing anything about the Referendum at the time. But I think that it represented a change in opinions and was an acknowledgment that the general public was aware and had an opinion — contrary to the loud bigots.

### 83. Johnny Bulun Bulun, about 18-years-old in 1967, was driving tractors in the Mangalala, Ramingining area, Northern Territory

Not much. Voting for election.

### 84. Lester Coyne, 30-years-old in 1967, was living in Albany, Western Australia and involved in the transport industry

At the time I was married, had one child and was very busy organising my life and my family, so I was really not aware of the Referendum or its importance. I had little or no interest.

The importance and impact of the Referendum was realised at a later date, but at the time it had little or no impact for me or my family, Mum, Dad, three brothers, two sisters.

Now, I think that at the time the Referendum was an attempt to correct and address an issue of major impact on Aboriginal people in Australia by non-Aboriginals — social conscience, world focus, views — enabling Aboriginals to vote, become citizens.

### 85. Dr Gordon Briscoe, historian, 29-years-old in 1967, was a clerk in the Canterbury Municipal Council, Sydney

I was an associate member of FCAATSI and I absolutely remember the Referendum. Because I was living in Sydney I participated and had an active interest in Aboriginal affairs around the Sydney area.

I did know that a Referendum was put in 1944 and it was defeated. Also, a group of people had met with the Menzies government back in 1961.

I also participated in the formulation of activities that worked towards the Referendum — mainly at Greenacre — such as raising money, manning booths, distributing leaflets — Vote 'Yes' — to Aboriginal families in the Bankstown area.

FCAATSI wanted to influence the way that the government spent money on Aborigines and at the time it was an almost impossibility to get into political structures — that is the States were virtually impenetrable and not open to any activist groups, and so FCAATSI wanted powers transferred to the Commonwealth.

At the time the welfare structure did not extend to those who weren't classified as Aborigines within the States: Aborigines were those that lived on missions and it didn't include 'half-castes', 'quarter–castes' etc. The focus of FCAATSI's campaign were those Aborigines. They were also asking the Federal government to change its definition of who was an Aborigine — this was in a subtle way, because the definition needed to be understood by those spending the money.

FCAATSI became more and more important as a lobby group, but they were used by the trade unions, the church and the ALP in opposition.

At FCAATSI meetings, Aboriginal people came in on a Friday and no organisational demands were made: they were merely asked to share their thoughts.

### 86. Muriel Smith, 34-years-old in 1967, was a housewife and living in Smithfield, New South Wales

Vote 'Yes' for Aboriginal. Giving of rights to be counted in the census.

Now the Referendum means to me that we were counted in the census, it allowed the Federal government to make special laws for us and took us out of the hands of the State governments.

### 87. Emily Walker, 29-years-old in 1967, was living on the outskirts of Brisbane, married and having her first child

I don't remember anything about the Referendum as I knew nothing about it at the time, especially because I was living in Queensland.

I was allowed to go to school because my grandmother and my mother both worked for white people — you know, doing the ironing, the cleaning etc. — so I was allowed to go to school because they worked for the white parents whose children attended the school. That was why I was allowed to go, but we weren't taught anything in school about Aboriginal history — so I never ever thought that I wasn't a citizen until that time.

I was told I had to vote because I was married to a white man. This is probably also why the Referendum at the time didn't make that much difference to my life — because I was married to a white man.

That whole time was a very confusing time: we weren't allowed to go into pubs, but in some places when I was with my husband I used to be served and others refused to serve us.

I don't really think that the Referendum achieved anything. It was the same basic thing — anything that the government did, didn't achieve anything. They did all the wrong things.

Even now the Referendum doesn't mean that much to me, not one thing. I know that I have to vote, otherwise I'll go to gaol.

Aboriginal people should have a choice — we are human beings. The Referendum didn't give US the choice, choices are always being made for us.

### 88. Terry Sutherland, 2-years-old in 1967, was living with his family in Uralla, New South Wales

Obviously I don't remember anything about the 1967 Referendum, but I do know that it wasn't when Kooris got the right to vote.

Now I think not only of the Referendum, but of the year 1967 as the time when I supposedly became a citizen of this country.

That aspect of the whole issue is really quite dumbfounding. Especially when I think of myself as an innocent two year old child who did not have the same rights as other two year old children at the time, who could not have the same expectations that non–Aboriginal children had, who could not expect to be able to grow up in a safe and secure environment, and who was not safe and secure in the rights that all children should expect — just the basic human right to live and be happy. That basic right was denied us for so long and was so vehement that it was a matter of government policy. Anyone would expect that a government would first and foremost endeavour to protect and nurture the children of its country.

It makes you think that white people at the time (and probably still now) must really have hated or feared people who were a different colour, who had a different culture, who had different beliefs and who had and chose to have a different lifestyle.

In these terms, the Referendum didn't really achieve anything. We may have started to be counted in the census and so practically be recognised as citizens, but Australia has a long way to go before we are really and truthfully recognised as its First Citizens and sincerely and truly accepted as such. After all we are this country's first children.

### 89. David Mowaljarlai, 42-years-old in 1967, was working as an orderly at Derby Hospital and living at Old Mowanjum, Western Australia

I didn't know one way or another if I could vote on the Referendum questions. We just did as the 'guardian' instructed.

When it came time for the census count we people were made promises. We were led to believe that the government was going to help us. We were told that we were going to have rights and things would be better.

We did what the white fella told us.

I don't believe the Referendum has achieved anything. It made things worse for my people. Drinking and those sorts of freedoms have caused things to be much worse.

I didn't come to know my rights or issues of voting until a long time after the Referendum.

In reflection, I feel my people have been cheated. I now understand what my people have LOST. It has made me all the more ready to fight for my culture and land.

### 90. Stephen R. Seiver, 21-years-old in 1967, was living in the Awabakal area, Newcastle

I was working and supporting my brothers and sisters at the time of the Referendum. I believed it meant citizenship rights and the end of 'dog tags' and rules made just for Aboriginal people.

When I was a child, I could not understand why my family was always in trouble. I just did not add the word 'Aboriginal' to our name.

I would think, 'if I could do something good, things would be better'. I had turned my hand to doing good things, with my life and for others. In some areas I did extremely well. I had even helped a girl overcome grief after an accident; I have taught a cripple to jump and somersault; I have stood up for a teacher in class; worked for Saint Vincent de Paul Society; maintained an apprenticeship.

I could say more, but all of this did not stop the trouble, because the trouble was, I was an Aboriginal. And doing good has nothing to do with keeping out of trouble. You see, being an Aboriginal means that you don't matter.

I don't think the Referendum achieved anything at the time, only Australians calling Australians — Australians.

I suppose the Referendum achieved being able to say that I am who I am, and being proud of who I am.

I hope that, building on the 1967 Referendum success, I, with others who are Aboriginals, will matter in the end, and thus no more trouble.

### 91. Edna Donovan, 35-years-old in 1967, was living with her family at Green Hills, New South Wales

I didn't know much about the Referendum campaign. I was busy having children and raising a family. Green Hills was a little community off alone from the rest of the world.

I voted in the election but never really knew the whole story of why some people had never been counted in the census or kept from voting. It still doesn't make sense to me.

I still don't think the Referendum achieved that much. Nothing has really changed for me, and now I know heaps of people who still don't vote, by choice.

Maybe the Referendum has let Aboriginal people have their heritage, because there was no heritage before, but I don't really think the Government listen or care.

### 92. Bill Humes, 22-years-old in 1967, was living in suburban Sydney and working in a bank. He was married and had a one-year-old child. He spent his weekends playing Aussie Rules football

Key Aboriginal and white Australians worked very hard to press for the Referendum. We owe them a debt of gratitude. These people were united in their aims.

In 1967 the Referendum meant that we had citizenship rights, voting rights and the right to enter a hotel and have a beer. It was also the recognition of Aboriginal people as Australians.

It was a great morale booster for Aboriginal and Torres Strait Islander people around the country.

The Referendum was also part of a worldwide awakening on civil rights, and as such Aboriginal people were becoming aware of their own worth and place in Australian society.

For me, it reinforced my political struggles and those of people I knew.

I see the Referendum and its results as a major point in Aboriginal and Australian history.

I did know that I could vote and I did. Previously I had voted in State and Commonwealth elections, and was on all the electoral rolls. I remember how good it felt voting this particular time.

I feel that the Referendum was a major milestone for Aboriginal and Torres Strait Islander people. At last there was full participation at the polls.

Citizenship rights were implemented and the course for Aboriginal Australia was well and truly set for full recognition and participation in all areas of life.

Many of the gains such as community organisations, education assistance, followed on from this. Other events such as street marches, protests and the Tent Embassy followed, but also the NACC and NAC that were forerunners to ATSIC. There were more forms of participation and co operation between government and community, including the Commonwealth Office of Aboriginal affairs then DAA.

### 93. Ray Wallace, 9-years-old in 1967, was attending school and living in Cairns

I remember Mum and Dad going to meetings and rallies with us kids in tow. Because of this it was very important for all of Australia (black and white) to recognise Aboriginal and Torres Strait Islander people.

In 1967 the Referendum opened 'the door' on Aboriginal and Torres Strait Islander peoples' basic rights.

If the Referendum hadn't happened in 1967, then it would have happened in another year. With or without the '67 Referendum, world politics would have seen that all peoples of Australia recognised and were given the same basic rights as each other.

To me now, the Referendum shows that since occupation of Australia by the 'Discoverers', it took 179 years for Australia's parliament to officially recognise Aboriginal and Torres Strait people.

The Indigenous people of Australia were denied all basic rights until after this Referendum.

# Part III

## Contemporary Aboriginal Perspectives

### Professor Larissa Behrendt

The campaign for the 1967 referendum highlighted the importance of ensuring equality for Aboriginal people. The posters showed a portrait of a black child and appealed to the electorate to give Aboriginal children the same opportunities that other Australian children enjoyed. In a country that has been reluctant to make changes to the Constitution, the 1967 referendum was an overwhelming success.

Forty years on, while much has improved, Aboriginal people still have poorer health, lower levels of education, higher unemployment and lower incomes than all other Australians. Clearly, the vision for a new era of opportunity and non-discrimination has not followed the constitutional change.

The referendum did two things: it allowed for Indigenous people to be included in the census and it altered the 'races power' to allow federal parliament to make laws about Indigenous people. While at the time, this change was seen as an important tool in allowing the federal government to pass laws to assist Indigenous people, it has turned out that the power can also be used to repeal or limit the rights of Indigenous people as well. For example, native title can be legislated but also repealed; heritage protection legislation can be enacted but can also be repealed; the Racial Discrimination Act has been stopped from applying to some aspects of native title.

It is easy to see in hindsight that the changes were not as effective as it was hoped they would be but the referendum remains an important moment in Australian history. The real achievement was the way the referendum united people across the political spectrum. It showed the results of a successful, decade long 'hearts and minds' campaign and it became a high point in the relationship between Aboriginal people and all other Australians. While social justice for Aboriginal people did not follow, it was an important step in furthering the political agenda for a new generation of Aboriginal activists.

**Kenny Laughton, author, Vietnam Veteran, former director of the Institute for Aboriginal Development**

The 1967 Referendum in my opinion was significant for several reasons. Aboriginal people finally became 'visible' to mainstream white Australia; we were counted in the following census. We became political and the Referendum itself was significant because it was one of the very few in Australian history that were passed. A vote of 97% in favour would be unheard of nowadays. I suspect if the same question were asked today the figures would be different.

Yet despite Australia's overwhelming wealth, after more than ten years of the Coalition government being in power, Aboriginal people still languish at the bottom rung of the socioeconomic ladder in their own country. I'd like to see the day when the common people (both black and white) in this so called Commonwealth of Australia, actually get some of this wealth from the global economy that is supposedly making us all richer.

**Dr Sue Gordon AM**

We all know the purposes of the amendments in the *Constitution Alteration (Aboriginals) 1967* legislation. The Commonwealth's object was to co-operate with the States to ensure that together they acted in the best interests of the Aboriginal people of Australia. However, paternalism continued throughout Australia and I believe still exists in some parts of Australia today, with States and Territories still not acting in the best interests of the Aboriginal people. I believe the original intent has all but been forgotten.

Interestingly, my first job as a 16-year-old was with the old Commonwealth Bureau of Census and Statistics in 1960 during a Census period and I had no idea that Aboriginal people, or Natives as we were called, were not included in the count. I was still a Ward of the State and subject to monitoring by the then Department of Native Welfare, having been forcibly removed from my mother in 1947.

So, where was I on 27 May 1967? I was employed at the Carnarvon Tracking Station as a teletype operator involved in Manned Space Flight Operations with the National Aeronautical and Space Administration (NASA). This job came about because of my Army training/service during 1960–64.

**Bob Randall, traditional owner of Uluru, author, singer songwriter**

When the campaign for the 1967 referendum was going on, it gave us all a hope that things could be better; both for Indigenous and non-Indigenous people. We thought it meant sharing of stories and knowledge; a more equal and better distribution of Australia's wealth and resources.

But it hasn't happened, and that's particularly true in Central Australia. We're still so dependant upon the generosity of the Australian government; that is, at their mercy.

The referendum has achieved little: a promise never fulfilled, a hope never met, and a desire for improvement that has never reached.

## Professor Mick Dodson

The 1967 referendum was a highly significant event in Australian constitutional history because it finally gave the Commonwealth power to make laws for Indigenous Australians. It also gave Indigenous people a great deal of hope that things would now improve and life would get better. I think the brave people who struggled to get the referendum through would be very disappointed that the changed constitution did not deliver as was expected by so many Australians. Too many national governments in the years since have repudiated the constitutional responsibility given them in 1967. We have made some little progress but sadly it has been piecemeal and appallingly slow. The saddest observation I think I can make is that I very much doubt whether such a referendum today would get the overwhelming support from the Australian people that it did in '67. I fear today it would not pass at all — that is the tragedy of 1967.

# Notes

## Preface

1.  Peter Sekuless, *Jessie Street: A Rewarding but Unrewarded Life*, University of Queensland Press, St Lucia, 1978, p. 163; Shirley Smith and Bobbi Sykes, *Mum Shirl: An Autobiography*, Heinemann, Melbourne, 1981, p. 72; Richard Broome, *Aboriginal Australians: Black Response to White Dominance 1788–1980*, Allen & Unwin, Sydney 1982, p. 178; Stuart Macintyre, *Winners and Losers: The Pursuit of Social Justice in Australian History*, Allen & Unwin, Sydney, 1985, p. xxi but compare pp. 130, 134; Robert Haupt, 'White Nightmare After a 20-Year Dreamtime', *Sydney Morning Herald*, 26 May 1987; Mike Secombe, 'Aboriginal Advances Threatened: Perkins', *Australian*, 27 May 1987; Barry Morris, *Domesticating Resistance: The Dhan–Gadi Aborigines and the Australian State*, Berg, Oxford, 1989, pp. 157, 175, 185, 193, 204, 211; Fay Gale, 'Aboriginal Australia: Survival by Separation', in Michael Chisholm and David M Smith (eds), *Shared Space: Divided Space*, Unwin Hyman, London, 1990, pp. 222–3; Tim Winton, *Cloudstreet*, McPhee Gribble, Melbourne, 1992, pp. 405–6, 411; PP McGuinness, 'Turn Back the Pages of History', *Australian*, 27 May 1992; *Sydney Morning Herald* (editorial), 27 May 1992; John Lahey, 'Memories of an Aboriginal Victory', *Age*, 27 May 1992; Gary Hughes, 'Blacks Assess 25 Years of Basic Rights', '25 Down', *Australian*, 27 May 1992; Pat Grimshaw, Marilyn Lake, Ann McGrath and Marian Quartly, *Creating a Nation*, McPhee Gribble/Penguin, Melbourne, 1994, p. 279; Paul Heinrichs, 'Stolen Lives', *Age*, 2 December 1995; Heather Goodall, 'New South Wales', in Ann McGrath (ed.), *Contested Ground: Australian Aborigines under the British Crown*, Allen & Unwin, Sydney, 1995, p. 108; Liberal Party, Aboriginal and Torres Strait Islander Affairs Policy Discussion Paper, <www.liberal.org.au/POLICY/ABORIGINAL/aborl.htm#>, 1996; *Socialist Alternative*, no. 13, 1996, p. 6; Tim Colebatch, 'The Hemline that Shocked the Nation', *Age*, 1 January 1996; Jamie Walker, 'Black Australia's Game Plan', *Australian*, 6–7 January 1996; 'Access Age', *Age*, 23 and 24 January 1996; Chairman of the Aboriginal History Committee, quoted *Australian*, 10–11 February 1996; Roberta Sykes, 'Aborigines' Sense of Siege', *Sydney Morning Herald*, 15 April 1996; Tim Bowden, 'The Man from Mer', *Australian*, 12–13 October 1996; *Australian* (editorial), 26–7 October 1996; Bill Bunbury, 'Unfinished Business, Part V', *Hindsight*, ABC Radio National, 3 November 1996; Dr Mahathir Mohammed, quoted *Australian*, 22 November 1996; James Button, 'A Land that Time Forgot', *Age*, 5 April 1997; Tony Stephens, 'Dynamic Duo Turned the Tide on Justice', *Sydney Morning Herald*, 12 April 1997.
2.  George Williams, 'Race and the Australian Constitution: From Federation to Reconciliation', *Osgoode Hall Law Journal*, vol. 38, no. 4, 2000, p. 662.
3.  The most valuable work in respect of the particular subject matter of this book has been that done by Sue Taffe. See her *Black and White Together: FCAATSI:*

*The Federal Council for the Advancement of Aborigines and Torres Strait Islanders 1958–1973*, University of Queensland Press, St Lucia, 2005, and 'The Role of FCAATSI in the 1967 Referendum: Mythmaking about Citizenship or Political Strategy?', in Tim Rowse (ed.), *Contesting Assimilation*, API Network, Perth, 2005, pp. 285–98. For other useful works, see John Chesterman and Brian Galligan, *Citizens without Rights: Aborigines and Australian Citizenship*, Cambridge University Press, Melbourne, 1997; John Chesterman, 'Defending Australia's Reputation: How Indigenous Australians Won Civil Rights, Parts One and Two', *Australian Historical Studies*, vol. 32, nos 116 & 117, 2001, pp. 20–39 & 201–21; Marilyn Lake, *Faith: Faith Bandler, Gentle Activist*, Allen & Unwin, Sydney, 2002; Bain Attwood, *Rights for Aborigines*, Allen & Unwin, Sydney, 2003; and John Chesterman, *Civil Rights: How Indigenous Australians Won Formal Equality*, University of Queensland Press, St Lucia, 2005. More generally, see Sue Taffe, 'Australian Race Relations: Diplomacy in a Policy Vacuum, 1961–62', *Aboriginal History*, vol. 19, pt 2, 1995, pp. 154–72; Jennifer Clark, '"Something to Hide": Aborigines and the Department of External Affairs, January 1961 – January 1962', *Journal of the Royal Australian Historical Society*, vol. 83, no. 1, 1997, pp. 71–84; Tim Rowse, *Obliged to be Difficult: Nugget Coombs' Legacy in Indigenous Affairs*, Cambridge University Press, Melbourne, 2000; Fiona Paisley, *Loving Protection?: Australian Feminism and Aboriginal Women's Rights 1919–1939*, Melbourne University Press, Melbourne, 2000; Peter Read, *Charles Perkins: A Biography*, revised edn, Penguin, Melbourne, 2001; Ann Curthoys, *Freedom Ride: A Freedom Rider Remembers*, Allen & Unwin, Sydney, 2002; Jack Horner, *Seeking Racial Justice: An Insider's Memoir of the Movement for Aboriginal Advancement, 1938–1978*, Aboriginal Studies Press, Canberra, 2004.

4. Paul A. Cohen, *History in Three Keys: The Boxers as Event, Experience, and Myth*, Columbia University Press, New York, 1997, p. xv.

5. Nicolas Rothwell, 'Plenty to be Ashamed of', *Australian*, 30–1 August 1997; Claire Miller, 'Pat Dodson in Attack on a Race Poll', *Age*, 29 November 1997; Janine MacDonald, 'Black Poll was "Pandora's Box"', *Age*, 2 January 1998; Andrew Clennell, 'Wik Poll Would Divide the Nation: Doug Anthony', *Sydney Morning Herald*, 3 January 1998; Zita Antonios, quoted Miriam Cosic, 'The Equaliser', *Australian Magazine*, 24–5 January 1998, p. 23; Gay Alcorn and Mark Baker, 'A Divided Nation', *Age*, 21 March 1998; Martin Flanagan, 'Howard's Vision on Race Fails All of Us', *Age*, 10 April 1998, 'Hanson Blue Undermines Racist Claims', *Australian*, 15 July 1998; Gustav Nossal, 'Let's Call it for Australia', *Age*, 29 November 1998; Cathy Pryor, 'Apology is Appropriate and Overdue', *Australian*, 29 November 1998; 'Our Story', *Sydney Morning Herald*, 2 February 1999; Gerard Brennan, 'The Defining Qualities', *Eureka Street*, vol. 9, no. 3, 1999, p. 18; Georgina Safe, 'Dots and Dances not Half the Story', *Australian*, 11 May 2001; Nic O'Malley, 'For Half her Life she Didn't Count', *Sydney Morning Herald*, 8 August 2001.

6. See, for example, Troy Lennon, 'Cl@ssmate Series 7 #6, History of Voting', *Daily Telegraph*, 6 March 2007; 'Six-Time Finalist in Fine Form', *North Shore Times*, 7 March 2007; Helen Musa, 'Prize Draws on Reconciliation Progress', *Canberra Times*, 10 March 2007; Greg Burchall, 'Message on Power Finds a Novel Voice', *Age*, 10 March 2007; Anne Fulwood, quoted 'Entrants an Insight into Sitter's Soul', *North Shore Times*, 16 March 2007; Tony Stephens, 'Reconciliation Pioneers Put Faith in the Young', *Sydney Morning Herald*, 21 March 2007; Queensland Premier Peter Beattie, Press Release Young South Africa Leaders Invited to Queensland, 22 March 2007.

## 1 The Constitution and the Power of Race

1. This argument has been related most recently by John Hirst in his *Australia's Democracy: A Short History*, Allen & Unwin, Sydney, 2002, pp. 183–4. For the evidence, see *Official Record of the Debates of the Australasian Federal Convention* (1891), Legal Books, Sydney, 1986, p. 66.

2. Ibid., p. 525.

3. JA La Nauze, *The Making of the Australian Constitution*, Melbourne University Press, Melbourne, 1972, p. 67; John Chesterman and Brian Galligan, *Citizens without Rights: Aborigines and Australian Citizenship*, Cambridge University Press, Melbourne, 1997, p. 69.
4. Sir Robert Garran to Professor AP Elkin, 22 July 1944, AP Elkin Papers, University of Sydney Archives, series 1/12/205.
5. Geoffrey Sawer, 'The Australian Constitution and the Australian Aborigines', *Federal Law Review*, vol. 2, no. 1, 1966, p. 17. See also Chesterman and Galligan, *Citizens without Rights*, pp. 61–2.
6. Ibid., pp. 60–1.
7. La Nauze, *Making of the Australian Constitution*, p. 68; Chesterman and Galligan, *Citizens without Rights*, pp. 73–4.
8. See also parallel provisions for allocation of seats and qualification for membership of parliament:
   section 24: The number of members [of parliament] shall be in proportion to the respective numbers of their people...
   section 25: if by the law of any State all persons of any race are disqualified from voting at elections for the more numerous House of Parliament of the State, then, in reckoning the number of people of the State or the Commonwealth, persons of that race resident in that State shall not be counted.
   section 30: Until the Parliament otherwise provides, the qualification of electors of members of the House of Representatives shall be in each State that which is prescribed by the law of the State as the qualification of electors of the more numerous House of Parliament of the State...
9. Pat Stretton and Christine Finnimore, 'Black Fellow Citizens: Aborigines and the Commonwealth Franchise', *Australian Historical Studies*, vol. 25, no. 101, 1993, p. 522.
10. *Commonwealth Franchise Act 1902*, section 4.
11. Stretton and Finnimore, 'Black Fellow Citizens', p. 527.
12. *Commonwealth Electoral Act 1925*, section 2(b).
13. *Commonwealth Electoral Act 1949*, section 3 (b) (aa).
14. *Commonwealth Electoral Act 1962* (An Act to give to Aboriginal Natives of Australia the right to Enrol and to Vote as Electors of the Commonwealth...).

## 2 The Commonwealth and Aboriginal Affairs

1. APNR Records, University of Sydney Archives, MS S55, series 6.
2. Enclosure in memorandum of 30 March 1928, NAA, A1, 36/6595.
3. Ibid. See DJ Mulvaney and JH Calaby, *'So Much that is New': Baldwin Spencer, 1860–1929, a Biography*, Melbourne University Press, Melbourne, 1985, pp. 274–5.
4. 'A Brief Statement of the Policy and Purposes of the APNR', 1928, APNR Records, series 4.
5. See Andrew Markus, *Governing Savages*, Allen & Unwin, Sydney, 1990.
6. *Report of the Royal Commission on the Constitution Together with Appendices and Index, Minutes of Evidence*, AGPS, Canberra, 1929, pp. 333–4, 552–3, 626, 918, 1124, 1599. See also Fiona Paisley, 'Federalising the Aborigines?: Constitutional Reform in the Late 1920s', *Australian Historical Studies*, vol. 29, no. 111, 1998, pp. 248–66.
7. *Report of the Royal Commission*, pp. 479, 478.
8. Ibid., p. 1125.
9. Ibid., p. 334.
10. Ibid., pp. 626, 1124, 1125.
11. 'Report of the Royal Commission on the Constitution', *Commonwealth Parliamentary Papers*, 1929–31, vol. 2, p. 303.
12. Ibid., p. 270.

13. William Cooper to the Minister for the Interior, Thomas Paterson, 31 October 1938, in Andrew Markus (ed.), *Blood from a Stone: William Cooper and the Australian Aborigines' League*, Allen & Unwin, Sydney, 1988, p. 48.
14. AP Elkin to Charles Duguid, 15 July 1958, AP Elkin Papers, University of Sydney Archives, series 5/2/18.
15. Elkin, 'The Future of the Aborigines', APNR Records, series 6.
16. *Commonwealth Parliamentary Debates: House of Representatives*, 17th Parliament, 1st Session, 1944, p. 152.
17. Commonwealth of Australia, *You and the Referendum*, AGPS, Canberra, 1944, pp. [9, 11].
18. LF Crisp, *Ben Chifley: A Political Biography* (1961), Angus & Robertson, London, 1977, p. 195. See also Paul Hasluck, *The Government and the People 1942–1945*, Australian War Memorial, Canberra, 1970, pp. 535–40.
19. *Herald* (Melbourne), 22 June 1945; HV Johnson to Elkin, 21 November 1945, Elkin Papers, series 4/2/214.
20. Commonwealth of Australia, *Conference of Commonwealth and State Ministers held at Canberra, 22nd to 25th January 1946: Proceedings of the Conference*, AGPS, Canberra, 1946, pp. 62–5; NAA, A609, 37/1/4.
21. Gillespie Douglas to Elkin, 31 January 1947, Elkin Papers, series 4/2/158.
22. *Sun*, 25 March 1946; *Australian*, 1 March 1947, 15 November 1949; *Herald*, 17 November 1949; Kim Beazley snr to Prime Minister Ben Chifley, 14 September 1949, NAA, A431/1, 1949/1591.
23. *Northern Standard*, 9 March 1951; Council for Aboriginal Rights, 'Constitution', 13 April 1951, CAR Papers, State Library of Victoria, MS 12913/5/6.

## 3   The Federal Council for Aboriginal Advancement and Constitutional Change

1. See Faith Bandler, *Turning the Tide: A Personal History of the Federal Council for the Advancement of Aborigines and Torres Strait Islanders*, Aboriginal Studies Press, Canberra, 1989; *1967: Citizens at Last?*, ABC Television, 1996; *The Fair Go: Winning the 1967 Referendum*, ABC Television, 1999; Marilyn Lake, *Faith: Faith Bandler, Gentle Activist*, Allen & Unwin, Sydney, 2002, pp. 69, 82; Reconciliation Australia, The 1967 Referendum: 40th Anniversary, www.acnet.mq.edu.au/anonymous@C331625408/-/p/67referndum/index.html, accessed 1 February 2007.
2. For a fine treatment of the Warburton Ranges controversy, see this part of a website created by Sue Taffe: <www.indigenousrights.net.au/section.asp?sID=1>.
3. *Age*, 6 February 1957; Anna Vroland, Notes of the Meeting, WILPF Papers, State Library of Victoria, MS 9377/1726/22.
4. *Analysis of Mr Rupert Murdoch's Article...*, Save the Aborigines Committee, Melbourne, 1957, pp. 2–3.
5. *Guardian*, 28 March 1957; *Advocate*, 25 April 1957, cited in *Analysis of Mr Rupert Murdoch's Article*, pp. 5–6.
6. *Mercury* (Melbourne), 28 March 1957.
7. Mark A Kibell et al. to Robert Menzies, 15 April 1957, NAA, A452/1957/245.
8. Jessie Street to Thomas Fox-Pitt, 3 March 1957, Jessie Street Papers, National Library of Australia, MS 2683/10/223.
9. Ibid.
10. See Andrew Markus, 'Under the Act', in Bill Gammage and Peter Spearritt (eds), *Australians 1938*, Fairfax, Syme & Weldon, Sydney, 1987, pp. 47–53, and *Australian Race Relations 1788–1993*, Allen & Unwin, Sydney, 1994, chap. 5.
11. Street to Brian Fitzpatrick, 4 March 1957, Street Papers, MS 2683/10/228.
12. Ibid.
13. Street to Fox-Pitt, 20 March 1957, Street Papers, MS 2683/10/251; Street to Shirley Andrews, 20 March 1957, CAR Papers, State Library of Victoria, MS 12913/2/7.
14. Sue Taffe, *Black and White Together: FCAATSI: The Federal Council for the Advancement of Aborigines and Torres Strait Islanders 1958-1973*, University of Queensland Press, St

Lucia, 2005, p. 34, and Collaborating for Indigenous Rights, www.indigenousrights. net.au/subsection.asp?ssID=11>.

15. SG Middleton to Street, 9 July 1956, Street Papers, MS 2683/10/99.

16. AP Elkin to Marian Alderdice, Acting Secretary, Aboriginal-Australian Fellowship, 25 June 1958, AP Elkin Papers, University of Sydney Archives, series 1/12/123.

17. See, for example, Peter Sekuless, *Jessie Street: A Rewarding but Unrewarding Life*, University of Queensland Press, St Lucia, 1978, pp. 182–3.

18. Street to Paul Hasluck, 15 September 1961, CAR Papers, MS12913/9/9; Street to Fox-Pitt, 2 February 1963, ASS Papers, Rhodes House Library, Oxford, series 22, G954/1; Street to Andrews et al., 7 July 1963, in Lenore Coltheart (ed.), *Jessie Street: A Revised Autobiography*, Federation Press, Sydney, 2004, p. 235.

19. Anthony G Amsterdam and Jerome Bruner, *Minding the Law*, Harvard University Press, Cambridge, Mass., 2000, pp. 111, 122, 133, 135, 138.

20. Sekuless, *Jessie Street*, pp. 175, 180.

21. Ibid., p. 175 (and adjacent page); Bandler, quoted Faith Bandler and Len Fox (eds), *The Time was Ripe*, Alternative Publishing Company, Sydney, 1983, pp. 11–12; Bandler, *Turning the Tide*, p. 9; *1967: Citizens at Last?*; *The Fair Go*.

22. Draft petition, Street Papers, MS 2683/28/16.

23. Petition, Brian Fitzpatrick Papers, National Library of Australia, MS 4965/1/5273.

24. Street to Fox-Pitt, 30 April 1957, Street Papers, 2683/10/285; *Tribune*, 1 May 1957; Bandler and Fox (eds), *The Time was Ripe*, pp. 12–16; Taffe, *Black and White Together*, p. 36.

25. Bain Attwood, *Rights for Aborigines*, Allen & Unwin, Sydney, 2003, pp. 122, 125, 152–3; Taffe, *Black and White Together*, pp. 1–11, 40, 42–3.

26. See ibid., pp. 5–11.

27. *Smoke Signals*, May 1958. See also *Advertiser* (Adelaide), 17 February 1958.

28. Minutes of the Adelaide Conference, 14–16 February 1958, in Bandler and Fox (eds), *The Time was Ripe*, pp. 97–8.

29. Taffe seems to advance this interpretation in her 'The Role of FCAATSI in the 1967 Referendum: Mythmaking about Citizenship or Political Strategy?', in Tim Rowse (ed.), *Contesting Assimilation*, API Network, Perth, 2005, p. 289.

30. Tim Rowse, 'Introduction', in Rowse (ed.), *Contesting Assimilation*, p. 17.

31. *Smoke Signals*, December 1958, pp. 3–4, July 1959, p. 1.

32. 'Report from the Joint Committee on Constitutional Review, 1959', *Commonwealth Parliamentary Papers*, 1959–60, vol. 3, pp. 54, 56.

33. Sue Taffe, 'Australian Race Relations: Diplomacy in a Policy Vacuum, 1961–62', *Aboriginal History*, vol. 19, pt 2, 1995, pp. 154–72; Jennifer Clark, '"Something to Hide": Aborigines and the Department of External Affairs, January 1961 – January 1962', *Journal of the Royal Australian Historical Society*, vol. 83, no. 1, 1997, pp. 71–84.

34. John Chesterman, *Civil Rights: How Indigenous Australians Won Formal Equality*, University of Queensland Press, St Lucia, 2005, pp. 19, 36, 39, 44, 88.

## 4  The 1962–3 Petition Campaign

1. Riley and Ephemera Collection, State Library of Victoria. This had some minor inaccuracies.

2. Draft petition, Jessie Street Papers, National Library of Australia, MS 2683/28/16.

3. Sue Taffe, *Black and White Together: FCAATSI: The Federal Council for the Advancement of Aborigines and Torres Strait Islanders 1958–1973*, University of Queensland Press, St Lucia, 2005, p. 93.

4. Gordon Bryant, 'Aboriginal Rights: National Campaign to Remove Discrimination from the Constitution', no date, Gordon Bryant Papers, National Library of Australia, MS 8256/185.

5. Shirley Andrews to Jessie Street, 14 June 1962, CAR Papers, State Library of Victoria, MS 12913/9/8.

6. Andrews to Brian Manning, 24 September 1962, George Gibbs Papers, Mitchell Library, MS 2662/2113.
7. Andrews to Tom Dougherty, 15 March 1962, CAR Papers, MS 12913/9/8; Bain Attwood, *Rights for Aborigines*, Allen & Unwin, Sydney, 2003, p. 169.
8. Bryant, 'After the Referendum — What?, *Smoke Signals*, vol. 2, no. 2, 1962, p. 3.
9. Taffe, *Black and White Together*, pp. 94–5.
10. Faith Bandler, Circular Letter, 24 September 1962, AAF Papers, Mitchell Library, MS 4057/7.
11. Aboriginal-Australian Fellowship, 'Public Meeting to Launch a Petition', 1962, and Andrews, 'Report on Meeting Held by FCAA to Launch a National Petition', 23 October 1962, CAR Papers, MS 12913/11/5.
12. Taffe, *Black and White Together*, p. 96.
13. Ibid., p. 98.
14. Council for Aboriginal Rights, Annual Report 1962–63, CAR Papers, MS 12913/7/3.
15. *Age*, 27 & 28 September 1963; Andrews to Street, 13 November 1963, CAR Papers, 12913/9/9.
16. Faith Bandler, *Turning the Tide: A Personal History of the Federal Council for the Advancement of Aborigines and Torres Strait Islanders*, Aboriginal Studies Press, Canberra, 1989, p. 98. This account incorrectly says the meeting occurred in 1965.
17. 'This is Your Life' (Faith Bandler), Network Seven, 1978, excerpt in *The Fair Go: Winning the 1967 Referendum*, ABC Television, 1999.
18. *Commonwealth Parliamentary Debates, House of Representatives*, 25th Parliament, 1st Session, 1964, pp. 1903–5, 1907.
19. Ibid., pp. 1916–17.
20. Ibid., pp. 1906–7, 1909.

## 5  The Coalition Government and the Demand for a Referendum

1. See Ann Curthoys, *Freedom Ride: A Freedom Rider Remembers*, Allen & Unwin, Sydney, 2002, especially ch. 8.
2. *Commonwealth Parliamentary Debates, House of Representatives*, 25th Parliament, 1st Session, 1965, p. 533.
3. *Age*, 12 April 1965; *Australian*, 20 April 1965, 12 & 20 May 1965; *Commonwealth Parliamentary Debates, House of Representatives*, 25th Parliament, 1st Session, 1965, pp. 543, 1594–6, 1613–14.
4. A few months later, Minister for the Territories Charles Barnes recommended the government intervene in the industrial case pressed by the North Australian Workers' Union for equal wages for Aboriginal stock workers in the Northern Territory largely on the same grounds: 'it would reduce the scope for national and international criticism of Australia's treatment of Aborigines' (Cabinet Minutes, 22 April 1965, NAA, A5827, item 741). For the cabinet's response to this, see John Chesterman, *Civil Rights: How Indigenous Australians Won Formal Equality*, University of Queensland Press, St Lucia, 2005, p. 84.
5. Cabinet Minutes, 7 April 1965, NAA, A5827/1, item 660.
6. Ibid.
7. Cabinet submission, 23 August 1965, and Cabinet Minutes, 30 August 1965, NAA, A5827/1, item 1009.
8. See also *Commonwealth Parliamentary Debates, House of Representatives*, 25th Parliament, 1st Session, 1966, pp. 121–5.
9. Sue Taffe, *Black and White Together: FCAATSI: The Federal Council for the Advancement of Aborigines and Torres Strait Islanders 1958-1973*, University of Queensland Press, St Lucia, 2005, pp. 95, 107, and 'The Role of FCAATSI in the 1967 Referendum: Mythmaking about Citizenship or Political Strategy?', in Tim Rowse (ed.), *Contesting Assimilation*, API Network, Perth, 2005, p. 291.
10. Queensland Elections Acts 1915 to 1962, section 27; Elections Acts Amendment Act 1965, section 27, (b)(v).

11. Chesterman, *Civil Rights*, pp. 19, 36.
12. Taffe, *Black and White Together*, p. 95.
13. 'Principles of Legislation for Aborigines and Torres Strait Islanders', CAR Papers, State Library of Victoria, MS 12913/11/5.
14. Lorna Lippmann to Don Chipp, 6 February 1966, quoted Taffe, *Black and White Together*, p. 105.
15. Lippmann, Circular letter to federal parliamentarians, 2 February 1966, Barrie Pittock Papers (personal collection).
16. Minutes, FCAATSI executive meeting, 21 February 1966, CAR Papers, MS 12913/10/1; Sue Taffe, personal communication to the authors, 21 March 2007.
17. Cabinet Minutes, 3 & 15 February 1966, NAA, A5839, items 9 and 24.
18. *Commonwealth Parliamentary Debates, House of Representatives*, 25th Parliament, 1st Session, 1966, p. 121; Cabinet Minutes, 12 August 1966, NAA, A5841/2, item 397; Harold Holt to Lippman, 3 March 1966, Pittock Papers; Taffe, *Black and White Together*, pp. 106–7.
19. Cabinet minute, 22 February 1967, NAA, A4940, C4257.
20. Cabinet submission no. 46, January 1967, NAA, A5842/2.
21. Ibid., no. 64, 31 January 1967, NAA, A5425.
22. Cabinet minute, 22 February 1967.
23. *Commonwealth Parliamentary Debates, House of Representatives*, 26th Parliament, 1st Session, 1967, pp. 107, 113, 115, 263.
24. *Age*, 17 & 22 May 1967.
25. *Smoke Signals*, vol. 6, no. 2, 1967, p. 6; *Sydney Morning Herald*, 27 May 1967.
26. *Age*, 16 May 1967; *Sydney Morning Herald*, 16 May 1967.

# 6 The Campaign for the 'Yes' Vote

1. Marilyn Lake, *Faith: Faith Bandler, Gentle Activist*, Allen & Unwin, Sydney, 2002, pp. 113–14.
2. 'Vote Yes for Aborigines', FCAATSI Papers, Mitchell Library, MS 2999, Y604; Rev. Gary Shearston, conversation with Bain Attwood, 22 November 2002.
3. Bain Attwood, *Rights for Aborigines*, Allen & Unwin, Sydney, 2003, p. 173.
4. *Age*, 25 March 1967; Minutes and Short Proceedings of the Annual General Meeting of FCAATSI, 26 March 1967, quoted Sue Taffe, *Black and White Together: FCAATSI: The Federal Council for the Advancement of Aborigines and Torres Strait Islanders 1958-1973*, University of Queensland Press, St Lucia, 2005, p. 110.
5. Minutes of General Meetings, NSW Vote Yes Committee, 2, 10 & 27 April 1967, 7 & 21 May 1967, FCAATSI Papers, box Y604; <www.indigenousrights.net.au/document.asp?ssID=30&isID=783>.
6. *Smoke Signals*, vol. 6, no. 2, 1967, p. 1.
7. *Age*, 27 March 1967; Jack Horner to editor of 'The Bridge', 22 April 1967, Circular letter, 10 May 1967, FCAATSI Papers, Y604; 'The Referendum', *Smoke Signals*, vol. 6, no. 2, 1967, p. 7; *Sydney Morning Herald*, 19 May 1967; *Australian*, 25 May 1967.
8. Vote Yes Information, 31 March 1967, Mamie Smith, Publicity Officer, National Directorate of Vote 'Yes' Committee, Circular letter, 4 May 1967, FCAATSI Papers, Y604; Press release, quoted Faith Bandler, *Turning the Tide: A Personal History of the Federal Council for the Advancement of Aborigines and Torres Strait Islanders*, Aboriginal Studies Press, Canberra, 1989, p. 107; Faith Bandler, 'What a Yes Vote Means for Aboriginals', *Australian*, 17 May 1967; *Sydney Morning Herald*, letter to the editor by Jack Horner, 22 May 1967.
9. Jack Horner, Radio Talk for Station 2GZ, Operation Referendum, Recommendations on Campaign Structure, 25 March 1967, Vote Yes Information, 31 March 1967, FCAATSI circular letter, April 1967, FCAATSI Papers, boxes Y600 & Y604; *Age*, 16 May 1967; *Australian*, 17 May 1967.
10. Operation Referendum, Recommendations on campaign structure, 25 March 1967, FCAATSI Papers, Y604.

11. CD Rowley, *The Remote Aborigines*, Australian National University Press, Canberra, 1970, p. 310.

12. Bandler, 'What a Yes Vote Means'; 'Aboriginal Rights and the Referendum', Gordon Bryant Papers, National Library of Australia, MS 8256/175; Horner to Father Fitzgerald, 9 May 1967, FCAATSI Papers, Y604.

13. Horner, Radio talk for 2GZ, Barry Cohen, FCAATSI circular letter, April 1967, FCAATSI Papers, Y604; 'Aboriginal Rights and the Referendum'; National Campaign Committee, What Can You Do, FCAATSI Papers, Y604; Vote Yes Information (3), 31 March 1967, Bryant Papers, MS 8256/175; *Australian*, 3 April 1967.

14. *Age*, 24 May 1967; *Sydney Morning Herald*, 10 May 1967.

15. *Age*, 11 & 25 May 1967; *Sydney Morning Herald*, 16, 17, 22 & 24 May 1967; *Herald* (Melbourne), 26 May 1967.

16. Morgan Gallup Poll, 19 May 1967.

17. *Australian*, 8 May 1967; *Sydney Morning Herald*, 13 May 1967; Joe McGinness, *Son of Alyandabu: My Fight for Aboriginal Rights*, University of Queensland Press, St Lucia, 1991, pp. 77, 80.

18. *ABC Television News*, Melbourne, 10 April 1967, ABC Archives, Melbourne.

19. ABC Television, *The Day of the Aboriginal*, 19 May 1967.

20. *Sydney Morning Herald*, 27 May 1967.

21. *Australian*, 25 May 1967.

22. *Sun*, 27 May 1967.

23. *Age*, 25 May 1964; *Sun*, 19 October 1966.

24. Quoted Bandler, *Turning the Tide*, p. 135.

25. Shirley Smith and Bobbi Sykes, *Mum Shirl: An Autobiography*, Heinemann, Richmond, 1981, p. 72.

## 7  The Poll and its Consequences

1. Commonwealth of Australia, *Referendums to be Held on Saturday, 27th May 1967*, Government Printing Office, Canberra, 1967, p. 16.

2. Scott Bennett, 'The 1967 Referendum', *Australian Aboriginal Studies*, no. 2, 1985, p. 29.

3. Parliament of the Commonwealth of Australia, *Statistical Returns in Relation to the Submission to the Electors of Proposed Laws for the Alteration of the Constitution*, 1968, Parliamentary Paper no. 125.

4. Bennett, 'The 1967 Referendum', p. 29.

5. Ibid.

6. Ibid.; *Statistical Returns*, 1968 – Parliamentary Papers nos 128 and 130.

7. Don Aitkin et al., *Australian Political Institutions*, 4th edition, Pitman, Melbourne, 1989, pp. 37–41.

8. Evelyn Scott, interview, 17 October 1996, FCAATSI Oral History Project, AIATSIS Library; Faith Bandler, interview, *1967: Citizens at Last?*, ABC Television, 1996.

9. Rodney Hall, interview, *The Fair Go: Winning the 1967 Referendum*, ABC Television, 1999, and quoted David Marr, 'The Betrayal', *Sydney Morning Herald*, 20 May 2000.

10. *Sydney Morning Herald*, 29 May 1967; *Australian*, 29 May 1967.

11. *Sydney Morning Herald*, 30 May 1967.

12. *Commonwealth Parliamentary Debates, House of Representatives*, 26th Parliament, 1st Session, 1967, p. 384.

13. CD Rowley, *The Remote Aborigines*, Penguin, Melbourne, 1972, p. 310, and *Outcasts in White Australia*, Penguin, Melbourne, 1972, p. 384.

14. See, for example, Scott Bennett, *Aborigines and Political Power*, Allen & Unwin, Sydney, 1989, p. 15.

15. Excerpt, *The Fair Go*.

16. *Australian*, 29 & 30 May, 5 June 1967; *Sydney Morning Herald*, 29 & 30 May 1967; *Commonwealth Parliamentary Debates, House of Representatives*, 26th Parliament, 1st Session, 1967, pp. 185–7, 196, 297, 384, 767–70.

17. Cabinet Submission, no. 432, 14 August 1967, NAA, A5425; Cabinet Decision, no. 507, 15–16 August 1967, NAA, A5840.
18. *Commonwealth Parliamentary Debates, House of Representatives*, 26th Parliament, 1st Session, 1967, pp. 973–4.
19. Aboriginal-Australian Fellowship Newsletter, September 1967, AAF Papers, Mitchell Library, MS 4057, box 4.
20. *Sydney Morning Herald*, 9 September 1967.
21. See Tim Rowse, *Obliged to be Difficult: Nugget Coombs' Legacy in Indigenous Affairs*, Cambridge University Press, Melbourne, 2000, especially ch. 1.
22. Gough Whitlam, Policy Speech, 13 November 1972, <www.australianpolitics.com/elections/1972/72-11-13_it's-time.shtml>.
23. We have adapted here an argument made by Tim Rowse in his *Obliged to be Difficult*, pp. 20–1.
24. *Commonwealth Parliamentary Debates, House of Representatives*, 26th Parliament, 2nd Session, 1968, pp. 15, 17, our emphasis.

## 8   Remembering and Forgetting the Referendum

1. See, for example, *Sydney Morning Herald* (editorial), 27 May 1992; Gary Hughes, 'Blacks Assess 25 Years of Basic Rights', *Australian*, 27 May 1992; John Lahey, 'Memories of an Aboriginal Victory', *Age*, 27 May 1992; John Stone, 'Convention is no Way to Reconcile the Past', *Australian Financial Review*, 5 June 1997; Janine Macdonald, 'Hanson was Wrong on Black Vote: Anthony', *Age*, 18 July 1998; *Australian* (editorial), 24 October 2002; Alan Ramsey, 'Gentle Vision a Signpost to Better Future', *Sydney Morning Herald*, 11 March 2006.
2. See, for example, Department of Aboriginal Affairs, *Information for Use During 1967 Referendum Commemoration*, AGPS, Canberra, 1987; ATSIC, *25 Years On: Making the Anniversary of the Aboriginal Referendum of 27 May 1992*, AGPS, Canberra, 1992; Australian Reconciliation Convention, *The Path to Reconciliation: Issues for a People's Movement*, AGPS, Canberra, 1997, pp. 6–7; *Walking Together*, no. 18, 1997, pp. 14–15; Council for Aboriginal Reconciliation, *Australians for Reconciliation Study Circle Kit*, AGPS, Canberra, [1997], sections 6.2 & 6.3.
3. Quoted Faith Bandler, *Turning the Tide: A Personal History of the Federal Council for the Advancement of Aborigines and Torres Strait Islanders*, Aboriginal Studies Press, Canberra, 1989, p. 135.
4. Ibid., pp. 1, 116, 123, 161.
5. Quoted Barry Cohen, 'Dreaming of Reconciliation', *Australian*, 27 May 1992.
6. See Peter Read, '"Cheeky, Insolent and Anti-White": The Split in the Federal Council for the Advancement of Aboriginal and Torres Strait Islanders — Easter 1970', *Australian Journal of Politics and History*, vol. 36, no. 1, 1990, pp. 73–83; and Sue Taffe, *Black and White Together: FCAATSI: The Federal Council for the Advancement of Aborigines and Torres Strait Islanders 1958–1973*, University of Queensland Press, St Lucia, 2005, ch. 7.
7. See ibid., pp. 125–8, 145–63.
8. See Bain Attwood, *Rights for Aborigines*, Allen & Unwin, Sydney, 2003, ch. 11.
9. See, for example, PP McGuinness, 'Turn Back the Pages of History', *Australian*, 27 May 1992.
10. See, for example, Peter Yu, quoted in Richard McGregor, 'Aborigines Bid for Native Title Fighting Fund', *Australian*, 6 April 1998.
11. *Australian*, 27 May 1987, 27 May 1992. See also *Sydney Morning Herald*, 26 May 1987, 27 May 1992; *Age*, 27 & 28 May 1987, 27 May 1992; *Land Rights News*, vol. 2, no. 3, 1987, p. 18.
12. *Age*, 28 May 1987.
13. Heather Goodall, 'The Politics of Information Control', *Oral History Association of Australia Journal*, no. 9, 1987, pp. 22, 23, 24, 28.
14. Barry Morris, personal conversation with Bain Attwood, 12 February 1996.

15. Noel Pearson, "Grist to the Legal Machine', *Australian*, 6–7 January 2007. We are indebted to Geoff Gray for bringing this comment to our attention.
16. *Australian*, 27 January 2007.

## 9  Reconciliation and Constitutional Change

1. For a discussion of this shift, see Bain Attwood, *Rights for Aborigines*, Allen & Unwin, Sydney, 2003, Parts IV and V.
2. For a consideration of the question of whether assimilation could ever be said to have come to an end, see Tim Rowse, 'Introduction', in Rowse (ed.), *Contesting Assimilation*, API Network, Perth, 2005, pp. 19–24.
3. Jeremy Beckett, 'Aboriginality, Citizenship and Nation State', *Social Analysis*, no. 24, 1988, pp. 3–18.
4. Our discussion here draws a good deal from Mark McKenna, *This Country: A Reconciled Republic?*, University of New South Wales Press, Sydney, 2004.
5. See Rosemary Hunter, 'Aboriginal Histories, Australian Histories, and the Law', in Bain Attwood (ed.), *In the Age of Mabo: History, Aborigines and Australia*, Allen & Unwin, Sydney, 1996, pp. 1–16.
6. 'The Position of Indigenous People in National Constitutions', *Constitutional Centenary*, vol. 2, no. 3, 1993, p. 4.
7. Lowitja O'Donoghue, in Council for Aboriginal Reconciliation and Constitutional Centenary Foundation, *The Position of Indigenous People in National Constitutions*, AGPS, Canberra, [1993], p. 42.
8. For a summary of these, see McKenna, *This Country*, pp. 32–3.
9. George Williams, 'Race and the Australian Constitution: From Federation to Reconciliation', *Osgoode Hall Law Journal*, vol. 38, no. 4, 2000, p. 662.
10. Larissa Behrendt, *Achieving Social Justice: Indigenous Rights and Australia's Future*, Federation Press, Sydney, 2003, p. 144.
11. Noel Pearson, 'An Optimist's Vision', in Noel Pearson & Will Sanders, *Indigenous Peoples and Reshaping Australian Institutions: Two Perspectives*, Centre for Aboriginal Economic Policy Research, Discussion Paper, no. 102, 1995, p. 8.

## 10  Race, Rights and the Constitution

1. Judith Brett, *Australian Liberals and the Moral Middle Class: From Alfred Deakin to John Howard*, Cambridge University Press, Melbourne, 2003, pp. 197, 200–1.
2. For a consideration of the background to the so-called history wars, see Bain Attwood, *Telling the Truth about Aboriginal History*, Allen & Unwin, Sydney, 2005, ch. 1; for Howard's race politics, see Andrew Markus, *Race, John Howard and the Remaking of Australia*, Allen & Unwin, Sydney, 2001.
3. Liberal Party, Aboriginal and Torres Strait Islander Affairs Policy Discussion Paper, <www.liberal.org.au/POLICY/ABORIGINAL/aborl.htm#>, 1996, accessed 3 February 1997.
4. For Hanson's comments, see *Australian*, 16 July 1998.
5. The Constitutional Convention 1998 *Final Report of the Convention*, vol. 1, ch. 7, 1998, <pandora.nla.gov.au/nph-arch/O1998-Nov-12/http://www.dpmc.gov.au/convention/report1/7comm3.htm#Preamble>.
6. Mark McKenna, *This Country: A Reconciled Republic?*, University of New South Wales Press, Sydney, 2004, p. 50.
7. Constitutional Convention, *Final Report*, vol. 2 appendix 4, <pandora.nla.gov.au/nph-arch/O1998-Nov-12/http://www.dpmc.gov.au/convention/report2/4wkgrps.htm>.
8. McKenna, *This Country*, p. 58.
9. *Parliamentary Handbook of the Commonwealth of Australia*, <www.aph.gov.au/library/handbook/referendums/r1999.htm>.
10. Gatjil Djerrkura, Lack of Proper Consultation Sinks Referendum, ATSIC Media Release, 8 November 1999.

11. *Sydney Morning Herald*, 28 May 1997.
12. *Australian Financial Review*, 6 January 1998.
13. Cabinet Minutes, 23 August 1965, NAA, A5827/1, item 1009.
14. Rt Hon. Harold Holt, 'Party Leaders Urge "Yes" Vote', *Smoke Signals*, vol. 6, no. 2, 1967, p. 6.
15. *Australian*, 1 January 1998; *Australian Financial Review*, 2 January 1998.
16. *Sydney Morning Herald*, 7 February 1998.
17. *Australian*, 10 March 1997, 10 June 1997.
18. *Sydney Morning Herald*, 6 & 7 February 1998.
19. Kartinyeri v The Commonwealth (1998), HCA 22 1 April 1998. For a discussion of the case in reference to the race power, see Justin Malbon, 'The Race Power Under the Australian Constitution: Altered Meanings', *Sydney Law Review*, vol. 21, no. 80, 1999, pp. 80–113.
20. George Williams, 'Race and the Australian Constitution: From Federation to Reconciliation', *Osgoode Hall Law Journal*, vol. 38, no. 4, 2000, p. 656–7.
21. *Australian Financial Review*, 2 April 1998.
22. *Australian*, 3 February 1998.
23. Ibid., 17 July 1998.
24. David Marr, 'Betrayal', *Sydney Morning Herald*, 20 May 2000.
25. In essence the argument we have advanced in this and the next paragraph is one made by John Chesterman, *Civil Rights: How Indigenous Australians Won Formal Equality*, University of Queensland Press, St Lucia, 2005, ch. 4.
26. Newspoll et al., 'Public Opinion on Reconciliation', in Michelle Grattan (ed.), *Reconciliation: Essays on Australian Reconciliation*, Black Inc., Melbourne, 2000, pp. 33–4.
27. See, for example, the writings of those employed by the Institute for Public Affairs (<www.ipa.org.au/publications/pubsbycategory.asp?category=Indigenous%20Affairs>).
28. See, for example, Gary Johns, 'Look for Strength in the Mainstream', *Australian*, 22 November 2001.
29. Melissa Castan, 'Reconciliation, Law and the Constitution', in Grattan (ed.), *Reconciliation*, p. 207.

# Index